SHAKESPEARE SURVEY

SHAKESPEARE SURVEY

AN ANNUAL SURVEY OF
SHAKESPEARIAN STUDY & PRODUCTION

9

EDITED BY
ALLARDYCE NICOLL

Issued under the Sponsorship of
THE UNIVERSITY OF BIRMINGHAM
THE UNIVERSITY OF MANCHESTER
THE SHAKESPEARE MEMORIAL THEATRE
THE SHAKESPEARE BIRTHPLACE TRUST

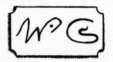

CAMBRIDGE UNIVERSITY PRESS

CAMBRIDGE
LONDON · NEW YORK · MELBOURNE

Published by the Syndics of the Cambridge University Press
The Pitt Building, Trumpington Street, Cambridge CB2 1RP
Bentley House, 200 Euston Road, London NW1 2DB
32 East 57th Street, New York, NY 10022, USA
296 Beaconsfield Parade, Middle Park, Melbourne 3206, Australia

ISBN: 0 521 06422 8

First published 1956
Reprinted 1966 1970 1975

Printed in Great Britain
at the University Printing House, Cambridge
(Euan Phillips, University Printer)

CONTENTS

[Notes are placed at the end of each contribution. All line references are to the 'Globe' edition, and, unless for special reasons, quotations are from this text]

LIST OF PLATES

STUDIES IN *HAMLET*, 1901–1955

BY

CLIFFORD LEECH

The criticism of *Hamlet* is marked by its extent, its variety and its frequent aggressiveness. A. A. Raven's *A Hamlet Bibliography and Reference Guide 1877–1935* (Chicago, 1936) listed 2167 items: in the last twenty years the tide has not slackened. The Prince has been seen as too sensitive for the rough world, as given to metaphysical speculation, as shocked out of normality by incest and murder, as an effective stage-figure resistant to psychological probing, as a man of sanguine temperament falling into melancholy adust, as the victim of an Oedipus complex, and as an altogether vigorous and right-thinking young man who would stir no suspicion in the mind of an immigration officer. The play presents itself to some as good craftsman's work; to others it is a palimpsest, with fragments of sources and early drafts unsatisfactorily showing themselves in the final version. For most critics the Prince dominates the play and their interest, but some would have us give at least comparable importance to other figures or would remind us that a dramatic poem exists primarily as a pattern of words. And it is possible, but rare, to be modest and tentative in writing of this play: more frequently we are offered a 'solution' which is, for good and all, to pluck out the play's heart and banish its mystery. Because of the vast extent of this critical writing, it can happen that such a 'solution' is an old acquaintance innocently offered as new. The extreme divergence of critical opinion may suggest a flaw in the play, that the dramatist did not come to a full awareness, or at least a full dramatic realization, of his central idea. After all, many of the critics of *Hamlet* have been men of deep understanding and great scholarship. But the aggressiveness of the critics, fantastic though it may sometimes appear, surely hints at the play's strength. We do not feel passionately committed unless our chosen cause seems important. The play lives in our minds as it does in the theatre. It inevitably becomes a starting-point for speculation and fantasy; it is a datum which we are compelled to incorporate within our private view of the world.

In this century the criticism of the play has had to endeavour to keep pace with textual study. Although we cannot claim to have reached a general agreement on the nature and provenance of the First Quarto, the dominant view since the appearance of G. I. Duthie's *The 'Bad' Quarto of Hamlet* (1941) has been that it is a memorial reconstruction derived, via a process of stage-abridgement, from the full text that lies behind the Second Quarto. Consequently all those critical studies that use the First Quarto as evidence of Shakespeare's first intentions in the writing of the play have now a somewhat old-fashioned air. Similarly, in recent years *Der bestrafte Brudermord* has rarely been seen as a straightforward derivative of the Ur-*Hamlet*. Yet critical studies that are partially dependent on out-moded textual theories cannot be dismissed from present-day consideration: though their explanations of how the full text came into existence may be suspect, their interpretations depend primarily on the impact that that text has made. In details here and there their arguments may have little importance for us, but we cannot for that reason reject their views as wholes.

In a short survey it is clearly impossible to do more than observe some of the more interesting features of the great landscape. Some few pieces of writing—*Shakespearean Tragedy*, *Art and Artifice in Shakespeare*, the commentary in J. Q. Adams's edition of the play, *What Happens in Hamlet*, Granville-Barker's *Preface*, T. S. Eliot's essay, Ernest Jones's *Hamlet and Oedipus*, the section on the play in D. G. James's *The Dream of Learning*—need far more space than can here be given to them. And other books and articles, almost numberless, have contributed something to a fairly diligent reader's view of the play: of these only a selection can be mentioned, some for their merit, others for their perhaps significant eccentricity.

BRADLEY AND HIS SUCCESSION

Before the appearance of *Shakespearean Tragedy* (1904), the dominant influences on the English views of *Hamlet* were those of Goethe (who symbolized the Prince as a china vase in which an oak disastrously grew), of Coleridge (who found him metaphysically given and unfit for action), and of Karl Werder (for whom Hamlet was an active person charged not merely with killing Claudius but with making his guilt plain to Denmark). Werder's views were published in his *Vorlesungen über Hamlet* (1875), but this book did not appear in English translation until 1907, when it was given the unfortunate title *The Heart of Hamlet's Mystery*. Meanwhile his arguments had been ably summarized and, on the whole, gently disposed of both by Bradley and by A. H. Tolman in *The Views about Hamlet and Other Essays* (Boston and New York, 1904). Tolman's essay, which is independent of Bradley, gives an excellent account of the state of *Hamlet*-criticism at the beginning of this century, and adds a number of judicious observations: in particular, he shows that Werder's view lacks warrant in the text and clashes with the evidence of the soliloquies, he sees the mouse-trap as "hardly more than a plausible excuse for doing nothing", he illustrates anti-revenge feelings in Shakespeare's time from Belleforest's version of the story and from Bacon's essay on revenge, and he shows that disputes concerning Hamlet's 'madness' depend largely on terminology. But Tolman's essay has exerted little influence, while Werder is the progenitor of an apparently unfinished line of interpreters: he attracts doubtless through his dogmatism, his insistence on the simple vigour of the hero and on the thorough healthiness of the play's atmosphere. He denies that Hamlet delayed, he finds it natural that the Ghost's word should need confirmation, he ingeniously shows that Hamlet followed simple prudence in denying shriving-time to Rosencrantz and Guildenstern. His efforts to re-interpret some of the soliloquies exhibit a mountain in labour.

For Bradley Hamlet was not the simple person that Werder made him, but he had not the giant-stature of Shakespeare's later tragic heroes. He was not constitutionally unfitted for action, for Bradley does not quarrel with the descriptions given by Ophelia and Fortinbras. He was inhibited by nervous shock and did not himself understand his delay. He could literally forget his duty of revenge and be as eager that the player should speak his words aright as he was that Horatio should scrutinize the reaction of Claudius. His assumption of an antic disposition was perhaps in part due to a fear of real distraction, in part a means of gaining a psychologically necessary freedom. He quietened his conscience by cultivating a doubt of the Ghost's word. On his return from England there was "a slight thinning of the dark cloud of melancholy", a fatalistic acceptance of the ways of Providence, a rather greater consciousness of his own power, but there was no stronger determination in him, no evidence that he would bring himself nearer to the act of revenge. Bradley found no reason to take at their face-value all of Hamlet's words in the prayer-scene (for by that point the character's inhibition has been made plain to us), but had no doubt of Gertrude's adultery (for the Ghost's words seem explicit enough). Critics who have parted company with Bradley have accused him of giving a too preponderant attention to the character of the hero, of treating the play like a nineteenth-century novel, of neglecting its poetry, and of being insufficiently versed in Elizabethan thought and stage-conditions. There is something to be said for each of these objections, yet no other account of the play has been so inclusive as his, so dependent on a scrutiny of detail and yet directed all the time towards the emergence of a tragic idea. At times he could admit puzzlement, as in the matter of Hamlet's relations with Ophelia. His views on many points must be subject to modification, have been provocative of further enquiry, but it is a rash man who rejects them out of hand. He saw *Hamlet* as one of four plays by Shakespeare that were comparable in authority with Greek tragedy, as a product of a deep consideration of the nature of things. The play has become smaller in the hands of some of Bradley's successors, so small that we must sometimes wonder at its power to make demands on us.

The influence of Bradley was very strong on W. F. Trench's *Shakespeare's Hamlet: A New Commentary with a Chapter on First Principles* (1913), yet Trench saw his book as an attack on Bradley's views. He wished to set up a more Coleridgean Prince, and saw Ophelia's and Fortinbras's words as respectively delusional and courtly. Nevertheless, Trench frequently exhibits the kind of analysis of behaviour, the kind of conjecture about what happens off-stage and outside the play's time of action, where Bradley is at his most vulnerable. He believes that Hamlet changed his mind about adding a dozen or sixteen lines to *The Murder of Gonzago*: in "O what a rogue" he decided to write a wholly new play, and in III, ii he used the name "Gonzago" in reference to the Player-King because he thought his mention of the poisoning had come too quickly. Similarly Trench suggests that Gertrude's account of Ophelia's death was sheer fiction, invented out of fear of Laertes. He seriously challenges Bradley's "disconcerting suggestions" concerning the whereabouts of Rosencrantz and Guildenstern before they were fetched to Elsinore. Yet there are good things in the book: Trench notes that Hamlet's moralizing in the closet-scene is spoken with the dead Polonius in the audience's view, and that there is something of arrogance and complacency in Hamlet's words here; he sees the irony in Hamlet's finding the leisure to fence so soon after proclaiming "The interim is mine"; and despite his generally Coleridgean view he sees Hamlet's *hamartia* in a readiness to "let himself go"—into the violent and the grotesque and the thought of suicide. Generally Coleridgean too is Stopford Brooke's account of the play in *Ten More Plays of Shakespeare* (1913), yet he could see that Hamlet was no remarkable philosopher: his thoughts, far from being of "exceptional range or excellence", are "the ordinary thoughts of his time in a cultivated youth with a turn for philosophy". For Stopford Brooke, in fact, Hamlet was distinguished from a host of men only by the beauty and authority of his utterance. This modification of Coleridge is useful, but Brooke's view of the play is a partial one. Denying even the verge of madness to the hero, he confesses himself puzzled by the treatment of Rosencrantz and Guildernstern, which he can see only as "a blot on the play".

Bradley is the strongest influence on J. Q. Adams's commentary in his edition (Cambridge, Mass., 1929). The antic disposition, he says, supplied Hamlet with "a surrogate form of *activity*", it offered the opportunity of humour, a useful antidote to grief, and it was a safety-valve for pent-up feelings. Hamlet felt no doubt of the Ghost until he spoke the words "About, my brain!" in his soliloquy at the end of Act II. The interposition of "To be, or not to be" in III, i demonstrates that for Hamlet the play is not truly "the thing". His sparing of the King in the prayer-scene is another unconscious subterfuge, but Adams makes the illuminating comment that Hamlet's desire for Claudius's damnation is in contrast to Othello's "I would not kill thy soul". Yet with all this there is an echo of Werder when Adams says that Hamlet must kill Claudius "with safety to himself", justifying the deed to the court and Denmark and not involving his mother in the disclosure. The Ophelia scenes are rather sentimentally presented, and there is an over-emphasis on Hamlet's healthier state of mind towards the end of the play: in claiming "How all occasions" as evidence of this, Adams overlooks the final, characteristic stress on "thoughts". He sees indeed that Hamlet's attitude to the dead Polonius gives the lie to a sentimental interpretation of the character, though he is inclined to minimize Hamlet's brutality here and elsewhere as well as his obscenities in the play-scene. Some oddities of interpretation include the suggestions that, when Hamlet says "We'll teach you to drink deep ere you depart", he is enthusiastically promising his friend 'a gay time', and that Hamlet sees Claudius as a possible seducer of Ophelia. Like Trench, Adams believes that Hamlet's plans for the play-scene were considerably revised towards the end of "O what a rogue". One does not feel that Adams's view of the play is, like Bradley's, of one piece: rather, he has been sensitive in many points of detail and his account derives strength from its secure placing in the Bradley tradition.

H. B. Charlton is, of course, a militant Bradleian, as is evident in his interpretation of *Hamlet* in *Shakespearian Tragedy* (1948). He effectively dismisses the idea that Hamlet needed to test the Ghost's word, and sees the Second Quarto placing of "To be, or not to be" as "a master-dramatist's revision". He notes that, when Hamlet's feelings are excited, he is given to exaggeration and to generalizing from a single particular ("Frailty, thy name is woman"), but, when his mind dwells on generalities, he forgets his own situation ("No traveller returns"). Charlton anticipates D. G. James in suggesting that the world of *Hamlet* shows "the critical inquisitiveness and the accompanying part sceptical, part agnostic forms of the modern mind". As far as it goes, Charlton's account of the play is acceptable, but we may wonder if he—or Bradley, for that matter—has sufficiently demonstrated why Hamlet's experiences have inhibited him from performing the act that he repeatedly purposes. Charlton is content, it appears, with the simple assertion that they do: he will have no dealings with Freudian conjecture.

THE TEXT

During this century there have been two authoritative brief statements on the development of *Hamlet* textual study. These have inevitably come from E. K. Chambers in *William Shakespeare: A Study of Facts and Problems* (1930) and from W. W. Greg in *The Editorial Problem in Shakespeare* (1942). Preceding Chambers there was the work of A. W. Pollard and J. Dover Wilson on the Bad Quartos in general, which in relation to *Hamlet* assumed a peculiarly elaborate form in Wilson's *The Copy of 'Hamlet' 1603 and The 'Hamlet' Transcript 1593* (1918): here the theory of First Quarto provenance was that the actor of "Voltemar" (who also played other small parts) made some use of a transcript, made for provincial performance, of a manuscript that Shakespeare had partially revised from the Ur-*Hamlet* or from an intermediate revision: "Voltemar" also had his own written part in his possession. Among rival theories may be noted those of F. G. Hubbard in his edition of the First Quarto (Madison, Wisconsin, 1920) and B. A. P. van Dam in *The Text of Shakespeare's Hamlet* (1924). Hubbard believed that the First Quarto was a complete play, dramatically effective, and consistent within itself, although he admitted that it may not have been holding the stage at the time of publication. He did not attempt to explain the relationship between the two manuscript versions of the play that he assumed to lie behind the First and Second Quartos. Editing the First Quarto on the assumption that its corruptions were only a matter of misprinting, he produced a text that Chambers has described as "quite incredible". Van Dam held to the view that the First Quarto was produced by stenography, but his evidence of anticipations and transpositions would today be seen to accord with a theory of memorial reconstruction. He had to explain the wide variations between the First and Second Quartos, and the First Quarto's not infrequent echoes of other Shakespeare plays and *The Spanish Tragedy*, by the assumption that the players were not "part-perfect". Yet he believed that the First Quarto could not have come from a pirate-actor, because such a man would have been in a position to avoid mistakes in proper names and correct mis-writings and transpositions. The Second Quarto, he thought, was printed from Shakespeare's manuscript after it had been used as a prompt-copy: van Dam needed to assume this because he believed that the Second Quarto contained actors' interpolations, though he admitted that the text was too long for "an ordinary performance". The Folio text was based on an intermittent collation of a late quarto with a transcript of the prompt-copy. In 1930, however, Chambers had little doubt that "the Second Quarto substantially represents the original text of the play, as written once and for all by Shakespeare" and that the First Quarto, the Folio version and *Der bestrafte Brudermord* are all derivatives from that: the First Quarto he saw as a reported text, with the possibility of contamination by the Ur-*Hamlet*; the Folio version was set up from a manuscript that had been used as a prompt-copy.

Dover Wilson in *The Manuscript of Shakespeare's Hamlet and the Problems of its Transmission* (1934) was primarily concerned with the nature of the copy used for the Second Quarto and the Folio. This very full enquiry led to the conclusion that the Second Quarto was set up from Shakespeare's autograph, which suffered at the hands of an inexpert compositor and a press-corrector who emended without reference to the manuscript: omissions were either inadvertent, dishonest (the compositor being anxious to have done), or tactful (in the "little eyases" passage): sometimes the First Quarto was consulted when the author's handwriting was especially difficult (hence the appearance of 'sallied flesh', as in the First Quarto). The Folio version was based on a transcript of the prompt-copy, and was thus a text of less authority. Wilson argued that the light punctuation of the Second Quarto was Shakespeare's own, and consequently that the Second Quarto phrasing of "What a piece of work is a man" should be accepted. This deduction was strenuously combated by Peter Alexander in his British Academy lecture *Shakespeare's Punctuation* (1945), which led to controversy between Wilson and Alexander in *The Review of English Studies* (January and July, 1947). Alexander did not deny that the Second Quarto punctuation was Shakespeare's, but suggested that it needs interpretation: "What a piece of work is a man" shows "commas with inversion" together with an omission of "external punctuation" (i.e. stops at the end of a separable sense-unit) which Alexander finds not un-common in Shakespeare texts. Wilson understandably replied that this kind of punctuation would defy a player's or prompter's power of interpretation, and suggested that the Folio-pointing was due to Burbage's perverted reading of the lines. Yet, if we assume, as Wilson and Alexander do, that the Second Quarto punctuation is Shakespeare's, someone did interpret it as meaning what Alexander claims it was intended to mean. Nevertheless, Alexander's case would be much stronger if we could assume that this prose speech was set out in verse-lining in Shakespeare's manuscript: we might then have no qualms about the possibility of "external punctuation" being omitted.

While not disputing Dover Wilson's view of the provenance of the Second Quarto, T. M. Parrott and Hardin Craig in their edition of the Second Quarto (1938) argued that the Folio text could not have been derived from the prompt-book: it was too long, they suggested, to have been acted as it stood. They suggested, therefore, that it came from a transcript of Shake-speare's manuscript which was made before the preparation of the prompt-book and was again transcribed for the Folio printers. This argument seems to depend too much on a rigid acceptance of the two-hour theory, and has probably been rendered unnecessary by more recent views of the provenance of the Folio text.

G. I. Duthie's *The 'Bad' Quarto of Hamlet* (1941) returned to the provenance of the First Quarto. As Greg justly points out, this book "contains in fifty pages an admirable survey of recent research on Shakespeare's text". It presents the First Quarto as a memorial reconstruction of the full text, made for provincial performance by the actor who played Marcellus and perhaps Lucianus (as previously suggested by H. D. Gray in 1915), the part of Voltemar being available for transcription: when the actor's memory failed, he wrote blank verse of his own made up of echoes from the full text and from other plays: occasionally he drew on the phraseology and other characteristics of the Ur-*Hamlet*, deriving from that source the names Corambis and Montano. *Der bestrafte Brudermord*, he believes, was derived from a further memorial recon-struction made for a continental tour by a company that included one or two who had acted the *Hamlet*-text used for the First Quarto: the reporters in this instance made some fresh use of the Ur-*Hamlet*. These views are, of course, speculative, but Duthie has in many instances provided plausible demonstrations of the First Quarto reporter's patch-work. In any event, his theories have yet to be seriously challenged. Greg in *The Editorial Problem* cautiously approved Duthie's views and accepted the autograph and prompt-book provenances of the Second Quarto and the Folio text, though he remarked, like Parrott and Craig, that the Folio text can hardly have been acted in its entirety.

Important new speculations concerning the text of *Hamlet* have recently been made. Miss Alice Walker in 'The Textual Problem of *Hamlet*: A Reconsideration' (*Review of English Studies*, October 1951) argues that the Second Quarto was printed from a corrected copy of the First Quarto as far as the end of Act 1, and that, as suggested by H. de Groot in *Hamlet, its Textual History* (Amsterdam, 1923), the Folio text was printed from a corrected copy of the Second Quarto. The manuscripts used to correct the printed copies were respectively Shakespeare's autograph and a transcript of the prompt-book. This would explain the length of the Folio text, which would thus not be based on an acting-copy. It would explain the agreements of the First Quarto and the Second Quarto (for Act 1) and of the Second Quarto and the Folio in unusual spellings and manifest errors. The obvious difficulty in this theory is that the Folio omits some two hundred lines of the Second Quarto, although it must, according to Miss Walker, have taken a good deal of material from the Second Quarto and not from the prompt-book: as appears more clearly in her book *Textual Problems of the First Folio* (1953), Miss Walker has to assume a measure of 'editing' in the Folio text, but it is difficult to see why that should have happened. This point has been taken up by Harold Jenkins in 'The Relation of the Second Quarto and the Folio Text of *Hamlet*' (*Studies in Bibliography*, 1955), who believes that only in some measure was a corrected Second Quarto the basis for the Folio text. He notes the Folio's many divergences from the Second Quarto, and suggests that the scribe who made a transcript for the printer may have had "a copy of the quarto at hand, or even open, in case of need" but that we cannot say how frequently he turned to it.

In 'A Definitive Text of Shakespeare: Problems and Methods' (*Studies in Shakespeare*, Coral Gables, Florida, 1953) Fredson Bowers attacked Dover Wilson's belief that the Second Quarto was set up by a single inexpert compositor, "an untutored dolt working beyond his normal speed": Bowers saw no evidence that only one compositor worked on the text, and argued that the number of skeleton-formes suggested composition speed was ahead of press speed and that a need for haste was therefore unlikely. Following this up, J. R. Brown in 'The Compositors of *Hamlet* Q2 and *The Merchant of Venice*' (*Studies in Bibliography*, 1955) deduces from evidence of spellings that the same two compositors worked on the Second Quarto and on *The Merchant*, which was also printed by James Roberts. Consequently the 'omissions' in the Second Quarto must have been due either to the illegibility of the manuscript or to the fact that they are really later additions to the text. Bowers in 'The Printing of *Hamlet*, Q2' (*ibid.*) accepts Brown's argument, relates it to the evidence of varying running-titles, and gives further consideration to the two compositors' stints. Miss Walker in 'Collateral Substantive Texts (with special reference to *Hamlet*)' (*ibid.*) notes that, though we are moving towards a new eclecticism in the editing of *Hamlet* and certain other plays, we still need to make up our minds which is the more authoritative text, for readings in the Second Quarto and the Folio may be evenly balanced against one another and we also need as much information as possible about transmission in order to formulate coherent principles for emendation. It is clear that an editor of *Hamlet* to-day must be equipped with a sound aesthetic judgement as well as with a full acquaintance with recent bibliographical methods.

DOVER WILSON AND GRANVILLE-BARKER

What Happens in Hamlet (1935) has probably had more influence on stage-practice than any other book by a Shakespeare scholar. It is best known for its insistence on the Ghost as constituting a problem for Hamlet and a largely Protestant audience, its suggestion that Hamlet in II, ii overheard Polonius's plan to "loose" Ophelia to him, and its ingenious reconstruction of the staging of the mouse-trap with Claudius's attention momentarily diverted. But twenty years after its publication these do not seem the strongest parts of the book. Hamlet was the first character in an Elizabethan drama to doubt a ghost's veracity: the dramatic tradition, untroubled by religious controversy, used ghosts as a convenient means of bringing news. Wilson, relating the Ghost in *Hamlet* to contemporary religious notions, is forced to see it as essentially a Catholic spirit. This has led to controversy between R. W. Battenhouse ('The Ghost in *Hamlet*: A Catholic "Linchpin"?', *Studies in Philology*, April 1951) and I. J. Semper ('The Ghost in *Hamlet*: Pagan or Christian?', *The Month*, April 1953), in which the mingled Christian and Senecan elements in the Ghost's constitution have become more evident. If Hamlet overheard Polonius's words about Ophelia, the audience would have to bear this in mind a long while. Wilson's view of the mouse-trap depends on the audience watching the dumb-show carefully, so that it will have in advance an easy grasp of the play's action, and simultaneously observing Claudius's inattention. Yet we must admit that this is more convincing than the view of Richard Flatter in *Hamlet's Father* (1949), that the dumb-show was acted on the upper-stage, out of sight of Claudius and Gertrude, who sat on their thrones on the inner-stage. The special value of Wilson's book to-day seems to consist in its wide-ranging ideas, its readiness to admit difficulty. He sees Hamlet as a man who delights in acting and in fooling his enemies, who behaves in a deranged fashion yet is ever conscious of it, who can convince himself but not us by his words in the prayer-scene, who in "How all occasions" achieves an unconsciously ironic conclusion by promising himself "bloody thoughts". T. S. Eliot's view of the play Wilson cannot bring himself to accept, finding Hamlet's awareness of Gertrude's incest cause enough for his behaviour, but, as in Bradley's case, we may wonder if this accounts for some of the peculiarities that Wilson has shrewdly observed. It is evident that this book is thoroughly in the Bradley tradition and, as such, can be an admirable guide to a producer. Nevertheless, some readers have fastened on a single point and made it, as Wilson does not, dominate the play: thus Bertram Joseph in *Conscience and the King: A Study of Hamlet* (1953) and Hugh Hunt in *Old Vic Prefaces: Shakespeare and the Producer* (1954), both manifestly indebted to Wilson, have been content to see Hamlet's delay as caused solely by his doubt of the Ghost.

Granville-Barker's *Preface* (1937) also owes much to Dover Wilson. Like J. Q. Adams's scene-by-scene commentary, this preface lacks a clear line of argument, but it is of the first excellence on many points of detail. Granville-Barker saw that Shakespeare inevitably took over the pretended madness, but fused it with something else, making an "alloy of sanity and insanity, pretence and reality": only in this way could Hamlet's character be fully developed and revealed. There was cruelty too in the character, the cruelty of a sensitive mind, "ever tempted to shirk its battle against the strong" in order to triumph over the weak. When Hamlet doubts, it is because "he has lost for a while the will to believe". The heart of the play is seen as a sceptical element in the hero's character, but Granville-Barker does not show how this keeps Hamlet from action: he does not, as D. G. James does, suggest an ethical uncertainty in Hamlet. Among the many good things here we find that "the old worldling" Polonius is epitomized in the kind of verse he speaks, that the standard five-act division spoils many effects of contrast and juxtaposition that Shakespeare must have had in mind, and that the Second Quarto and Folio sequence of scenes represents probably a revision and certainly a better version than that of the First Quarto.

If at times one regrets the way in which later commentators have fastened on a single point of Wilson's and made too much of it, one may be more astonished at a simple attempt to put him right. Thus A. J. Green in 'The Cunning of the Scene' (*Shakespeare Quarterly*, October 1953) believes that the mouse-trap and its dumb-show must have gone exactly as Hamlet intended, and the actors must all have played their parts brilliantly (despite "pox, leave thy damnable faces"), for Hamlet was a capable man of action who "cannot have planned carelessly". *What Happens in Hamlet* will survive this.

The 'Historical' School

No one could accuse Dover Wilson or J. Q. Adams or Granville-Barker of being indifferent to the circumstances in which Shakespeare wrote, but their approach to *Hamlet* and other major plays of its time has been dependent on the belief that they are exceptional works, not to be totally 'explained' by reference to dramatic fashions and methods or common trends of thought. These things, however, are given a special stress by the critics that now concern us. The best of these remain conscious of *Hamlet*'s stature, and there are many who have helped to a fuller understanding of the play. We cannot say that this movement in *Hamlet*-criticism is a mere reaction to Bradley, for its presence is felt in the nineteenth century, yet there is no doubt that Bradley's lack of concern with the Elizabethan playhouse provoked revolt and strengthened an existent tendency. John Corbin in *The Elizabethan Hamlet: A Study of the Sources, and of Shakespeare's Environment, to show that the Mad Scenes had a Comic Aspect now Ignored* (1895) indicated his approach in his title, and suggested that Hamlet's brutality was to be explained as a legacy from the Ur-*Hamlet*. But the 'historical' approach was further developed in C. M. Lewis's *The Genesis of Hamlet* (New York, 1907). Lewis's main thesis was that in the extant play we have an amalgam of Belleforest, Kyd and Shakespeare. It is not subject to æsthetic judgement because it is not an entity. If we want Shakespeare, we must subtract Belleforest and Kyd. Lewis is good on what may be called the 'growingness' of the play: he suggests that, as Shakespeare worked on it, he deepened Hamlet's philosophic inclination, his hint of moral scruple, his agnosticism. But the book as a whole is unsatisfying because Lewis disregards the sense of unity that the play in performance can give, despite the problems that may arise as we afterwards brood. And he does not relate the growing complication to the mingling of the splendid and the pathological that is a general mark of Shakespeare's work in the opening years of the seventeenth century. A. A. Jack's *Young Hamlet: A Conjectural Resolution of some of the Difficulties in the Plotting of Shakespeare's Play* (1950) was based on lectures given some fifty years before its publication. It resembles Lewis's book in its view that Shakespeare began his version as a straightforward revenge-play, which through revision came to bear the weight of philosophic thought. Jack differed from Lewis in regretting that Shakespeare had not left his first draft untouched, but he had excellent things to say on the play's emotional effect, seeing it—even in its final form—as primarily a theatre-play, not troubling the depths of our minds as the later tragedies do. J. M. Robertson's *The Problem of "Hamlet"* (1919) and *"Hamlet" Once More* (1923) similarly present the play as a palimpsest: Kyd, it is suggested, wrote a two-part *Hamlet*; Shakespeare attempted to fit Kyd's material into a single play; Kyd had already complicated things by imposing a Senecan ghost-revelation and the play-within-the-play on the old tale in which madness was assumed for safety's sake; Shakespeare added a pessimism of his own, and a hero who shows the effect of "psychic shock" despite preserving the readiness for action that he had displayed in earlier versions.

E. E. Stoll has written often on *Hamlet*, but his two major contributions are in *Hamlet: An*

Historical and Comparative Study (Minnesota, 1919) and *Art and Artifice in Shakespeare: A Study in Dramatic Contrast and Illusion* (1933). In the earlier work he was anxious to present the Prince in a heroic light, and to insist on the ready intelligibility of the play to an Elizabethan audience. He saw "To be, or not to be" as a mere generalizing soliloquy, like the Duke's words on death in *Measure for Measure*, like many speeches and choruses in Greek tragedy—having little or no relation to the context: the Greek analogue is hardly convincing, for Aristotle, rebuking irrelevance in choric passages, describes it as a quite recent development. Stoll justifiably refuses to see Hamlet as a merely pathological figure, and he gives an excellent account of the sheerly theatrical excitement of the last scene of the play. At one point he admits that Titus and Hieronimo, "like most Elizabethan revengers", both feigned madness and were mad, and adds: "Even in *Hamlet* Shakespeare has not handled the situation so carefully as to preclude some question on this head." This, of course, goes against the dominant thesis of his book, that *Hamlet* is the story of a simple hero. In *Art and Artifice* Stoll's account of the tragic effect reminds us of the worlds of opera and epic: he is often illuminating in bringing out the dramatic orchestration by means of contrast, suspense, iteration; the idea of drama he presents depends on juxtapositions rather than processes. He is surely right to differentiate between tragic and philosophic writing, to see that in *Hamlet* there is "no piercing of the veil", that we remain primarily in a world of particulars; yet it is strange that he does not see this world of particulars in more human terms, with contradictions and strife within the single dramatic figure. It is notable that he says nothing of Hamlet's bawdy and brutal talk, and he is capable of strangely misunderstanding a play close to *Hamlet* in time and theme, when he says that Chapman's Clermont delays merely for dramatic effect, "with no inner reason". From Stoll we have learned much concerning Shakespeare's artistry, but he has told us little of what the tragedies are about.

In *Character Problems in Shakespeare's Plays: A Guide to the Better Understanding of the Dramatist* (1922), L. L. Schücking presents Shakespeare as taking over the action of the Ur-*Hamlet* and adding or developing Hamlet's melancholy: there is thus, he considers, no point in talking of his delay. Hamlet's pessimism, his antic disposition, his wish for Claudius's damnation are due either to the original story or to his adherence to the fashionable melancholy type. In line with the general argument of this book, Schücking says we must believe Laertes on the nature of Hamlet's love and Gertrude, not the Clown, on the manner of Ophelia's death. Schücking's *The Meaning of Hamlet* (1937) is less challenging, and provides a useful analysis of Hamlet's behaviour. In particular it stresses the Renaissance and non-Christian element in the play. His British Academy lecture, *The Baroque Character of the Elizabethan Tragic Hero* (1938), develops the idea of Hamlet as a melancholy figure and links him with the violent exaggerations of baroque. This is a corrective to the straightforward blamelessness of Stoll's Hamlet, but Schücking in one place admits that Shakespeare differs, in general, from his contemporaries in his 'psychological realism', his following of 'Nature': this should make Schücking readier than it does to see that Hamlet's conduct has a way of hanging together, as that of a Marston hero does not. We are merely affronted when Antonio kills Julio; we are disturbed when Hamlet insults Ophelia. We look, therefore, for a special reason for Hamlet's railings, and we are not content to see them as part of a baroque presentation of a melancholy man. Here as elsewhere Schücking observantly notes what is in the play, but for explanation of its presence offers us only large descriptive terms.

G. F. Bradby's *The Problems of Hamlet* (1928) is an odd book, with a number of obvious errors of fact. In describing all Hamlet's unattractive features as survivals from an earlier version, Bradby overlooks the range of conduct in the later tragic heroes, the 'psychological realism' of the mingling of brutality and nobility in Hamlet, the consequent and profound truth to fact. Yet he is good on the discrepancies in the presentation of Horatio, and interestingly suggests that the extant texts of the closet-scene conflate two separate endings. A. J. A. Waldock in *Hamlet: A Study in Critical Method* (1931) offers a most useful summary of *Hamlet*-criticism from the eighteenth century and shows himself attracted to C. M. Lewis's view of the play as a palimpsest. What is missing here, perhaps, is a sense of *Hamlet*'s place in Shakespeare's development and in the general development of Elizabethan drama. Around the turn of the century plays seem to have become more inclusive, Jonson and Marston as well as Shakespeare manifesting a desire to put every available element into a single play. In Shakespeare, moreover, this seems accentuated through an up-welling of barely understood thoughts and feelings. Though we must not dismiss the effect of earlier versions on the extant *Hamlet*, we should recognize that the relative formlessness of *Hamlet* and *Troilus and Cressida*, as of *The Poetaster*, *Cynthia's Revels* and the *Antonio* plays, is symptomatic of the change from Elizabethan to Jacobean drama. Miss Lily B. Campbell in *Shakespeare's Tragic Heroes: Slaves of Passion* (1930) presents Hamlet as destroyed through the excess of his grief: the "lesson of tragedy" is that reason should balance passion, as it does in Horatio and Fortinbras: Hamlet is a sanguine person, reduced to melancholy adust. This is altogether a strange book, in which the assurance of the writing does not help it to win conviction. Miss Campbell can say: "I truly believe that if a Papist and King James and Timothy Bright had seen the play, as they all probably did, each would have gone home confirmed in his own opinions about ghosts." Yet the Ghost's early appearances are seen by several people, which would not suit Bright, and the Ghost proves a speaker of truth, which would be difficult for James. In J. W. Draper's *The Hamlet of Shakespeare's Audience* (Durham, North Carolina, 1938) we have a mingling of shrewd observation and simple devotion to a 'historical' thesis. According to Draper the background of *Hamlet* is essentially realistic, so each character must be such as an Elizabethan would expect to find in a corresponding position in actuality. Polonius is a worthy and able prime minister, Claudius and Rosencrantz and Guildenstern have much to be said for them. Hamlet's doubt about the Ghost is the sole reason for his delay: when the Ghost blamed him in the closet-scene, it was because ghosts could not see into the mind. We may feel that Draper is right in seeing *Hamlet* as based on a struggle between the one and the many, of an individual against a corrupt society, but that he glides by the disturbing element in the play—Hamlet's grossness and cruelty, his speculations about the cosmos, the element that has made E. M. W. Tillyard in *Shakespeare's Problem Plays* (1950) link it with the dark comedies. Draper has usefully insisted on the Elizabethan character of *Hamlet*'s background, though exaggerating the degree of normality of setting required in a tragedy, but his concept of the Elizabethan age seems a selective one. He is free, however, from the perversity of Salvador de Madariaga, who in *On Hamlet* (1948) was so determined to see Hamlet as a typical Renaissance prince that the character became for him a monster of egoism. Contrariwise, J. V. Cunningham in *Woe or Wonder: The Emotional Effect of Shakespearean Tragedy* (Denver, Colorado, 1951) saw Hamlet as dominated by reason and guided to a point of decision by Thomistic notions. And we are in a kind of Stoll-underworld with R. P. Janaro, who in

'Dramatic Significance in *Hamlet*' (*Studies in Shakespeare*, Coral Gables, Florida, 1953) urges on us the belief that Hamlet is not one man but five, each used in appropriate dramatic situations.

A different kind of 'historical' study appears in the attempt to see *Hamlet* as a tract for Shakespeare's time, incorporating detailed references to political events. Miss Lilian Winstanley in *Hamlet and the Scottish Succession* (1921) would equate the play's characters with leading figures of the time, but complicates and diminishes her argument in suggesting that Hamlet was simultaneously Essex and Darnley and James (also represented by Fortinbras), Polonius was both Burleigh and Rizzio, Claudius both the Elder and the Younger Bothwell. This would surely require leisure for an Elizabethan spectator to work out. Abel Lefranc in *A la Découverte de Shakespeare* (Paris, 1945) accepted Miss Winstanley's theories and in particular stressed points of connexion between *Hamlet* and Darnley's murder. Dover Wilson in *The Essential Shakespeare* (1935) saw a close connexion between the play and the Essex revolt, as did E. S. Le Comte in a cautious and sensible article, 'The Ending of *Hamlet* as a Farewell to Essex' (*ELH*, June 1950). That Shakespeare wrote so courtly a play as *Hamlet* with certain contemporary happenings in mind is not unlikely, but this contributes little to the tragedy's total significance: the allusions, in any event, could not be too blatant and may well be beyond our determination.

THE FREUDIANS

An account of the Freudian views of the play is given in Kenneth Muir's 'Some Freudian Interpretations of Shakespeare' (*Proceedings of the Leeds Philosophical Society* (*Literary and Historical Section*), July 1952). Freud himself in 1900 saw the Oedipus complex as the unconscious motive for Hamlet's delay, and this has been developed with assiduity and fine intelligence by Ernest Jones, most satisfactorily in *Hamlet and Oedipus* (1949). Jones considers the objection that his interpretation depends on viewing Hamlet as a real person, not as a figure in a play, and retorts that critics and spectators have always done this. We might add that the dramatist, though necessarily presenting a simplification, has imagined a whole character and implied it: we may have a sense of this 'whole' and investigate it, though we are of course dependent on a personal impression and assume that it is also the author's. In giving a full account of previous interpretations, Jones makes us aware that the play has appeared to mean something important, though not something easily definable, to a wide variety of men. He suggests that Shakespeare himself did not fully comprehend the reason for Hamlet's delay, that the writing of *Hamlet* was bound up with the execution of Essex (a father-figure), the death of John Shakespeare, and the conjectural infidelity of Mary Fitton. He gives an excellent picture of Hamlet occupying himself with any other matter than the task of revenge—"just as on a lesser plane a person faced with a distasteful task, e.g. writing a difficult letter, will whittle away his time in arranging, tidying, and fidgeting with any little occupation that may serve as a pretext for procrastination". Hamlet, he points out, gives a variety of motives for his delay (cowardice, doubt of the Ghost, desire for Claudius's damnation): indeed the latter two are not mentioned until circumstances (the arrival of the players, the sight of Claudius at prayer) have made them appropriate. The main criticism that can be legitimately made of the book's argument is that it presents *Hamlet* as too exclusively a personal tragedy. Though the play is less 'cosmic' than the other major tragedies—its references to heaven, though frequent, are a little perfunctory—it does suggest a cosmic framework for the action, it is more than a presentation of an individual's (or even Everyman's) neurotic condition. Jones is too ready to see Shakespeare, "the first modern", as equating "Character" and "Fate". Moreover, all the Hamlet-stories and related myths are seen here as enshrining the Oedipus complex, yet it is only in Shakespeare that the irresolution of the hero appears. Is this because Shakespeare was more nearly aware of the basic implications of the story? We need not, however, see the whole play in terms of the Oedipus complex in order to feel that Jones has made one of its components more graspable.

The Freudian influence is clearly strong on T. S. Eliot's essay (1919). He sees Hamlet's emotion as "inexpressible, because it is in *excess* of the facts as they appear": though Dover Wilson retorted that the idea of incest was a powerful enough cause, that may not explain the wide-ranging character of Hamlet's aggressiveness and speculation or provide the link between "psychic shock" and inability to carry out one particular task. Eliot also sees Shakespeare as not fully aware of the nature of his problem in writing the play, as at times "manifesting the buffoonery of an emotion which he cannot express in art". Linked with the Freudian inter-preters, too, is Gilbert Murray's British Academy lecture, *Hamlet and Orestes: A Study of Tradi-tional Types* (1914), where it is suggested that the Greek dramatists and Shakespeare were drawing on primitive myth, the hero representing a Winter-figure. Murray does not account for the fact that the hero's enemies (Aegisthus and Clytemnestra; Claudius) have done wrong, but perhaps this may be seen as a sophistication inevitable on the development of myth into poetry. In an account of a case-history, *Dark Legend: A Study in Murder* (1947), Frederic Wertham has related to *Hamlet* the story of a young Italian immigrant in America: he suggests a strong impulse to matricide in Hamlet, far stronger than his desire for revenge on his uncle: this impulse, which Hamlet manages to control, is bound up with an Orestes complex seen in an excessive attachment to the mother-image, a general hatred of women, homosexual poten-tialities, ideas of suicide, and guilt-feelings. This has the advantage that we do not have to assume, as with Freud and Jones, a hostility of Hamlet to his father. Because, in fact, Wertham does not attempt too full a probing of Hamlet's character, it is easier to see his account as presenting a motive available for Shakespeare. It should be observed that Wertham sees the Orestes and Oedipus complexes as "not mutually exclusive", but in his references to the play, as in the case-history he presents, he stresses only the first. Freudian views also underlie Wulf Sachs's *Black Hamlet: The Mind of an African Negro revealed by Psychoanalysis* (1937), which presents a real-life echo of the situation-pattern in the play, although the most difficult elements in the situation described seem to come from black-white tension in Africa rather than from anything that Shakespeare consciously or unconsciously employed. Michael Innes in *The Hawk and the Handsaw* (in *Three Tales of Hamlet*, 1950) wears all these things lightly: he engagingly suggests that Hamlet's delay was the direct result of his encounter with a Freudian doctor who had previously attempted to minister to Lady Macbeth.

SOME INDEPENDENTS

It is convenient to divide *Hamlet*-critics into groups, but a good deal of cross-fertilization has taken place and a number of critics will not fit easily into any of the groups so far named. In this last section, therefore, some mention must be made of a large body of work, ranging from the influential studies of *Hamlet*-imagery in Caroline Spurgeon's *Shakespeare's Imagery and what it tells us* (1935) and W. H. Clemen's *The Development of Shakespeare's Imagery* (1951) to A. S. Cairncross's fantasy that the complete text of *Hamlet* was written in 1588–9 (*The Problem of Hamlet: A Solution*, 1936), William Empson's small suggestion that "How all occasions" was in the nature of an encore to be given when a performance was going especially well ('*Hamlet When New*', *The Sewanee Review*, Winter and Spring 1953), D. S. Savage's whimsy that the references to pirates in *Hamlet* should be taken as references to the printing of the First Quarto (*Hamlet and the Pirates: An Exercise in Literary Detection*, 1950), and Jean Paris's laborious analysis of the play as a presentation of three sons, each reacting differently to the task of vengeance (*Hamlet, ou les Personnages du Fils*, Paris, 1953).

A. Clutton-Brock's *Shakespeare's 'Hamlet'* (1922), though at times sentimental and over-written, brings out the richness and complexity of the Prince, and suggests, vaguely, that the play presents a notion of the dramatist's values. Hamlet "has too rich a nature to be narrowed into a vendetta", and this richness is at odds with the attempted concentration on revenge: he has a "double consciousness", is subject to a "conflict between the permanent attitude and the practical task", and strives in vain to harmonize them. Clutton-Brock becomes slightly Freudian when, quoting Eliot, he suggests that a dramatist needs not so much knowledge of motives as sensibility and an awareness of people as people. Very different is the picture of Hamlet and his setting given by G. Wilson Knight in *The Wheel of Fire* (1930) and *The Imperial Theme* (1931). Knight sees Hamlet as a man who has unanswerable views about the vanity of living, who is impelled to destroy but not to achieve, who can be cruel. His world, on the other hand, is normal, with Claudius a good enough fellow who has sinned and whom Hamlet drives to further sinning. But the Ghost gives a "devilish command", the priest is "churlish", the account of Purgatory is harsh: we must accept Hamlet's views as right, and regret that we must. Knight makes us remember that we feel at home in Elsinore, as Hamlet does not; the Prince is a hero, and the company of heroes can be difficult to bear. For Granville-Barker in his British Academy lecture, *From 'Henry V' to 'Hamlet'* (1925), the play showed the first clear emergence of the "daemonic" Shakespeare, as distinct from the popular playwright: hence its moralising and its formlessness. In another British Academy lecture, *Hamlet: The Prince or the Poem?* (1942), C. S. Lewis saw Hamlet as mortal man "with his mind on the frontier of two worlds" and found the details of action and motive of small significance: yet he admitted, only to brush aside, the thought that Shakespeare made an effort to "psychologize" Hamlet. Roy Walker's *The Time is Out of Joint: A Study of Hamlet* (1948) presents Hamlet as a man inclined to pacifism. G. R. Elliott in *Scourge and Minister: A Study of Hamlet as a Tragedy of Revengefulness and Justice* (Durham, North Carolina, 1951) sees him as suffering from pride, unable to scrutinize his task or to realize that his nature shrinks from killing a sovereign ruler, but ultimately coming to a correct frame of mind for the killing, in which he was truly heaven's "scourge and minister": so the delay was right. Despite the brooding evangelism of his commentary, and his unusual view that the Folio text represents a Shakespearian revision of the Second Quarto, there is much in Elliott's book that sharpens the apprehension of the separate moments of the play.

Two recent books have contributed powerfully to our understanding. D. G. James's *The Dream of Learning: An Essay on The Advancement of Learning, Hamlet and King Lear* (1951) stresses Hamlet's scepticism and the link that this makes between him and us. Remembering the debate on "value" in *Troilus and Cressida*, James sees in Hamlet an uncertainty concerning the nature of things and the principles of conduct. As for the delay:

Is there anything mysterious about a man who has come to no clear and practised sense of life, and who in the face of a shocking situation which quite peculiarly involves him, shuffles, deceives himself, procrastinates, and in his exasperation cruelly persecutes the person he loves best in the world?

James sees something a little callow in Hamlet at times, in his excusing himself to Laertes and his claim to have loved Ophelia more than forty thousand brothers: the play is less than *Lear*, because it is concerned, not with life itself, but with "a mind arrested in dubiety before the awful problem of life". Perhaps in this book there is too easy an assumption of a clear purpose in Shakespeare's mind, but it makes remarkably evident one reason for the play's wide appeal: Hamlet, the neurotic, the death-willer, the hero, is primarily (for us surely, for Shakespeare perhaps) the sceptic with a Christian inheritance. Peter Alexander in *Hamlet Father and Son* (1955) would reinstate Hamlet too simply as the hero. He attacks the notion of *hamartia*, understandably enough, but disregards Hamlet's brutality and bawdy. He sees the antic disposition as intended to make Claudius aware of Hamlet's enmity, for he "will not come on his enemy silently and suddenly from behind". The book would be more convincing if Alexander did not vaguely accept the notion of *catharsis*, talking of "reconciliation" and "redemption" without a clear indication of how they are brought about. The hero's imperfections do not justify his destruction, but they link him with us and they give us the notion of a human involvement in the tragic chain of events: Cordelia does not deserve her hanging, but she contributes to the sequence that includes it; Gloucester's begetting of Edmund was surely a venial affair, but the blinding lay at the end of the course; Hamlet (we have it on his authority) deserved a whipping, but instead he killed and died.

Hamlet, written by more than one, perhaps written by Shakespeare more than once, has a smack of each of us in it: Stoll gives us its theatrical excitement, Bradley and Ernest Jones the working of the protagonist's mind, D. G. James its twentieth-century appeal, Dover Wilson and Schücking its special reverberations for its first audience, Granville-Barker its available meaning for a producer. Simplification must be recognized for what it is.

ENGLISH HAMLETS OF THE TWENTIETH CENTURY

BY

E. MARTIN BROWNE

This is a personal record; it is not a complete one. Its source is memory, reinforced by the study of some of the critical comment written at the time. Its purpose is to discover, if that is possible from such limited evidence, some of the significant developments in the treatment of the play during this century.

The first time I saw *Hamlet* was at Drury Lane in 1913. It was Forbes-Robertson's farewell season—a genuine farewell for once, since he never appeared again except in charity performances during the First World War, and *Hamlet* was not among the charity plays. His impact upon a boy who already knew and greatly loved the play was tremendous: and though the memory is dim, it corresponds very closely with that described by the great critics. "Mr Forbes-Robertson takes the part quite easily and spontaneously" says Shaw on the 1897 opening of the production. Forbes-Robertson "enjoys (Shakespeare) and understands his methods of expression". I suspect that this sense of the actor being at one with the author, as well as of "his well-known grace and accomplishment", is the reason why the far-off impression remains for me one of such deep and happy satisfaction. The only parallel from my experience as a young playgoer is Matheson Lang's magnificent Othello. Lang seems to have been far less successful as Hamlet, just as Forbes-Robertson was in Othello: which leads to the reflection that the supreme success in Shakespeare is made by the actor who first of all "understands his methods of expression" and secondly is suited to the particular leading role.

Clement Scott picks out two salient characteristics of Forbes-Robertson's performance. "Consummate good breeding" is the first: and it seems as though this may well have been the first Hamlet for a long time to bring out the humour of the part. Not, perhaps, the sardonic humour which has been fully exploited since 1930, but the whimsical humour of the gentleman —which Forbes-Robertson's Hamlet supremely was. Scott adds to this "a mind deeply sensitive to religious impression", and instances his speaking of "To be, or not to be" and most especially something which is still vivid in my memory, the speech to Horatio just before the duel, "there's a special providence in the fall of a sparrow...".

Archer, writing of the 1913 revival, describes Forbes-Robertson as "an accomplished gallant of the Renaissance, a sort of Sir Philip Sidney, transported by a strange anachronism into the uncongenial atmosphere of a barbarous Teutonic court". Perhaps he has hit on yet another reason why this Hamlet so captured the heart. I remember how the characters seemed suddenly to recede during the fourth act, in which Hamlet did not appear: and this may well have been due not entirely to Forbes-Robertson's pre-eminence but also to the removal of that figure in the 'traditional' Hamlet dress, who by suggestion provided a bridge leading from the remote Viking period—'Early Norman' would be our nearest equivalent—of the scenes and costumes to the time of its author, and so on to our own.

Scott speaks of "the three recognized intellectual forces who have advocated the natural as opposed to the conventional Hamlet—the Hamlet of the scholar and student—as against the Hamlet of the stage and the actor": Fechter, Henry Irving and Forbes-Robertson. All three performances, however, were enclosed in the "barbaric Teutonic court": and perhaps the contrast pointed by their very 'naturalness' was one cause of a change in the fashion of the play's decor.

The text "as arranged for the stage by Forbes-Robertson" was published for the first production. It is notable as being fuller than was then usual—most of Shakespeare's text was given in the three and a half hours' playing time, largely because the addition of 'stage business' was ruthlessly checked. The omissions are indicative of the actor's instinctively gentle approach to the part: the most curious is the speech "Now might I do it pat..." the excision of which leaves the scene to the King alone (a barren waste it seems); and the most characteristic are such harshnesses as "I'll lug the guts into the neighbour room". The most outstandingly meritorious change is the restoration of Fortinbras at the end, breaking the nineteenth-century habit of bringing down the final curtain on "The rest is silence".

I never saw Sir Henry Irving, but in seeing H. B. Irving's Hamlet I evidently saw a reading of the part very close to his father's, though the actor's gifts may have been of a different order. Here was an intellectual prince, tortured by "the time out of joint". His father's moments of "vivid, flashing, half-foolish, half-inspired hysterical power" (as Edward Russell describes them) were largely absent; the "forcible" quality to which Archer refers was that of passion rather than genius: and the play suffered badly from cuts, mostly inherited from Sir Henry. The other Hamlet of this period which I saw was Martin-Harvey's, which at Covent Garden was set in curtains, very effectively used.

The theatre's public in the First World War was not in the mood for Shakespeare: the three longest runs were *Chu Chin Chow, Romance* (with Doris Keane) and *A Little Bit of Fluff*. The wartime *Hamlets* I have referred to were both revivals of earlier productions, and my next contact with the play was through the O.U.D.S. I spent the Long Vacation of 1923 producing it at Angmering-on-Sea in Sussex with a cast mostly composed of O.U.D.S. members; Robert Speaight, aged 19 and just going up to Oxford, was the Hamlet. In the following February, the O.U.D.S. itself put on the play. Gyles Isham (my Ghost at Angmering, whose march was more truly that of "the majesty of buried Denmark" than any I have seen) made a good impression as Hamlet. He was more the soldier than the dreamer, but a young man (when Hamlets were as often as not middle-aged) of fine speech and natural distinction. Far more significant than the performance, however, was J. B. Fagan's production.

How little one perceives, while they are taking place, the changes in which one has a part! Here is *The Times*' description of Fagan's setting: "...a stage of open and simple design. It is bridged by a wide arch (an architectural false proscenium) round the pillars of which are two short spiral staircases. The play moves without interruption before and behind this arch, with little other decoration but plain backcloth and curtains." The reviewer goes on to admire the lighting, and especially the way in which "at those instants when the word's magic is most powerful...our minds are concentrated on the words, and the words only".

Did I think of Gordon Craig when I saw it? I don't remember doing so: but I do remember the sense of freedom that the acting gave, and the pace and sweep of the production. This was what we had aimed at in our Sussex village hall with a set of plain curtains and a 'traverse' and gas lighting for which special dimming arrangements were made! William Poel, who was already interested in young Robert Speaight, came to see us, and we dimly realized that he was one source of the new approach to Shakespeare which we had seen exemplified in the admired work of Granville-Barker and of Fagan himself.

Shakespearians have of late years acknowledged their debt to Poel and Granville-Barker and, however often their teaching may be set at naught, these two masters have permanently changed our approach to the staging of the plays. I wonder, though, whether we realize the measure of our debt to Craig. After all, however we may long for an open stage, we still have to produce Shakespeare in theatres with a proscenium: and it was Craig who uncluttered the space inside the frame so that the actors, not the scene-painter, could form the picture. I have been looking through Mander and Mitchenson's photograph album *Hamlet through the Ages*. In the first decade of this century, Germany and Russia suddenly produce designs in space and line and mass, while on the same page England is still immured in scenic detail. It is only in the 1920's and 1930's that Craig's influence is clearly seen in the English designs. English audiences have always liked decoration in their theatre: but they now accept that imaginative freedom as regards place which is the visual reflection of the poet's own treatment of it.

Fagan's is one of the first examples of the 'permanent set' for *Hamlet*. This has since become the generally accepted solution of the problem of how to suggest changes of place without breaking the continuity of action. I well remember the satisfaction which this first experience afforded: but I remember too that already one was saying to oneself "how ingenious!" as each new change appeared. Now that the practice is thirty years old, we see the danger of that very cleverness, and realize once again how the eye may too readily welcome a distraction from "the words, and the words alone".

Fagan set the play in the early sixteenth century, when Wittenberg had just been founded: the costumes were based on Dürer drawings. This was another big change—a civilized Teutonic court instead of the "barbarous" one of old. The play had come home to the Renaissance where it was born; Poel's doctrine was to be thanked for this (even though his own waywardness led to Robert Speaight appearing as a Napoleonic Coriolanus in 1931). There was a great gain in reality: the diction of all the characters now suited with their appearance.

The next year, 1925, is also notable in my *Hamlet* history: it contains my first seeing of Ernest Milton's Hamlet at the Old Vic, John Barrymore's visit to the Haymarket, and the 'modern dress' production by Barry Jackson. I am always grateful to Milton because he first made me aware of the full emotional depths of the character. Having never seen Henry Irving, I had to wait till now to find myself carried away by the horror and the pity of Hamlet's situation. There were mannerisms perhaps, but there was an overwhelming sweep of emotion in key with the high poetry of the play—and also, again freshly to me, with the harsh brutalities which sometimes escape from the overcharged heart. John Barrymore's production lives for me more through the heart-rending Ophelia of Fay Compton and the settings of Robert Edmond Jones than through the Hamlet himself. The great American designer created a spacious castle in an early medieval period: here was a blending of the earlier dating of the play with modern practice in design, which James Agate not unjustly declared to be "the most beautiful thing I have ever seen on any stage". Barrymore's every line was studied with care and faultless taste, the performance was full of perceptive touches: and yet—it lacked the compulsive inner fire. He was too much the star for me: the young disciple of Poel and Barker was alienated by the pause allowed after every utterance of Hamlet's, to give it time to sink in!

Quite another kind of performance followed a few months later, and proved to be one of the landmarks among this century's *Hamlets*. Barry Jackson let a fresh wind blow by putting the play into modern dress. Tradition in the theatre hardens all to quickly: and this was just what we needed to save us from becoming set in our ways. The 'modern dress' of the middle 1920's was hard on the women, for it happened to be the ugliest they have thought up in this century—waists at their lowest and skirts at their shortest. But this was an advantage for the immediate purpose: it removed all vestiges of 'tragic dignity'. The actors were stimulated by the freedom from convention to probe the hearts of their characters, and a fine set of performances resulted. Colin Keith-Johnston as the "Hamlet in plus-fours" very quickly made us see his problem as immediate to ourselves; Frank Vosper as Claudius, smiling in his evening dress and decorations, was a really plausible villain, who had palpably ensnared Dorothy Massingham, the sullen, sensuous queen. Polonius gained most of all: Bromley Davenport made him both real and amusing as a neatly bearded courtier whose mistakes in judgement are the worldly man's failures to understand an other-worldly problem. Gone was the tedious old fool of tradition—gone never to return, for subsequent productions in period costume have learnt, in this as in much else, from the modern-dress experiment, as witness George Howe in Gielgud's *Hamlet* and Alan Webb in Guinness's (1951).

I went to a matinee of this production, and was so enthralled that I went again at night. I was indeed moved by the acting, which was true and fine and often seemed much more poignant than it might have done at the remove made by period clothes. But still more I valued what *The Times* rightly calls "an opening out of fresh light upon the play". From time to time we need such a cleansing of our brains, where the lines of *Hamlet* say themselves over before the actor speaks them in a sort of fog of jumbled memories and associated ideas. Guthrie did it again in 1938 at the Old Vic, with a Ruritanian production and the young Alec Guinness as Hamlet.

One bad result, however, this production had: it encouraged the anti-poetic tendency in Shakespearian acting. At that time, Shakespearian actors were suspect by the managers casting modern plays: the current style of writing demanded a clipped, monosyllabic delivery which was quite unsuitable for the fine words of a poet. The young actors naturally cultivated the modern way of speaking and tried to adapt Shakespeare to this. The verse was deliberately twisted out of shape to conceal its rhythm, and rhyme where it occurred was deliberately 'walked over'; the very basis of the poet's art was destroyed by such interpreters. We are still suffering today from the after-effects of this attack.

In 1926 I played Voltimand in the 'Entirety' (with Milton as Hamlet). For several years past the Old Vic had given a matinee at which the uncut text was played, and which was always sold out. The 'entirety' had been done long before, by Frank Benson in 1900, and it had taken a generation to make people realize how much clearer the play becomes when Shakespeare's exposition is not interfered with—and how much shorter the play *seems* to its audience when the proper balance is kept between tense scenes and those which relieve the tension. Even a small-part actor was able to realize this in rehearsal. The Vic used the complete text in Guthrie's 1937 and 1938 productions and *The Times'* reviewer comments that, "as always when this is done, its sweep and coherence allow of no check or irrelevance". When are we to see another 'entirety'? True, it is more difficult than it was to keep an audience to a late hour: but the opera can do it, so why not Shakespeare?

After three years in America, my first visit to an English theatre in 1930 introduced me to John Gielgud's Hamlet. This was at the Queen's, whither Harcourt Williams's production had been transferred for a limited run. Harcourt Williams was at the Old Vic from 1929 to 1934 and, with Gielgud for the first two years as leading man, established perhaps the highest standard of Shakespearian acting ever seen at that theatre. He had himself graduated as an actor with Ellen Terry and H. B. Irving, and had also worked with Barker, so that the two streams of Shakespearian interpretation were united in a single sensitive artist. His productions were simple—the Vic had very little money: but because they went for the essentials, simplicity proved a blessing. In this *Hamlet*, he gave to an actor of twenty-six (with a good team in support, notably Martita Hunt as the Queen) the chance to show himself, in a clear, unfussy production, as the greatest Hamlet of his age.

About the truth of that categorical statement I have no doubt. I have seen all the four English productions in which he played the part. People sometimes say that he never quite touched the original (1930) rendering: I believe that this is because they were seeing him in the part for the first time. Certainly the impact of that evening was unforgettable: and in seeing the subsequent productions I was never so swept away. But I had with Gielgud's Hamlet the experience which stamps a work of art as of supreme quality. At every seeing, new beauties revealed themselves: so that long after the magic of surprise was quite gone, the deeper magic of imagination went on working.

Two impressions remain most vividly from 1930. First, the youth of the Prince. My first Hamlet was sixty when I saw him. Gielgud is four years younger than I am: and though I had always loved the play so deeply, I had never felt it speak so piercingly to myself from the stage. It was not that his youthfulness was pathetic, but that it accentuated his loneliness and the difficulty of coping with a world of older people: and the mother-son relationship with Martita Hunt's brilliantly stupid Queen was made startlingly real. The other new impression was of wormwood—the iron that had entered into Hamlet's soul. A sensitive young man had suddenly seen the ugliness that can be found in human life: it nauseated and embittered him.

This was not a 'sympathetic' Hamlet, but a character at once forceful and poetic. Gielgud balanced the two elements to make his Hamlet a person, as the performance matured through the three subsequent productions of 1934, 1936 and 1944. The later performances became a little more deliberate; perhaps by producing the play himself he inevitably lost some of the spontaneity of 1930, but this was off-set by a gain in dignity and in the profound understanding of the reflective passages in particular.

To describe Gielgud's Hamlet is, however, a work of supererogation, for we possess a record unique, so far as I know, in stage annals which has been far too little appreciated. Rosamond Gilder, who was editorially connected with *Theatre Arts* during the period of its pre-eminence, published in 1937 a book called *John Gielgud's Hamlet*. It was 'a record of performance' based on a detailed study at many visits to the 1936–37 production in New York, and told in narrative form. "The Hamlet of this description, however, is always John Gielgud, not an abstract, theoretic or imagined Hamlet....I did not ask John Gielgud what he thought about Hamlet; I watched what he did on the stage...." Gielgud checked and criticized her interpretation of his performance and added some notes on *The Hamlet Tradition*. This book is, in my opinion, equal in importance with those of the very greatest critics in the huge literature of *Hamlet*: for it is a record of the result produced from Shakespeare's work by the person for whom, after all, he wrote it—a great actor. It provides detailed evidence that the actor's performance does in fact constitute a commentary on the text: and a commentary with the most valid claim to authority in that, while the literary critic may indulge in personal speculation, the actor must make his interpretation convincing both to himself as the character and to hundreds of spectators who judge its validity directly from the experience he communicates.

Gielgud comes of a great theatrical family, and is steeped in tradition. He says that, reading how Irving acted the scene with Horatio and the soldiers in which he learns of the Ghost's appearance, he found a perfect guide to the playing of the scene. This is typical of his approach to tradition: the pupil, he says, will learn "from the master's approach to character, and from every moment in his performance in which he reveals or clarifies the text".

This is Gielgud's supreme gift—to bring forth every line, every movement designed by the dramatist, as if new-born. The result is a Hamlet at once firmly based in tradition and yet completely of our age. His fine speaking of the poetry never became incantation, and the quieter passages had a subtlety of meaning comparable to that achieved in a modern conversational play. The conception of the character was complete and clear, so that no obscure moments were left to be carried off by the excitement of the climaxes; the logic of the dilemma faced by the abnormally sensitive and intelligent man in an evil world was limpid from beginning to end, and the tragedy had a terrifying inevitability.

Other Hamlets of the time showed perhaps all the more clearly because of their proximity to Gielgud's how hard it is to present the complete character. (This is, I suppose, why criticism of the play has always been full of controversy.) Leslie Howard, for all his graces, had formed for himself no sustained view of Hamlet's character. Laurence Olivier's well-defined view of it seems, from *The Times*' account, to have come into its own at Elsinore. The custom of staging the play in the great courtyard each summer had been established by 1937, and Olivier, playing the part there, seemed to belong to the Castle's history: "...heroism on the winding staircases where defenders holding to the niches in the walls with their left hands and keeping their sword arms free, contested their ground step by step". This performance, created at the Old Vic, was full of athletic grace and vital fire, nor did it lack tenderness and pity. It delighted the eye and moved the heart—but it left the mind dissatisfied. Impatient of reflection, this Hamlet did not reveal the reasons for his delay, and left one with the feeling that the actor was blind to one side of the character's nature. This became a certainty in the film when he described *Hamlet* as "The tragedy of a man who could not make up his mind". The winding staircases of Elsinore, rather than the tragedy of Shakespeare, were the inspiration of a film and a performance which had many touching and thrilling moments but never penetrated the heart of Hamlet's mystery.

Perhaps, in looking for such penetration, I am in a small minority, and certainly the stage-history of *Hamlet* consists more of actors' personalities than of Hamlet's own. Each actor, maybe, is his own Hamlet: and certainly there is much to enjoy in seeing how each new one will turn out. Since the war, we have had a remarkable variety. The most satisfying to me was Michael Redgrave's, because the lines were delivered with such full and detailed understanding and such beauty of intonation, while the character, if not so fully consistent as Gielgud's, was convincing as an interpretation of Shakespeare. The production came from a period (1950) at the Old Vic when the settings usually contained some clumsy blocks which from time to time got in the actors' way: but apart from this, Hugh Hunt kept a clear and swift movement through most of the play.

During the war, Robert Helpmann created to Tchaikowsky's music a *Hamlet* ballet. The scholarship of George Rylands provided the inspiration for a work which seemed to me to have a touch of genius. As a drowning man is supposed to see in a flash the whole of his past life, so Hamlet, whom as the curtain rose we saw borne by the four captains to the stage, reviews his tragic story—with a strong bias towards the Freudian commentaries of German critics. The Name of Gertrude and Ophelia who, in different shades of green, are forever changing places in Hamlet's eyes, is Woman. The Prince is a neurotic: not mad in the good old-fashioned sense, perhaps, but certainly not normal. This ballet might well have been an absurdity or a bore: but a sound basis of scholarship with fine taste and invention (notably in Leslie Hurry's decor) combined to make it memorable.

When Helpmann essayed the play in 1944, the ballet was perhaps too recent: his command of the verse was certainly not equal to his mastery of movement. In 1948 he showed himself an accomplished actor with a sure touch when he played the part at Stratford-upon-Avon in Michael Benthall's production. This was a piece of colourful theatre, and Helpmann's acting was of the theatrical kind. Was the meaning of every line clear? Perhaps not: but the emotion was powerful. Had the wheel come full circle, taking us back to the Hamlets of Victorian days?

Alec Guinness made a determined bid to prevent this from happening. For the Festival of Britain 1951, Henry Sherek presented him as Hamlet in a production made by himself and Frank Hauser. The characters, dressed in early Jacobean costume at its most exaggerated, were shown in actuality as at the date of Shakespeare's writing the play: no romance, no poetry was allowed to blur the story of Renaissance villainy and intrigue in which this Hamlet found himself involved. Nor was he himself guiltless: "I am very proud, revengeful, ambitious"—these were exaggerations, perhaps, but not without foundation: and the persuasiveness which the performance certainly had derived from one's assurance that the actor was at all times honest with himself in creating the character. This is Guinness's shining virtue, and it is matched by an admirable lucidity of delivery. The over-elaborate production, which was dogged by mishaps, did not give him a proper chance: and this was a pity, because his performance should have given us the same stimulus as the modern-dress one of 1925 and forced us to think freshly of the play.

But when all is done, such treatment can, I think, only be a corrective: it cannot be finally satisfactory. Hamlet must be convincingly real as a person: but he must also be more than just a person. The play is a poem, and it is a tragedy: Hamlet is the hero. "Nothing extenuate" says another hero at his death, and in characterizing Hamlet the actor should obey that rule: but it is "a noble heart" which cracks when Hamlet dies, the heart of one created by the poet to epitomize that piece of work, a man.

The poet—yes, he is the creator: and in the last analysis the actor who most fully interprets the poet is the one who satisfies us. Is this not why Gielgud and Forbes-Robertson seem to emerge as the twin stars in my Hamlet firmament? Shaw writes of Forbes-Robertson, "he plays as Shakespeare should be played, on the line and to the line, with the acting and utterance simultaneous, inseparable and in fact identical". We have, in my *Hamlet*-going life, broken free of certain deadening elements in the tradition of Shakespearian acting. Have we not in doing so lost to some extent the understanding of the nature of dramatic poetry? The poet writes his verse so that its musical form heightens his dramatic effect. If that is fully realized, the actor has no need to look for anything new to do in a familiar part; it contains already an infinite variety of fresh inspiration in the marriage of sound with sense. The most recent *Hamlet* production at the Old Vic was not encouraging in this regard. Producers are still afraid that the modern audience has not got, or will not exercise, the auditory imagination which will make them receptive of poetic speaking. Actors do not give much study to the art, and it is too little taught in dramatic schools. Yet audiences for poetry are numerous and increasing, and actors do most of the poetry-reading: what they discover there they will surely come to practise on the stage. I still hope that Shakespeare, the poet-dramatist, will get another chance.[1]

[1] Since this article was written, I have seen Paul Scofield in Peter Brook's production of *Hamlet*, which has the distinction of being the first British offering to be seen in Moscow. Scofield alternated with Helpmann in Benthall's 'Victorian' production at Stratford (1948), but I did not see him then. His Hamlet in 1955 is pre-eminently a real man: the prince is subordinated to the human being. At the early performance I saw much of the detail of Shakespeare's poetry, and many of his psychological subtleties were missing: but what was portrayed was invariably true and moving. Alec Clunes' Claudius was outstanding: he made the difficult prayer-scene completely convincing, and showed us every movement of the character's mind.

THE DATE OF *HAMLET*

BY

E. A. J. HONIGMANN

Of all Shakespeare's plays *Hamlet* has attracted far more popular and critical attention than any other, and it is natural that we should want to know when it was written. No apology need be offered for the attempt to determine as precisely as possible the date of a work so outstanding in the annals of the theatre.[1]

That the text of the *Hamlet* we know belongs to the years 1598–1601 is generally agreed, the majority of modern scholars being in favour of 1601. Yet no recent survey of the available evidence has been made and, when we do examine this evidence carefully, it looks as though Shakespeare more probably produced the tragedy either late in 1599 or early in 1600.

Stylistic "internal" evidence does not help us, since the dates of the other plays written roughly at the same time are, on the whole, more uncertain than the date of *Hamlet* itself. We may, therefore, confine ourselves to the "external" facts. A fairly safe downward date is provided by the absence of *Hamlet* from the list by Francis Meres published in the autumn of 1598, and an unimpeachable upward date by the entry of the play in the Stationers' Register on 26 July 1602. The other evidence, from which a date between these limits has to be sought, is not so easy to interpret.

1. *Gabriel Harvey's Note.* In his copy of Speght's edition of *Chaucer* 1598, Harvey referred to *Hamlet* in an autograph note:

> The Earle of Essex much commendes Albions England: and not unworthily for diuerse notable pageants, before, & in the Chronicle. Sum Inglish, & other Histories nowhere more sensibly described, or more inwardly discouered. The Lord Mountioy makes the like account of Daniels peece of the Chronicle, touching the Vsurpation of Henrie of Bullingbrooke. which in deede is a fine, sententious, & politique peece of Poetrie: as proffitable, as pleasurable. The younger sort takes much delight in Shakespeares Venus, & Adonis: but his Lucrece, & his tragedie of Hamlet, Prince of Denmarke, haue it in them, to please the wiser sort.[2]

Both on the title-page and on the last page of the book Harvey signed his name and added the date 1598. This, nevertheless, does not mean that Harvey wrote all the marginalia in the book in 1598, for, as L. Kirschbaum observed,[3] Harvey sometimes added new notes in his books when he re-read them on later occasions—as one would expect. Some commentators, however, have thought that the allusion to *Hamlet* might be more precisely dated on the strength of other dateable details in Harvey's note, which continues with a eulogy of the poetry of Dyer and Raleigh:

> [Dyer's] Amaryllis, & Sir Walter Raleighs Cynthia, how fine & sweet inuentions? Excellent matter of emulation for Spencer, Constable, France, Watson, Daniel, Warner, Chapman, Siluester, Shakespeare, & the rest of owr florishing metricians.[4]

It was argued that Harvey, a close friend of Spenser, must have known that Spenser died in London in January 1599, and thereafter would not call him "florishing". But to this argument others countered that January 1599 cannot be taken as a safe *terminus ante quem* for Harvey's note because Watson, who is listed with Spenser, died in 1592. Though H. J. C. Grierson dismissed the "accidental inclusion of Watson's name in a hastily set down list",[5] Harvey's apparent mistake with Watson made the commentators uneasy about him; and the alternative suggestion that "florishing" meant "popular" or "sought after"[6] could not remove the feeling that there was something amiss with the note, for some of the metricians specified were certainly little in demand, if the complete absence of reprints of their books is any indication.[7]

Fortunately it can be shown that Harvey did not make a mistake about Watson. Evidently he used the word "florishing" in a technical sense, as frequently elsewhere:

Tria viuidissima Britannorum ingenia, Chaucerus, Morus, Juellus: Quibus addo tres florentissimas indoles, Heiuodum, Sidneium, Spencerum.

Poësie, a liuelie picture: and a more florishing purtrature, then the gallantest Springe of the yeare.

Eutrapeli stylus maxime viuidus, longeque omnium floridissimus.[8]

Many other examples could be quoted to corroborate that "flourishing", when used by Harvey to describe a writer, generally referred to style and not to popularity. As there is no verb in the sentence about "florishing metricians" it seems reasonable to suppose a verb in the past tense: Dyer's and Raleigh's poems *have been* excellent matter of emulation for Spenser and the rest. Uneasiness about Harvey's tenses would then be unjustified.

In the *Hamlet* note Harvey also writes of the Earl of Essex in the present tense (Essex was executed in February 1601); and he names Lord Mountjoy, who would normally be called by his new title after 1603, when he became Duke of Devonshire. I believe that the distrust aroused by Harvey's "mistake" about Watson is partly responsible for that sometimes displayed regarding these other possible "upper limits". Though Moore Smith, the first editor of the *Marginalia*, said firmly "that the note was certainly written before February 1601, and possibly in the latter part of 1598",[9] L. Kirschbaum has replied that a dead man's opinion can be quoted in the present tense,[10] and even that the creation of the Duke of Devonshire cannot be considered as an "upper limit" for Harvey's note, since (according to Kirschbaum) Elizabethans were not always careful about titles. Kirschbaum argued further that there is

one unimpeachable case which *proves* that Harvey did use the present tense in setting down a dead man's critical opinion, an evidential passage so apposite that it completely destroys the validity of the Essex reference as a limit in dating the note.

Another series of marginalia supplied the "proof":

In the beginning of the assemblie of Ladies. In a ballad 343...

Two cristall stones artificially sett in the botom of the fresh well: in the romant of the Rose. 123...

M. Digges hath the whole Aquarius of Palingenius bie hart: & takes mutch delight to repeate it often.[11]

Here, according to Kirschbaum, the numbers with the Chaucer notes refer to the foliation of the 1598 *Chaucer*: yet Thomas Digges died in 1595, and is quoted in the present tense.

Kirschbaum's point would be strong if Harvey had indeed referred to the 1598 *Chaucer*. But the numbers agree equally well with the 1561 *Chaucer*—and that destroys the more important part of his argument. Nevertheless, it must be admitted that a parallel is not essential to prove that the present *could* sometimes serve for the past.

In the sentence in question, however, the ultimate significance of Harvey's present tense may not be irretrievably lost. For "Essex much commendes" comes in the middle of a paragraph of similar statements in which the present tense and the word "now" are repeated to bear witness to the literary taste current at the moment. Harvey enumerates works "now freshest in request", i.e. he is concerned with up-to-date opinion. Though the commendation of a *dead* earl could conceivably deserve mention in a list such as Harvey's, it would be out-of-date and therefore out-of-place. The logical conclusion is that Essex was probably still alive when *Hamlet* pleased the wiser sort.

This conclusion can be supported by an argument deriving from H. J. C. Grierson.[12] Harvey's note on *Hamlet* seems to continue one in which "the King of Scotland" is mentioned (giving 1603 as upper limit), and "Lord Mountioy" (also giving 1603 as upper limit) is named in the *Hamlet* note itself. Though Kirschbaum has raised objections,[13] 1603 therefore seems a safe upper limit for the *Hamlet* note. If Harvey wrote after Essex's death he must consequently have written very shortly after. Though the present tense might be employed to give the opinion of dead men in academic controversy, it would be peculiar to find Essex quoted in the present in a gossipy note shortly after his sensational death.

It is just possible, of course, that Harvey had in mind the Ur-*Hamlet* of *c*. 1589 and not Shakespeare's revision. Many have regarded this lost *Hamlet* as Kyd's, but others have thought it an early work of Shakespeare himself.[14] In contrasting *Venus* and *Lucrece* Harvey seems to make a moralistic and not an artistic distinction: *Lucrece* will have pleased the wiser sort because it condemned lust, whereas *Venus* approved of it—not because it was a greater work of art. As works of art there is not much to choose between the two. Could Harvey then have praised *Hamlet* as well on purely moral grounds? If so, the immature Ur-*Hamlet* could have been meant. We may ignore this difficulty, I think, by recalling that the contemporary remarks about the Ur-*Hamlet* that survive are mostly derisive, which makes it unlikely that the wiser sort would have delighted in it on any grounds.

Taking all these considerations into account, we may tentatively date Harvey's note before February 1601.

2. *The "little eyases"*. In the First Folio text of *Hamlet* there occurs a passage about "little eyases" (II, ii, 352–79), which clearly alludes to the War of the Theatres and therefore could not have been written before the middle of 1601. In the Quarto of 1604 the passage is missing. We must consequently decide whether the 28 lines were interpolated in the Folio or cut from the Quarto.

Though there has been no lack of declarations in favour of the priority of the one or the other text, few detailed examinations of the problem have been published. Dover Wilson thought that the Quarto omitted the passage.[15] W. J. Lawrence thought that in the Folio the "little eyases" section

is not connective. Hamlet's last speech is not a reply to Rosencrantz's last. Originally, it was evoked by Rosencrantz's 'No indeede are they not.' Hamlet, then, asked no questions about the players' unpopularity, but simply went on to give another illustration of public caprice.[16]

This seems to me to be splitting hairs. Both texts read connectively—and that could almost be regarded as the decisive factor in establishing which came first. Dover Wilson pointed out that there are five longish passages in the Folio not found in the Quarto, and that three of these "omissions" from the Quarto "have left frayed edges" behind them.[17] If we put aside the "little eyases" passage, being the subject in dispute, then three out of four of the omissions from the Quarto caused disconnected dialogue. The fourth instance (IV, v, 161–3), moreover, occurs in a different type of context from the others, where Ophelia interrupts the normal flow of talk with her songs: here the dialogue consists of frayed edges, and one more or less would not show. In short, we may say that imperfect joints are to be expected with long omissions from the Quarto—what could be more natural?—and that nevertheless the absence of the "little eyases" lines does not seem to have damaged the texture of ideas in this rendering:

Ham. How chances it they trauaile? their residence both in reputation, and profit was better both wayes.
Ros. I thinke their inhibition, comes by the meanes of the late innouasion.
Ham. Doe they hold the same estimation they did when I was in the Citty; are they so followed.
Ros. No indeede are they not.
Ham. It is not very strange, for my Vncle is King of Denmarke, and those that would make mouths at him while my father liued, giue twenty, fortie, fifty, a hundred duckets a peece, for his Picture in little, s'bloud there is somthing in this more then naturall, if Philosophie could find it out.[18]

To explain the absence of the passage from the Quarto as an accident of the printing-house[19] is unsatisfactory, for the 'omission' seems too neat to be just an accident. To argue, on the other hand, that the passage was deliberately cut from the Quarto text because no longer topical[20] is equally unconvincing, since it was allowed to stand in the (prompt-copy) Folio text—and, after all, Shakespearian quartos do not seem to have been tampered with in this way as a rule. What is known of the provenance and transmission of the Quarto and Folio texts should favour the view that the "little eyases" lines were an afterthought in 1601. That this conclusion was reached independently by J. R. Brown in the latest and very valuable re-examination of the text of the Quarto gives it more consequence than will emerge in my sketchy reasoning.[21]

3. *Inhibition and innovation.* As important as the "little eyases" themselves, are the "inhibition" and "innovation" mentioned just before (II, ii, 346–7). Since "innovation" and its cognates were given the sense of "political upheaval" on the rare occasions when Shakespeare used them (which was only four times), it has been urged that in *Hamlet* too "innovation" must have this sense:[22] and then the Essex rebellion (8 February 1601) would best fit the facts. To this there are two objections. Firstly, the Essex rebellion did not lead to an "inhibition", for Shakespeare's company was asked to play at court only a fortnight later.[23] Secondly, the pirates of the First Quarto of *Hamlet* understood "innovation" to mean "novelty" and not "political upheaval":

Yfaith my Lord, noueltie carries it away,
For the principall publike audience that
Came to them, are turned to priuate playes,
And to the humour of children.[24]

3-2

Since no political upheaval of this period seems to have led to an inhibition I think that the pirate was right. What "noueltie", then, was intended?

On 22 June 1600 the Privy Council decreed that the many London playhouses were to be limited to two, that the two companies there were to perform only twice a week, and that any playhouse owners or actors who resisted this order were to be committed to prison.[25] This was an inhibition with a vengeance, and many have held that the *Hamlet* lines allude to it. Others, however, pointed to a later Privy Council order of 31 December 1601, in which it was stated that the 1600 order was not properly executed, the Justices of Middlesex and Surrey being requested to amend their apathy:[26] it was argued that if the 1600 order was ineffective it could not be regarded as an inhibition.

Whatever the ultimate repercussions of the 1600 order, there can be little doubt that it must have caused unquietness in theatrical circles immediately it was made public, when it could not be foreseen what line of action the Justices would take. It was by far the most unpleasant anti-theatrical move in the years to which *Hamlet* can be approximately assigned. The complaint of an inhibition in *Hamlet* therefore seems to imply June–July 1600, when a few at least of the smaller companies may have prudently withdrawn from London.[27]

It is quite true, of course, that the Privy Council ordered that theatres should be "plucked down", and that no more than two companies should be allowed in London, before 1600—as in the minutes of 28 July 1597, and of 19 February 1598.[28] But in the order of December 1601 the Council writes of the order of "about a yeare and a half since" as its principal regulation, not referring to any others, and the whole tenor of the 1600 order suggests that a fresh start was being made so as to settle matters once and for all. If the Council looked upon its 1600 order as its most important inhibition to date, we too may do so all the more readily.

It has been objected, again, that the 1600 order could not be meant, since the "tragedians of the city" are Shakespeare's own company, which was allowed to stay in London. But are they Shakespeare's company? The tragedians have been forced to travel, yet the purport of the "little eyases" passage is to comment on the continuing controversy between the children and the (Shakespearian) company at the Globe.[29] If we agree that the tragedians are not the Chamberlain's men, as I think we must, this too supports the view that the 1600 order is the "inhibition", as there was no other occasion between 1598 and 1601 when Shakespeare would feel impelled to speak up for the smaller adult companies (the order of 31 December 1601 is too late, for Shakespeare's attack on the boy-actors surely materialized before the War of the Theatres was fizzling out).

More useful in helping us to arrive at a decision is Hamlet's continuation—"It is not very strange; for mine uncle is king of Denmark..." (II, ii, 380 ff.). Both in the Quarto and the Folio these words follow the statement that a once popular adult company has become unpopular, with the reflection that this is not very strange, since the change from unpopularity to popularity, as in the case of Claudius, is also familiar. Shakespeare, however, does not confine himself to one company of actors and one king—he has two of each. Claudius is now king, but there were "those that would make mows at him while my father lived". In the figures of the kings, Shakespeare continues the exposition of theatrical affairs, Claudius standing for the boy-actors; for, as we know, the public did make mows at the "musty fopperies of antiquity" performed by the boys when they resumed their activities *c.* 1599.[30] The kings are not really a suitable analogue to the War of the Theatres, however, for Old Hamlet would have to represent Shakespeare's company, which was not dead but competing vigorously with the boys. On the other hand the "tragedians of the city" *were* dead—in so far as they had left London and no longer competed there—so that one suspects that the parallel of the two kings was originally intended as a comment on their fate. This again suggests that the "little eyases" were a late insertion in the text.

The "innovation", if not political, must have been theatrical—as the context makes sufficiently clear: and the great theatrical novelty *c.* 1600 was the renewal of acting by the boys. The "inhibition" of 1600 was directly due to the "multitude of plaie howses",[31] which was naturally made worse by the children. Although the children played in "private houses" this was a mere quibble to get round the law, and anti-theatrical opinion classed them as no better than "common players".[32] Thus the "innovation" of the children might be viewed as the cause of the 1600 "inhibition" (especially by their professional enemies). In the Quarto, Shakespeare said so in passing; when the children later "berattled" the common stages and a rebuke was deemed necessary, the least irksome means to this end would have been to expand a play which already dealt with the subject: in short, to add the "little eyases" lines which are not found in the (foul paper) Quarto but survive in the (prompt-copy) Folio text.

4. The "*humorous man*". W. J. Lawrence thought that "the humorous man shall end his part in peace" (*Hamlet*, II, ii, 335–6) refers to the trouble brought about by the original conclusion of *Every Man Out of his Humour*,[33] and Sir Edmund Chambers added "Lawrence may be right".[34] Lawrence therefore dated *Hamlet* in 1600.

Jonson dated *Every Man Out* in 1599 in the 1616 Folio, and the play made fun of *Julius Caesar* (? spring/summer, 1599), and of *Histriomastix* (? autumn, 1599), which suggests autumn/winter, 1599 as the likeliest date for it. As Lawrence also believed that the "inhibition" in *Hamlet* (II, ii, 346) was the order of June 1600, he evidently thought that *Hamlet* took half a year or more to write. Though I do not feel that "the humorous man" was necessarily a joke at Jonson's expense—the phrase can be accounted for on other equally plausible grounds[35]—the hypothesis of a protracted period of composition is not unappealing.

5. '*Hamlet*' and '*Julius Caesar*'. In *Hamlet*, III, ii, 104–11 Polonius is asked about his acting "i' the university". Polonius says that he once acted Julius Caesar:

> I did enact Julius Caesar: I was killed i' the Capitol; Brutus killed me.

Now it happens that *Julius Caesar* is one of Shakespeare's few plays that can be dated with some confidence—namely, in the spring/summer of 1599.[36] As *Hamlet* belongs to more or less the same period it is natural to assume that the rather forced allusion to Caesar could have been partly due to the fact that *Julius Caesar* was in repertoire when *Hamlet* was produced.

The impression that *Hamlet* followed *Julius Caesar* is borne out by two coincidences. First, the two actors who played the original Hamlet and Polonius—almost certainly Burbage and Heminges—must have taken Brutus and Caesar in *Julius Caesar*, if we can trust modern casting-methods and the researches of present-day scholars into "Shakespeare's personnel".[37] Polonius would then be speaking on the extra-dramatic level in proclaiming his murder in the part of Caesar, since Hamlet (Burbage) will soon be killing him (Heminges) once more in *Hamlet*.

Second, the completely gratuitous anecdote about playing "i' the university" seems to corroborate that the passage in question contains extra-dramatic meanings. Shakespeare does not allude to playing in the university in any other work, while the First Quarto of *Hamlet* is the only early text of Shakespeare to announce on the title-page that it had been performed at a university:

As it hath beene diuerse times acted by his Highnesse seruants in the Cittie of London: as also in the two Vniuersities of Cambridge and Oxford, and else-where.

It may be objected at this stage that if the "little eyases" are claimed to be an interpolation—then the "Julius Caesar" passage could have been added later too. The text of the Second Quarto provides an adequate reply: the "Julius Caesar" passage is not omitted from it—unlike the "little eyases". As it is generally agreed that the Quarto was printed from Shakespeare's foul papers one would not expect a "later insertion" to be found in it.

If we are willing to allow that *Hamlet* followed *Julius Caesar* we can narrow the date-limit for *Hamlet* by a year. That the composition of the two plays overlapped is not very likely in this case, they being so similar (a noble, introspective hero has to commit a murder for which he feels no enthusiasm, and so on). One can imagine Shakespeare writing a comedy and a tragedy simultaneously: but would he take up Hamlet until he realized that he had not exploited his theme to the full with Brutus? This reasoning leads us to the autumn of 1599 as the *terminus a quo* for *Hamlet*.

6. '*Hamlet*' *and Marston*. Literary parallels are always a last resort for chronologers. Often, of course, supposed parallels are not parallels at all; but those between Marston's *Antonio's Revenge*, 1602, and *Hamlet* are too many and too arresting to allow of any explanations except imitation one way or the other.[38] *Antonio's Revenge* was dated "in the early winter of 1599" by Sir Edmund Chambers,[39] the Prologue providing the indication of season:

> THE rawish danke of clumzie winter ramps
> The fluent summers vaine: and drizling sleete
> Chilleth the wan bleak cheek of the numd earth,
> Whilst snarling gusts nibble the juyceles leaves,
> From the nak't shuddring branch.[40]

Here the references to "drizling sleete" rather than to snow, and to "juyceles leaves" still to be seen on the trees, suggest the *early* winter.

But the Prologue for *Antonio's Revenge* must have been written when the tragedy was ready for the stage, and therefore the composition of the play can be assigned to the autumn (early winter) of 1599. As either *Hamlet* or *Antonio's Revenge* was most probably completed before the other was begun, and as Shakespeare would hardly have dashed off *Hamlet* in the autumn of 1599 immediately after *Julius Caesar* and yet preceding *Antonio's Revenge*, it seems warrantable to assume that Marston's tragedy came before Shakespeare's. There are several jumps in this reasoning, the most dangerous being that the *year* for *Antonio's Revenge* (1599) is not a certainty. But as the conclusion towards which we are driven does not quarrel with the other facts, we may entertain it, with all due caution: the conclusion, that is, that the winter of 1599 should be considered the *terminus a quo* for *Hamlet*.

Various parallels to *Hamlet* are also to be found in Marston's *Malcontent* 1604 (a play which may belong to the year 1600),[41] and one of these has been claimed as proof that in this case

Marston was the debtor.[42] Hamlet's famous apostrophe of man is echoed by Mendoza's apostrophe of woman:

sweet women, most sweete Ladies, nay Angells...in body how delicate, in soule how witty, in discourse how pregnant, in life how wary, in favours how juditious, in day how sociable, and in night, how?[43]

As everyone knows, Shakespeare adapted a Renaissance commonplace. But no one seems to have observed that Marston may also have followed a tradition. Two typical 'parallels' will serve as examples:

the most excellent and great God (principally Architect, of this worldly frame) hauing with al beautie bedecked the celestiall regions...in the end made man, being of al worldly creatures the most miraculous, ...if a man addict himself only to feeding and nourishment, hee becommeth a Plante, if to things sensuall, he is as a brute beast, if to things reasonable & ciuil, he groweth a celestial creature: but if he exalt the beautiful gift of his mind, to thinges inuisible and diuine, hee transfourmeth himselfe into an Angel; and to conclude, becommeth the sonne of God.[44]

women...models of heauen, and Goddesses on earth...Women are in churches, Saints: abroad, Angels: at home, deuills: at windowes Syrens: at doores, pyes: and in gardens, Goates.[45]

The turn of phrase in the two plays, however, makes it extremely inprobable that both their speeches were independently inspired. Since the *Hamlet* passage falls in line with a much more important tradition it might seem logical to date it first. But why does Hamlet add "man delights not me: *no, nor woman neither*, though by your smiling you seem to say so" (II, ii, 321–3)? It seems just possible that Hamlet's afterthought implies the precedence of Marston's speech—and therefore the *Malcontent* of 1600, if there was one, cannot really help us with the date of *Hamlet*.

7. *Ostend.* Dover Wilson's publications on *Hamlet* in the 1930's convinced Sir Edmund Chambers that his own date for the play (1600) was wrong, and in *Shakespearean Gleanings* (1944) Chambers agreed that 1601 was more likely.[46] Chambers was persuaded on account of the "little eyases" passage which, he admitted, must belong to the summer/autumn of 1601. But he did not moot the possibility that the passage might be an interpolation. Moreover, Chambers felt, the "innovation" in *Hamlet* (II, ii, 346), must have been a political upheaval. Here he ought to have added that the First Quarto pirate interpreted "innovation" as "noueltie" (see above, p. 27). The first part of Chambers's paper seems to have been written rather hurriedly. Although he was won over to 1601, however, he devoted the greater number of his pages to the rejection of the supposed "Ostend allusion" in *Hamlet*, IV, iv:

> We go to gain a little patch of ground
> That hath in it no profit but the name.
> To pay five ducats, five, I would not farm it....

Wilson had elaborated the theory that the siege of Ostend (begun in June 1601) is referred to, and therefore it is important for us that Chambers, accepting his date, could not assent to the theory.

8. *Parallels*. Beside being the most frequently imitated and echoed play of the age, *Hamlet* is also full of striking phrases which are themselves borrowed from popular usage. Even today many of these have not been spotted by the editors. For instance, Polonius's advice that one should grapple one's friends to one's soul with hoops of steel (I, iii, 63) may be indebted to a proverb—or to Thomas Churchyard:

friendship is most fit to knit the joints and minds of men together, and bind them about with such brazen bands, that no bars of iron may break, no policy of people may put asunder....[47]

Hamlet's tag "this goodly frame, the earth" (II, ii, 310) may be lifted out of Sir Richard Barckley's *Discourse of the Felicitie of Man* (1598)[48], the felicity of man being actually the subject of Hamlet's speech; yet the tag was a commonplace long before:

the foundation of the world is in a manner worne out, and also this goodly frame ready to fall vpon our shoulders....[49]

As F. P. Wilson noted, Hamlet's "sea of troubles" (III, i, 59) had already appeared in Barckley's *Discourse*[50]—indeed, this was a favourite cliché in 1598:

let them...throw *Pelion* and *Ossa* the Giants weight vpon vs, we know we shall rise againe. By these practises both you my Lords, and you good people may easily discerne, that this world is a very sea of trobles.[51]

> And from the dungen of the darke abysse,
> Wherein the Ocean Seas of troubles flowe,
> I doe ascend.[52]

The very vocabulary of the play still needs much elucidation. Memorable lines, such as "When we have shuffled off this mortal coil" (III, i, 67), have been claimed to contain words with new meanings, as witness Dover Wilson's note:

'shuffle off' means 'shirk' or 'evade' (cf. *Tw. Nt.* 3, 3, 16); its modern sense of disencumbering oneself hastily of some garment or wrap is derived from *Hamlet*.[53]

But the word "shuffle" occurred in clothing contexts in the Vestiarian Controversy in the 1560's:

to be shufflyd in a surples, whiche the Popes clergye wear, were rather a confusion then an order....[54]

In brief, we cannot trust 'parallels'. Those drawn up above were almost certainly common property before Shakespeare: even though several of the books quoted were printed in 1598 we cannot attach any significance to this date.

9. *Conclusion*. Now to sum up the various arguments. It seems that *Hamlet* was written after Meres's *Palladis Tamia* (September 1598), after *Julius Caesar* (spring/summer, 1599), and perhaps after *Antonio's Revenge* (? early winter, 1599) and *Every Man Out of his Humour* (1599, probably autumn/winter); the "inhibition" in *Hamlet* II, ii, 346 is most easily explained as an allusion to the Privy Council order of June 1600. At the other end, *Hamlet* was entered in the Stationers' Register in July 1602; allusions to the War of the Theatres take us back to 1601

and, if these allusions are insertions, as I have contended, to before the middle of 1601, Gabriel Harvey's note suggesting a date prior to February 1601. All in all we may say that *Hamlet* seems to have been written after late 1599 and before the summer of 1601, perhaps before February 1601; and the most likely date of composition seems to be late 1599 to early 1600.

NOTES

1. I am indebted to the Editor for his very helpful suggestions, many of which I have used.
2. *Gabriel Harvey's Marginalia*, ed. G. C. Moore Smith (Stratford-upon-Avon, 1913), p. 232.
3. 'The Date of Shakespeare's *Hamlet*', *Studies in Philology*, XXXIV (1937), 168–75.
4. *Op. cit.* p. 233.
5. Review of *Gabriel Harvey's Marginalia*, *Modern Language Review*, XII (1917), 218–21.
6. Moore Smith, *op. cit.* p. x; W. J. Lawrence, 'The Date of Shakespeare's *Hamlet*', *Shakespeare's Workshop* (Oxford, 1928), ch. VI, p. 99; F. S. Boas, 'The Date of *Hamlet* & Gabriel Harvey's "Marginalia"', *Shakespeare & the Universities* (Oxford, 1923), p. 258.
7. No second edition of any work by Thomas Watson is recorded in *S.T.C.*
8. *Gabriel Harvey's Marginalia*, pp. 122, 159, 160. Cf. *O.E.D.*, flourish, *verb*, 7.
9. *Op. cit.* p. xi.
10. Kirschbaum, *op. cit.* pp. 172 ff.
11. *Gabriel Harvey's Marginalia*, pp. 160–61; cf. Kirschbaum, *op. cit.* pp. 172–3.
12. *Op. cit.* pp. 218–21.
13. *Op. cit.* p. 174. The reader should also be referred to H. D. Gray's argument that Harvey's note belongs to the year 1605 ('The Date of *Hamlet*', *Journal of English and Germanic Philology*, XXXI (1932), 51–61). Gray supposed that Harvey meant the third Earl of Essex. But the third earl was only fourteen or fifteen in 1605, which ought to have disqualified him from a place in a survey of the most enlightened literary opinion such as Harvey's; and in 1605 Mountjoy had become Devonshire. None of Gray's reasons for a late date is very strong, while those against it are considerable.
14. Cf. 'Shakespeare's "Lost Source-Plays"', *Modern Language Review*, XLIX (1954), 298–300.
15. *The Manuscript of Shakespeare's "Hamlet"* (Cambridge, 1934), I, 96 ff.
16. *Op. cit.* pp. 107–8.
17. *Op. cit.* I, 97.
18. *Hamlet*, Q2, sig. F2b.
19. J. Dover Wilson, *op. cit.* I, 97.
20. *Id.* I, 98.
21. J. R. Brown's article in *Studies in Bibliography. Papers of the Bibliographical Society of the University of Virginia*, VII (1955), 31.
22. See F. S. Boas, *Shakespeare & the Universities* (Oxford, 1923), p. 23 n.
23. Chambers, *William Shakespeare*, I, 65.
24. Sig. E3a.
25. Chambers, *The Elizabethan Stage*, IV, 329–32.
26. *Id.* IV, 332–4.
27. In this paragraph I have followed W. J. Lawrence (*Shakespeare's Workshop*, ch. VI).
28. Chambers, *The Elizabethan Stage*, IV, 322, 325.
29. The "little eyases" lines discuss the War of the Theatres in the present and in the past, but the past does not mean that the war is over. There is some recapitulation of what has recently happened, but the present tenses prove that the struggle was still going on: "little eyases...*are now* the fashion, and so berattle the common stages...*that many...dare scarce come thither*", "there has been much to-do on *both sides*: and the nation *holds* it is no sin to tarre them to controversy".
30. See Chambers, *The Elizabethan Stage*, II, 20.
31. *Id.* IV, 329–33.

32. *Id.* II, 508, 511.

33. *Id.* ch. VI.

34. Chambers, *William Shakespeare*, I, 423.

35. It has been suggested that in enumerating the stock character-types of the stage, Hamlet speaks ironically of the chief characters in the play (II, ii, 332–9): the king (Claudius) shall be my sovereign—for a while; the adventurous knight (Laertes) shall show off his swordsmanship; the lover (Hamlet) shall not sigh gratis; the humorous man (Polonius) shall be allowed to finish his never-ending speeches—and later "rest in peace"; the clown (gravedigger) shall make men laugh; the lady (Ophelia) shall reveal what is on her mind in her songs, which halt the blank verse. This interpretation would resolve the need for a topical innuendo in "the humorous man".

36. See E. K. Chambers, *William Shakespeare*, I, 397.

37. See T. W. Baldwin, *The Organization and Personnel of the Shakespearean Company* (1927), pp. 228–9; Eduard Castle, 'Zu dem Problem: Shakespeare und seine Truppe' (*Shakespeare Jahrbuch*, XVII (Weimar, 1940), 57–111), who prints nineteenth-century actor-lists in which Hamlet and Brutus were assigned to one actor, and Polonius and Caesar to another actor. C. J. Sisson reminds me that Shakespeare might have intended a reference to the *Caesar Interfectus* which was acted at Oxford *c.* 1582 (E. K. Chambers, *The Elizabethan Stage*, III, 309), rather than to his own play. If this were the case the Burbage-Heminges theory would have to be abandoned; but I find the possibility of a reference to *Julius Caesar* more attractive.

38. See F. Radebrecht, *Shakespeares Abhaengigkeit von John Marston* (Coethen, 1918), pp. 24 ff.

39. E. K. Chambers, *The Elizabethan Stage*, III, 430. Donald J. McGinn, in 'A New Date for *Antonio's Revenge*', *PMLA*, LIII (1938), 129–37, dated Marston's play in the winter/spring of 1600/1601, after *Hamlet*. If he is right, my point here would have to be discounted: but McGinn's dating forces him to ignore the chronological implications of "*Anno Domini* 1599...*Etatis suæ* 24" in *Antonio and Mellida* v. i, which I am reluctant to do.

40. *The Plays of John Marston*, ed. H. Harvey Wood (1934), I, 69.

41. E. K. Chambers, *The Elizabethan Stage*, III, 432; also H. R. Walley, 'The Dates of *Hamlet* and Marston's *The Malcontent*', *Review of English Studies*, IX (1933), 397–409, and E. E. Stoll, 'The Date of *The Malcontent*: A Rejoinder', *Review of English Studies*, XI (1935), 42–50.

42. *The Works of John Marston*, ed. J. O. Halliwell (1856), II, 300.

43. *The Malcontent*, I, v (Marston, ed. Wood, I, 154–5).

44. Annibale Romei, *The Courtiers Academie* (1598), pp. 47–8.

45. John Florio, *Florios Second Frutes* (1591), sigs. Z3a–Z4a.

46. 'The Date of *Hamlet*' (*Shakespearean Gleanings*, pp. 68–75).

47. *A Sparke of Friendship* (1588) (see *The Harleian Miscellany* (ed. 1808), III, 263).

48. P. 4.

49. R. Harvey, *An Astrological Discourse* (1583), p. 42.

50. F. P. Wilson, *Shakespeare and the Diction of Common Life* (British Academy Shakespeare Lecture, 1941), p. 6.

51. S. Gosson, *The Trumpet of Warre. A Sermon* (1598), sig. F1a.

52. T. Rogers, *Celestiall Elegies* (1598), quatorzain 12, in *A Lamport Garland*, ed. Charles Edmonds (1881).

53. *Hamlet*, ed. J. D. Wilson (Cambridge, 1948), p. xxxiv.

54. The copy of the book which I have seen (B.M. 3932, a. 48 (5) sig. C1ᵛ) had lost its title-page.

HAMLET AND THE COURT OF ELSINORE

BY

R. A. FOAKES

The court of Elsinore which is the focal point of all the action in *Hamlet* has a dual character, realized largely by means of style and imagery. The good values of the court are presented through its honour and dignity, through qualities associated with the majesty and eloquence of style in the play; the unpleasant side of the court through the imagery that springs from and extends the significance of the action. These aspects are important in setting the tone and establishing the themes, for they are made actual on the stage from the beginning, and the final revelation of evil is brought about through the conflict between them. Writers on the imagery of *Hamlet* have given a gloomy picture of the play's atmosphere as one in which poison, disease and corruption are 'dominant';[1] this is misleading, for though corruption underlies the play's action, it exists chiefly in Hamlet's imagination: as a result, it is latent rather than actual, like the murder of Hamlet's father, which is not seen, but remains always in the background. The oppositions between the honour and the prison-like nature of the court are at least as important in creating the atmosphere of *Hamlet*, and a consideration of them suggests a more balanced picture. For corruption is significant only in relation to what is good or fine, and plays in which it is dominant, as several Jacobean examples testify, tend to be horrific or grotesque.

One of the most prominent features of *Hamlet* is the ceremonious and stately diction of the court. When the major characters speak in public they have generally a leisured way of speaking, using many words to say little, freely amplifying and illustrating, as when the King complains of Hamlet's excess of grief:

> 'tis a fault to heaven,
> A fault against the dead, a fault to nature,
> To reason most absurd; whose common theme
> Is death of fathers, and who still hath cried,
> From the first corse till he that died to-day,
> 'This must be so'.　　　　　　　　　　　　(I, ii, 101–6)

or when Hamlet welcomes the news that the players are coming:

> He that plays the king shall be welcome; his majesty shall have tribute of me; the adventurous knight shall use his foil and target; the lover shall not sigh gratis....　　　　(II, ii, 332–5)

This rhetorical way of speaking appears in the devices of Hamlet's excuse to Laertes, "Was't Hamlet wrong'd Laertes? Never Hamlet", in the marked pompousness of the verse Rosencrantz and Guildenstern use for intercourse with the King, and in the formal balance of such lines as:

> *King.*　　Thanks, Rosencrantz and gentle Guildenstern.
> *Queen.*　Thanks, Guildenstern and gentle Rosencrantz.　　　　(II, ii, 33–4)

The artifice becomes conscious in the affectation of Osric, in the slow end-stopped bombast of the play within the play, and in the language of Polonius. It is a 'public' manner of speaking,

35

which tends to sound similar in the mouths of different characters, and preserves an outward stateliness and formality in the court.

While it is more or less habitual to the practised courtiers like Polonius, Laertes or Osric, it may also afford a screen behind which truth can be concealed, and there is a strong contrast between the public and private speech of several characters, notably Claudius and Hamlet.[2] Claudius, for instance, has a more direct and personal manner when praying, trying to obtain information, or plotting with an accomplice, but for the most part he is shown speaking in public, as when he asks Rosencrantz and Guildenstern to watch Hamlet, and says[3]

> Something have you heard
> Of Hamlet's transformation; so call it,
> Sith nor the exterior nor the inward man
> Resembles that it was.... (II, ii, 4–7)

This is the courtly mode of speaking, and the same cadence is echoed a little later in the same scene, in a speech for which Gertrude rebukes Polonius:

> your noble son is mad:
> Mad call I it; for, to define true madness,
> What is't but to be nothing else but mad? (II, ii, 92–4)

It is the vice of Polonius that he exaggerates the worst features of the style, and on this occasion the King and Queen are eager for fact and have no time for rhetoric; "More matter, with less art", cries Gertrude.

Other elements in the play contribute to this formal, rhetorical tone. There is endless moralizing and sententiousness; Claudius is ready with long-winded and commonplace advice for Hamlet, and so are Polonius for Laertes, Laertes for Ophelia, and Hamlet for the players. Many characters besides Polonius are stored with proverbs or 'sentences'.[4] Set speeches and formal descriptions abound, such as Horatio's account of events in Denmark, the Ghost's tale of the murder, Hamlet's speech on man, Gertrude's description of Ophelia's death, Hamlet's story of the sea-battle. The use of hendiadys, commoner in this play than in any other of Shakespeare's,[5] also gives weight and amplification to the style; often the words barely modify each other, but simply duplicate the sense, "food and diet", "cheer and comfort", "pith and marrow", "book and volume", "grace and mercy", "lecture and advice", "duty and obedience", so that the effect is one of slight pompousness, of using two words where one would be enough.

All these formal elements are present in some of the 'public' speeches, such as the court flattery of Rosencrantz. The pomp and spaciousness of such diction is part of the atmosphere of *Hamlet*. The court of Elsinore is a place of ostensible stateliness and nobility; affairs of state, dealings with ambassadors, preparations for war, enter into the action, and many of the 'pictures' the play presents on the stage, its direct images, are static or nearly so, like the pictorial effect of the dumb-show in the play scene, of Hamlet's contemplation of Claudius praying, of the pictures in the closet-scene, and of the skulls in the graveyard-scene.[6]

This dignity is enhanced by the frequent imagery of war, not the hurly-burly, clamour, movement and destruction of war—there are no battles in the play—but war with an air of chivalry, reflected in the personal challenges which old Fortinbras had made to Hamlet's father, and Laertes makes later to Hamlet. War is a pursuit of honour, and the exercise of arms is a courtly accomplishment. 'Honour' governs also in Laertes's quarrel with Hamlet; when Hamlet apologizes, Laertes is "satisfied in nature", but

> in my terms of honour
> I stand aloof; and will no reconcilement,
> Till by some elder masters, of known honour,
> I have a voice and precedent of peace. (v, ii, 257–60)

There is, too, a very real warlikeness about the state of Denmark; this extends from the opening scene, in which the soldiers standing on guard against possible attack from Norway are startled by the "martial stalk" of the armed Ghost, to the return at the end of the play of Fortinbras "with conquest come from Poland". Imagery of war is common in the language of most characters, of Hamlet especially, who, in addition, asks to hear of the Trojan war from the Players, and reports his share in a sea-battle with pirates. Even Gertrude, the "imperial jointress to this warlike state", can describe Hamlet's wild looks in these terms:

> as the sleeping soldiers in the alarm,
> Your bedded hair, like life in excrements,
> Starts up, and stands an end. (III, iv, 120–2)

A martial bearing in life, "An eye like Mars, to threaten and command", and martial honours in death are the marks of nobility, and it is appropriate that Hamlet's body should be carried off ceremoniously:

> Let four captains
> Bear Hamlet, like a soldier, to the stage...
> The soldiers' music and the rites of war
> Speak loudly for him. (v, ii, 406–11)

There are other courtly accomplishments; one is the bookishness of Hamlet and the "scholar" Horatio, which links with the many classical references, and with the appreciation of the actors and their plays by Polonius and Hamlet; the latter's advice to the players may stem from the "saws of books" that "youth and observation" have copied in his mind. Books twice play some part in the action, first when Hamlet enters reading, to be disturbed by the questions of Polonius, and later when Ophelia pretends to be reading while waiting for him. Music and games are also important, and all go together to make that "rose and expectancy of the fair state" which Ophelia saw in Hamlet:

> The courtier's, soldier's, scholar's, eye, tongue, sword. (III, i, 159)

Significant, too, is the strong religious emphasis in the play for its part in establishing the grace and ceremony of Elsinore, and the main impression is of dignity, pomp and pompousness, so that Laertes' complaint that his father has been given an obscure funeral stirs sympathy; it is wrong that such a high official and dignitary should receive

> No trophy, sword, nor hatchment o'er his bones,
> No noble rite nor formal ostentation. (IV, v, 214–15)

For all its spaciousness in diction, the court of Elsinore is closed and secretive. Only rarely does the action move into the open air; and in these scenes there is no sense of unoppressed space as on the wind-swept heath in *King Lear*, and no change of location, such as *Othello* shows with its transition from Venice to Cyprus, and *Macbeth* with its excursion into England. *Hamlet* is unusual among Shakespeare's plays, and unique among the tragedies, in maintaining a rough unity of place: the court is the focus of all the action, and no characters truly escape from it. Denmark, or more strictly Elsinore, is indeed a prison, as Hamlet says; he is not allowed to return to Wittenberg, and suffers restraint in more ways than one. When eventually he does leave the court, he goes under the close guard of Rosencrantz and Guildenstern and, if the intentions of Claudius were to be carried out, would be journeying to his death. On the way to England he is taken prisoner, ironically, by pirates, who treat him with more respect than did the king. The only other character of importance to depart the court is Laertes, and Polonius sends Reynaldo to spy on him in Paris. The Ghost comes from prison to warn Hamlet, from where he is "confined to fast in fires", and forbidden "to tell the secrets of my prison-house". Even Claudius, burdened by conscience, is imprisoned in spirit if not in body:

> O limed soul, that, struggling to be free,
> Art more engaged! (III, iii, 68–9)

In addition, Hamlet is under constant watch, spied on by Claudius and his agents Rosencrantz, Guildenstern, Polonius, and even by Ophelia, who is employed as a decoy in the nunnery scene; and in turn Hamlet and Horatio spy on Claudius in the play-scene. From the opening scene, with its group of characters keeping "this same strict and most observant watch", spying is one of the main characteristics of *Hamlet*. Claudius makes Hamlet stay in Denmark in "the cheer and comfort of our eye", and with Polonius hides so that "seeing unseen" he may watch him; in more than one sense is Hamlet "the observed of all observers". This mutual observing reflects what seems to be a universal need to see in order to believe, as in the opening scene,[7]

> I might not this believe
> Without the sensible and true avouch
> Of mine own eyes, (I, i, 56–7)

or in Hamlet's desire to see Claudius reveal his guilt,

> For I mine eyes will rivet to his face. (III, ii, 90)

But what is seen has to be interpreted, and may still not reveal the truth; it may indeed be a deliberate attempt to mislead. Polonius reaches the wrong conclusions in spite of his zeal in looking into Ophelia's love for Hamlet:

> If I had play'd the desk or table-book,
> Or given my heart a winking, mute and dumb,
> Or look'd upon this love with idle sight;
> What might you think? (II, ii, 136–9)

In his plans to murder Hamlet, Claudius tries to ensure that his stratagem will not be detected, that what is seen will be misinterpreted; but although he takes care to avoid trouble from the multitude "who like not in their judgement, but their eyes", and to prevent a mistake that would let "our drift look through our bad performance", his plans fail. Hamlet continually endeavours to see reality, and strip off false appearances; he employs the actors who "hold the mirror up to nature" to reveal what really happened at the death of his father, and in the scenes with Ophelia and his mother his aim is similar. The scene with Ophelia,

I have heard of your paintings...God has given you one face, and you make yourselves another...

(III, i, 148–50)

is poignant because he is mistaken, and the closet scene terrible because of the doubts it leaves. Hamlet sets up a glass where Gertrude may "see the inmost part" of herself, and cries, showing her the two portraits of his father and Claudius,

> Have you eyes?
> Could you on this fair mountain leave to feed,
> And batten on this moor? Ha! have you eyes?   (III, iv, 65–7)

She confesses, "Thou turn'st mine eyes into my very soul", but the confusion between the shows of things and the truth remains; for only Hamlet sees the Ghost:

> *Hamlet.* Do you see nothing there?
> *Gertrude.* Nothing at all; yet all that is I see.   (III, iv, 131–2)

Polonius is killed while spying and Ophelia is spurned because she acts as a decoy; perhaps they would both have done better to follow Hamlet's advice, "Let the doors be shut upon him, that he may play the fool no where but in's own house", and "Get thee to a nunnery"; they would have been safer behind locked doors, imprisoned. In the last scene, when Hamlet recognizes treachery, he cries, "Ho! let the doors be lock'd", and the stage becomes a prison indeed for the final slaughter; at the end he dies, giving a new beauty and relevance to an old image:

> as this fell sergeant, death,
> Is strict in his arrest....   (V, ii, 347–8)

For, as is continually brought out in action and image, the court of Elsinore is a prison, a place of spying and watching. All the characters must try to deceive each other, and in particular Hamlet and Claudius must conceal their true motives and aims. To do this, all indulge in play acting, make use of the artificial ceremonious court diction, and in their behaviour, as Polonius says,

> with devotion's visage
> And pious action we do sugar o'er
> The devil himself.   (III, i, 47–9)

Claudius recognizes the contrast between his deed and his "most painted word", Hamlet puts on an "antic disposition", and deceit affects everything. All those who spy on Hamlet have something to conceal from him, as he keeps the discovery of the Ghost secret:

> If you have hitherto conceal'd this sight,
> Let it be tenable in your silence still.   (I, ii, 247–8)

Laertes persuades Ophelia that Hamlet's vows are false; Reynaldo may "put on" Laertes what forgeries he pleases, and Ophelia is made to "colour" her loneliness by reading. All put up a barrier of deceit, innocence, even madness, and the players who come to the court symbolize the state of affairs there, as their playlet represents what has happened there.

Behind the appearance, feigned or real, the spying and counter-spying are carried on, so that Hamlet thinks of himself both as hunted:

> why do you go about to recover the wind of me, as if you would drive me into a toil?
>
> (III, ii, 361–2)

and as a hunter, setting a trap in the play within the play, or a falconer:

> We'll e'en to't like French falconers. fly at any thing we see.   (II, ii, 449–50)

Laertes falls into his own snare, "as a woodcock to mine own springe"; Polonius "hunts the trail of policy", and the Danish rabble surges after Laertes like a pack of hunting dogs:

> How cheerfully on the false trail they cry!
> O, this is counter, you false Danish dogs!   (IV, v, 109–10)

All these aspects of the play's language spring from action, and indicate the more unpleasant features of the Danish court. The prison-like close watching and secrecy of Elsinore is all designed to reveal, prevent the discovery of, or hide the evil Hamlet is trying to expose. A sense of this evil, of "rank corruption mining all within" is conveyed in imagery of sickness, the nastier aspects of sex and food, dirt and weeds. Sickness seems to extend through the play as Francisco's "I am sick at heart" in the opening lines is caught up in the "heart-ache" of Hamlet's soliloquy in III, i, and again just before the duel, "thou wouldst not think how ill all's here about my heart". As Hamlet probes in order to test the Ghost's words and is betrayed by all except Horatio, the whole universe comes to seem "thought-sick at the act" of his mother's marriage with Claudius. Even the living are rotten and diseased in Denmark, as the gravedigger says in his significant reply to Hamlet's question, put amid the dirt and decay of the graveyard, "How long will a man lie i' the earth ere he rot?"

> I' faith, if he be not rotten before he die—as we have many pocky corses now-a-days, that will scarce hold the laying in—he will last you some eight year....   (V, i, 180–3)

The court of Elsinore is then at the same time a place of nobility, chivalry, dignity, religion, and a prison, a place of treachery, spying and, underlying this, corruption. Both of these aspects are equally real and important. In the creation of both the play-scene is central, as it is central in time and action. Its dialogue of stiff rhymed couplets is the most formal and stately in the play, with its continual generalization:

> But what we do determine oft we break.
> Purpose is but the slave to memory....
> The great man down, you mark his favourite flies;
> The poor advanced makes friends of enemies.
> And hitherto doth love on fortune tend;
> For who not needs shall never lack a friend,
> And who in want a hollow friend doth try,
> Directly seasons him his enemy....   (III, ii, 197 ff.)

and its formal personifications, Phoebus, Tellus, Neptune, Hymen; but these are only extreme forms of features found elsewhere in *Hamlet*, the habit of generalizing, common especially to Polonius and to the courtly figures, the frequent personification, much of it memorable, as of frailty (I, ii, 146), occasion (I, iii, 54), brevity (II, ii, 90), fortune (II, ii, 228 ff.; 515 ff.), death (v, ii, 347, 375).[8] The player's speeches, with their suggestion of an old-fashioned, stilted style, are only an extension of the stilted courtly diction, which occasionally suggests parallels with the diction of much earlier plays. An example is the three-fold amplification in a speech of Claudius,

> His liberty is full of threats to all;
> To you yourself, to us, to every one.
> Alas, how shall this bloody deed be answer'd?
> It will be laid to us, whose providence
> Should have kept short, restrain'd and out of haunt
> This mad young man....   (IV, i, 14–19)

which is reminiscent of a characteristic feature of earlier plays,

> Our truth to you, nor yet our wakeful care
> For you, for yours, and for our native land.
> Wherefore, O King, I speak as one for all...
> Whose honours, goods and lives are whole avow'd
> To serve, to aid and to defend your grace....   (*Gorboduc* I, ii, 108 ff.)

> I thank you all and here dismiss you all,
> And to the love and favour of my country
> Commit myself, my person and the cause....
>   (*Titus Andronicus* I, i, 57–9)

In *Hamlet* the use of such devices is deliberate, and no necessary indication that Shakespeare was rewriting an old play. Many old plays were resurrected on the stage and in print at the time *Hamlet* was written, and no doubt Shakespeare was taking advantage of a vogue for parody and imitation of them. The parody of *The Battle of Alcazar* found in *Poetaster*, the play-scraps in Pistol's language, and the imitation—often serious, sometimes for comic effect—of *The Spanish Tragedy* and other early plays in Marston's *Antonio's Revenge*, all testify to a renewed interest in old plays. *Titus Andronicus* was re-issued in 1600, *Soliman and Perseda* in 1599, *The Spanish Tragedy*, with additions for a fresh stage presentation, in 1602. There was then some purpose in Shakespeare's recalling an older diction in parts of *Hamlet*, now and then in the language of the court, and particularly in that of the players. For to audiences attuned to stylistic variations, as few are now, and aware too of a current fashion for old plays, the contrast between the artificiality of this diction and the sudden outbursts when it is broken down, must have been very striking. Hamlet continually tries to achieve this breaking-down, and in the case of Claudius's fine words and stately behaviour does it only through the extreme artifice of the players' "poison in jest". The deceit and evil of other characters, Polonius, Rosencrantz, Guildenstern and Gertrude, are also revealed in the process of breaking down the poise and outward formality of the court diction.

Yet this formality embodies or is connected with all the good values of the court; the destruction of it is the destruction of something good, of the dignified courage with which Claudius outfaces the Danish rabble, of those qualities which go to make Horatio:

> blest are those
> Whose blood and judgement are so well commingled,
> That they are not a pipe for fortune's finger
> To sound what stop she please. Give me that man
> That is not passion's slave....
>
> (III, ii, 73–7)

Dignity is broken down by release of passion, and in bringing about that breakdown in others, in Claudius who flings out from the play-scene "frightened with false fire", and "marvellous distempered...with choler", and in Gertrude, who is made to recognize her lust, Hamlet also releases passion in himself. He becomes angry with Gertrude, who cries

> Upon the heat and flame of thy distemper
> Sprinkle cool patience.
>
> (III, iv, 123–4)

He kills Polonius rashly, stirring up the "fire and spark" of passion in Laertes; and reveals too often in himself

> The flash and outbreak of a fiery mind,
>
> (II, i, 33)

as when, in the nunnery scene, it is his own faults that are revealed, not the cold, passionless Ophelia's, whose nature is that of water, as

> a creature native and indued
> Unto that element.
>
> (IV, vii, 180–1)

These conflicting aspects of *Hamlet*, formality and corruption, point to an interpretation of the play. Hamlet has to fight continually to see what lies behind appearances, behind the court formality, in order to find out the truth about his father's death. Everywhere he finds or thinks he finds corruption of some kind behind the formal grace, so that he mistrusts the court diction and all the good values with which it is associated. When he turns on Ophelia,

> *Ophelia.* ... their perfume lost,
> Take these again; for to the noble mind
> Rich gifts wax poor when givers prove unkind.
> There, my lord.
> *Hamlet.* Ha, ha! are you honest?
>
> (III, i, 99–103)

there is no need to assume that he has overheard the plot to release her to him; she addresses him with the aphoristic speech characteristic of her father, and that in itself is enough to arouse his suspicion and hostility. Soon only the blunt Horatio, more an antique Roman than a Dane, the one character lacking in subterfuge, remains faithful to him. Perhaps the most terrible feature of his recognition of corruption everywhere is his recognition of it in himself too; where others deceive he must deceive too, where others act he must put on an antic disposition, where the inmost desires and passions of others must be revealed, so must his own passions be roused. And where there is no legal punishment for his father's death, he must stoop, driven by the universal wrong, and "being thus be-netted round with villanies", to revenge. He must share the corruption of others in spite of his nobility, and recognize in himself the common features, "We are arrant knaves all". In this perhaps lies a clue to the tragedy, that in revealing the evil in others, Hamlet arouses evil passions in himself; that however clear the evidence may seem, the truth may still escape, as Hamlet forgets himself in rash anger on seeing Laertes's grief, which, after all, is genuine:

> I am very sorry, good Horatio,
> That to Laertes I forgot myself;
> For, by the image of my cause, I see
> The portraiture of his; I'll court his favours:
> But, sure, the bravery of his grief did put me
> Into a towering passion.   (v, ii, 75–80)

For Hamlet is forced to judge the actions and behaviour of the other characters, when it is only in the next world that, as Claudius knows,

>   the action lies
> In his true nature; and we ourselves compell'd,
> Even to the teeth and forehead of our faults,
> To give in evidence.   (iii, iii, 61–4)

NOTES

1. See W. Clemen, *The Development of Shakespeare's Imagery* (1951), where disease and poisoning are called the "leitmotif of the imagery", and C. F. E. Spurgeon, *Shakespeare's Imagery and what it tells us* (1935), p. 316, "the idea of an ulcer or tumour as descriptive of the unwholesome condition of Denmark morally is...the dominating one".

2. U. M. Ellis-Fermor noted the contrast between the 'public' and 'private' imagery of Claudius in *The Frontiers of Drama* (1945), p. 88.

3. So in the Folio; the quartos read "so call it".

4. M. P. Tilley, *A Dictionary of the Proverbs in England in the Sixteenth and Seventeenth Centuries* (1950), lists 140 he has found cited in some form in *Hamlet*, as compared with 90 in *Othello* and fewer in the other tragedies (except for the early *Romeo and Juliet* which has 120).

5. If pairings of adjectives, nouns and verbs are counted, where the effect is partly one of rhetorical duplication, there are 247 examples in *Hamlet*.

6. These are set in contrast to incidents of violence, for instance Claudius's sudden exit from the play-scene, or the quarrel in the grave with Laertes; but the general effect of them is much more static than of the equivalent direct impressions in *Macbeth* with its dancing witches, the disorder of the banquet, the continual riding and movement ending with a sequence of battle scenes; or of those in *King Lear* with its violent storm scenes.

7. The words "watch" (eleven times), "eye" (ten times), and other words of seeing echo through the first two scenes of the play.

8. These formal personifications contrast with the frequent near-personifications in scenes of great passion, such as are found in the closet-scene, "an act that blurs the grace and blush of modesty" (iii, iv, 40); "sense to ecstasy was ne'er so thralled" (iii, iv, 74); "reason pandars will" (iii, iv, 88); "from the body of contraction plucks the very soul" (iii, iv, 46–7): these are active, characterized by verbs of movement or violence, but the formal personifications like "Frailty, thy name is woman" are static.

HAMLET'S 'SULLIED' OR 'SOLID' FLESH:
A BIBLIOGRAPHICAL CASE-HISTORY

BY

FREDSON BOWERS

One of the most debated of all textual problems in Shakespeare is that of Hamlet's reference to his "too too solid flesh". Are we to read this as *sallied*, following the Second Quarto? Are we to adopt the Folio's *solid*? Or are we to consider *sallied* as a misprint for *sullied* and boldly indulge in emendation?

The traditional reading is the *solid* of the Folio, but J. Dover Wilson has offered a vigorous defence of *sullied*. This, he argues, is what Shakespeare wrote, and he suggests that what he calls the misprint *sallied* was taken over by the Second from the First Quarto. He also points to the Second Quarto's *slight sallies* at II, i, 39 and to *unsallied* for *unsullied* in *Love's Labour's Lost*, V, ii, 352—all, in his opinion, exhibiting the same error of *a* for *u*. *Sullied flesh* is for him the key to the soliloquy, for it shows Hamlet thinking of his mother's incestuous marriage as a personal defilement. *Solid flesh*, he declares, is absurd associated with *melt* and *thaw*, whereas on various occasions Shakespeare uses *sully* with the image, implicit or explicit, of dirt upon a surface of pure white, like snow. An example would be *Winter's Tale*, I, ii, 326–7, "sully the purity and whiteness of my sheets".[1]

The critical, or literary, argument in favour of *sullied* has, however, fallen short of acceptance. While Wilson is sure that *sullied* best fits the tone of the "To be or not to be" soliloquy, others are equally certain that this word ill fits the context and that *solid* was the adjective which Shakespeare had in his original manuscript.

When so much is a matter of opinion, little certainty can obtain. However, once we begin to pursue a somewhat different line of enquiry, certain strands of the problem may become clearer. That *sally* is a legitimate form of *sully*, and not a misspelling, seems to be the growing opinion of linguists.[2] Moreover, that the Oxford English Dictionary does not list *sally* is not real evidence that the word does not exist: almost surely the compilers overlooked the three occurrences in Shakespeare because they used edited modernized texts. And when we find the same form elsewhere in the sense of *sully*, in Dekker's *Patient Grissil*, "Then sally not this morning with foule lookes" (I, i, 12), we can perhaps no longer appeal to coincidence in error, misreading of handwriting, and so on, but accept *sally* as a legitimate variant of *sully*, and not—as Wilson believed—as a misprint for it.

The early editors, who did not understand the relationship of the three *Hamlet* texts, could select Folio *solid* only on literary grounds. But the fact that some degree of corruption in the Second Quarto must be attributed to the influence of the First Quarto introduces other than purely literary considerations, and it is well to see how the case stands up to a somewhat more rigorous examination than is usually given it. Contamination from the First Quarto definitely exists in sheets B–D of the Second Quarto, which contain all but the last seven lines of Act I. In his *Manuscript of Shakespeare's Hamlet* (1934), I, 159–61, Wilson gave it as his opinion that the

Second Quarto compositor was well aware of the degenerate nature of the First Quarto text and that he consulted it only infrequently and with due caution when he could not decipher a reading in his manuscript. According to Wilson there are only twenty-five readings in Act I of the Second Quarto that have resulted from the First Quarto's influence. Most of these turn out to be eccentric spellings or punctuations, and Wilson selects only five in all that he feels represent actual corruption foisted on the Second from the First Quarto. Of these five, three are really spelling errors (*horrowes*, I, i, 44; *cost*, I, i, 73; *sallied*, I, ii, 129), and hence only two remain as real verbal contaminations (*of a most select*, I, iii, 74; *interr'd*, I, iv, 49), to which he later added three more.[3]

The six most prominent post-Wilson editors, all necessarily aware of the possibility for contamination in the Second Quarto from the First Quarto, are able to concur in only two of Wilson's five supposed substantive corruptions and in none of his added three; and since this concurrence is only in rejecting *horrowes* and *cost*, not much is proved.[4] Yet all save Craig-Parrott side against Wilson in believing that Folio *solid* must be correct. The fact is that in the twenty or so years after Wilson's pioneer monograph, five major editors (omitting Craig-Parrott as rigid followers of the Wilson hypothesis) have been able to agree only on *sallied* and thus have made it the single substantive contamination from the First in the Second Quarto text.

Viewed dispassionately, the textual situation does not enforce this word's being isolated as a manifest contamination any more than several other strong candidates; and certainly the Second Quarto's meaning is not so difficult or inappropriate as to force one to stretch textual probabilities unduly in order to avoid it. It may be that editors would have looked more kindly on *sullied* if Wilson had not mistaken the spelling as a misprint and hence listed *sallied* among the corruptions from the First Quarto. It was perilously easy, as a consequence, to feel that Wilson's arguments were partial and that the real contamination lay in the word itself and not merely in its spelling. This view would be the easier to hold since there is no evidence from their texts that the listed editors made any attempt to carry the facts about the First Quarto contamination beyond the rather unsatisfactory state in which Wilson had left them.[5] Hence it is clear that the bibliographical knowledge of the Second Quarto corruption from the First Quarto had no editorial influence on the post-Wilson state of the text save, ironically, to confirm editors in their critical preconception that *solid* was a better word than *sullied*.

Various considerations may be raised against this singular editorial treatment. A strong one is the fact that the peculiar form the line takes in the First Quarto shows that rightly or wrongly the actor reporting the First Quarto version (or the editor) thought it was *sallied*. When he recited "O that this too much grieu'd and sallied flesh Would melt to nothing", we can be quite sure that *sallied* is no compositorial error or actor's simple mis-hearing for *solid*: the balancing word to *grieu'd* and one that participates in the modification by *too much* would be nonsensical as *solid*. If the First Quarto line is corrupt in this word, therefore, we must believe that the corruption arose when the actor lost his memory for *solid*, recovered it approximately as *sallied*, and thereupon twisted the line to suit the new meaning. On the other hand, if *sallied* is correct, we have this key word shaping the half-remembered form of the rest of the line.

Another strong consideration develops from the propositions we can now lay down. *Solid* can be defended only on one of two logical premises:

  1. In Shakespeare's manuscript *solid flesh* was written much like *sallied* and was so misread

45

by the scribe who copied the actor's part (and presumably the prompt book); and on the evidence of the First Quarto the actor was never corrected. When, therefore, at I, ii, 129 the compositor of the Second Quarto came to read the word in what was presumably the same basic manuscript, he (*a*) made the same mistake, or (*b*) was uncertain about the word and consulted the First Quarto, taking its form from that document; and when, later, he came to II, i, 39 the same handwriting difficulty led him to mistake manuscript *sullies* for *sallies*.

Only a remarkably gullible person could believe this furious coincidence and persistence of error under variable conditions, the more especially since only in *Love's Labour's Lost* was the difficulty repeated. Hence only the second proposition remains:

2. (*a*) *Solid* stood in the manuscript behind the Second Quarto, and *sallied* in the First Quarto is an actor's memorial corruption. When the Second Quarto compositor came to I, ii, 129, for one reason or another—dependent upon the theory held as to the exact means by which the First Quarto contaminated the Second Quarto—he picked up *sallied* from the First Quarto.

(*b*) When he came to II, i, 39, the sense was not especially clear to him and, either by misreading the handwriting or by misinterpretation—perhaps accompanied by his memory of earlier *sallied flesh*—he set the form *sallies* instead of *sullies*.

There are difficulties in this proposition. First, it is surely obvious that in dealing with such a rare word appearing twice in one play, we may not appeal to separate and divided error. It seems incredible that there is no connexion between *sallied* at I, ii, 129 and *sallies* at II, i, 39. Hence if *sallies* means *sullies*, as it surely does, *sallied* must mean *sullied*. To escape this conclusion one must believe (*a*) manuscript *solid* was misread *sallied* by the Second Quarto compositor and manuscript *sullies* was misread *sallies*; (*b*) *sallied* is a First Quarto corruption taken over by the Second Quarto, and *sallies* is an independent misprint for *sullies*; or (*c*) the corruption *sallied* influenced the Second Quarto compositor to misread *sullies* as *sallies*.

The odds against the first are certainly serious, and at best its improbability is marked. The second is not much more probable, since it offers two different causes to explain identical double error. The third is logically the most defensible but it can be demonstrated to be wrong. Once we depart from Wilson's view and accept *sally* as a quite possible variant spelling for *sully*, the whole idea of a misprint vanishes, and no reason exists to suppose that the first could have influenced the second. But there is evidence more relative.

We can now prove on physical evidence that no connexion can possibly obtain. Bibliographical analysis now shows not only that sheet E in which (sig. E1ᵛ) the second *sally* appears in the Second Quarto was printed on a different press from sheet C containing on sig. C1 "this too too sallied flesh", each being machined at approximately the same time,[6] but also (as necessarily follows), that each was set by a different compositor.[7] Since the second *sally* was set by the second compositor from manuscript, the appearance of the first *sally* in *sallied flesh*, set by the first workman, can have had no possible influence on the other. Hence if one word is right, as must be so, the other must also be right as well, and the contamination explanation for *sallied flesh* fails as a matter of simple logical impossibility. If we cannot believe that *sallied* was picked up from the First Quarto in error, there is no argument by which *solid* can be maintained.

It stands that bibliographical research separating the typesetting and the printing of the two sheets as the work of two different compositors and presses can be applied directly to settle this celebrated Shakespearian crux. Double handwriting error by two compositors is improbable enough, but it is surely impossible in this case given the First Quarto's *sallied flesh*. Hence since Polonius's *sallies* must have been written in the manuscript, it is mere fantasy to hold that *solid* was present in the manuscript for Hamlet's soliloquy but by one cause or another the compositor corrupted it to the rare form *sallied*, and this by the purest chance was repeated by a different compositor from his manuscript in another sheet. On the evidence of the appropriateness of the black on white image for *sully* and of the *thaw* and *melt* for flesh compared to snow; on the belief that Hamlet's feeling his flesh to be soiled by his mother's incestuous marriage is not a far-fetched idea;[8] on the linguistic suggestion that *sally* is not a misprint for *sully* but a legitimate though rare form; on the evidence that the First Quarto actor remembered his part as reading *sallied*; and finally on the bibliographical evidence that the same word in its rare variant form was set by two different compositors in the same play and therefore the two appearances have no possible connexion with each other,[9] one can now expose an error in criticism and by the application of the mechanical evidence of bibliography establish the text for an individual reading.

NOTES

1. The original arguments in *The Manuscript of Shakespeare's Hamlet* (1934), II, 307–16, are summarized, with some addition, in the New Cambridge *Hamlet*, pp. 151–2 and, in the revised later printing, p. 294.

2. However, the linguistic opinion is not based on strictly linguistic grounds. If I read Kökeritz aright (*Shakespeare's Pronunciation* (1953), p. 242 and n.), he is unwilling to take a definite position and cannot solve the problem. He starts by seeming slightly to favour the *unsallied* in *Love's Labour's Lost* as a misprint (he does not know of the Dekker *sally* and, curiously, fails to consider Polonius's *sallies*). He then splits the ticket and offers the opinion that this *unsallied* nevertheless suggests that the *sallied* of *Hamlet* should be interpreted as *sullied*; on the other hand, it may be an unrounded form of *solid*. Kökeritz's manifest confusion stems from the fact that such *u:a* alternative forms have not been recorded; hence as a linguist he would clearly prefer to find almost any escape.

In his review of Kökeritz in *Language*, XXIX (1953), 560–1, Professor A. A. Hill proved himself to be perhaps the first scholar willing to grasp the nettle firmly. At my request, he has subsequently amplified his position, which he describes only as "the evidence and a statement of the kind of method a linguist would use in attacking the problem". He continues in his letter:

(*a*) There is no sound change, dialectal or otherwise, which would result in giving variants in the shape of *sully-sally*. I would add only that since we don't know all about the history of English, it is always possible that we might find somewhere a dialect in which such a sound change occurred. What is involved is a sound change from *schwa*, which occupies the exact centre of the three columns and three rows of the nine English vowel phonemes, to the position in the centre of the bottom row. Such a change is therefore perfectly thinkable, but as I said above, remains unknown.

(*b*) If *sallied* is to be recorded as the result of sound change, it would be possible to assume that it is a development of unrounding and forwarding of the low back vowel ordinarily spelled 'o'. This would point to *sallied* as a variant of *solid*, but the possibility leads only to a blind alley, since, as I stated in the Kökeritz review I know of no instance in which the verbal ending usually spelled *-ied* alternated with the *-id* ending of such adjectival forms as *solid*, *frigid*, and the like. The result of the consideration of *sallied* as a possible variant due to normal English processes, then, is to make it seem extremely unlikely that any sound change can have produced the variant.

(*c*) Next, as to the possibility of a series of mis-readings of *u* as *a*. A number of scholars have built up a theory that Shakespeare's handwriting was such as to confuse these two letters. Unfortunately, all the evidence for such a confusion that I have seen—there may be other evidence that I have not seen—rests on the series of *sally-sully* variants. Thus to use the theory of confusion in Shakespeare's handwriting as an explanation for *sally-sully* is perfectly circular.

(*d*) There are three examples of *sally* in Shakespeare involving three compositors and presumably two different batches of printer's copy. There is a fourth quite independent example in Dekker. To assume a misreading of *a* for *u* thus requires four separate assumptions.

(*e*) To assume an Elizabethan word *sally*= *soiled* is only one assumption and is therefore simpler. Since it is axiomatic that we cannot assume that we have recorded the whole of the Elizabethan vocabulary, there is nothing in such an assumption which is in any way radical—unless one believes that it is radical to postulate a word not recorded in dictionaries.

(*f*) If *sally* is a genuine word, it is not the result of sound change. It can, however, be explained as a borrowing from French *sale*, and its later disappearance in turn is explained by its homonymity with *sally*, 'issue forth to attack'.

3. In the New Cambridge edition Wilson adds *rootes* for *rots* (I, v, 33); *Heauens* for *Heauen* (I, v, 113); and the omission of *Looke you* before *I will goe pray* (I, v, 132).

4. These six are Kittredge, Craig-Parrott, Harrison, Campbell, Alexander, and Sisson. For example, only Kittredge agrees with Wilson that the First Quarto has contaminated the Second Quarto in *roots* and that Folio *rots* is correct. Only three of the six (Kittredge, Harrison, and Alexander) concur that *interr'd* is a corruption taken over from the First Quarto and that Folio *enurn'd* is the true Shakespearian reading. More complete facts about the readings and their editorial treatment in Act I will be found in my 'Textual Relation of Q2 to Q1 *Hamlet*', *Studies in Bibliography*, VIII (1956), 64–6.

5. The evidence itself, without further interpretation, is sufficient to show that Wilson's explanation for the method of contamination is incorrect. It is interesting to see that though his treatment of the text was based on information about contamination from the First Quarto, a relationship unknown to the Old Cambridge editors, his choice of readings in this immediate connexion did not differ materially from their traditional text. Of his original five corruptions the Old Cambridge editors had varied only in their preference for *solid* over *sullied*; and of the supplementary three found in his edition, only his choice of Folio *rots* disagreed with the Old Cambridge preference for *roots*.

6. Bowers, 'The Printing of *Hamlet* Q2', *Studies in Bibliography*, VII (1955), 41–50.

7. John Russell Brown, 'The Compositors of *Hamlet* Q2 and *The Merchant of Venice*', *Studies in Bibliography*, VII (1955), 17–40.

8. This stain from his mother attacks his natural honour. For the important distinction between natural and acquired honour in Elizabethan concepts, and the belief that acquired honour cannot be maintained if natural is destroyed, see my 'Middleton's *A Fair Quarrel* and the Duelling Code', *Journal of English and Germanic Philology*, XXXVI (1937), 40–65.

9. For example, if from the fact that the two occurrences in *Hamlet* of the spellings *somnet* (for *summit*) are set by different compositors we may establish that *somnet* was the manuscript spelling, the same principle should work for *sally*. It is amusing to contemplate that this same *somnet* form was rejected as a misprint in Thomas Pyle, 'Rejected Q2 Readings in the New Shakespeare *Hamlet*', *ELH*, IV (1937), 114–46.

HAMLET AT THE GLOBE

BY

GEORGE F. REYNOLDS

How *Hamlet* was given at the Globe is a somewhat troublesome inquiry, not because it makes any particularly difficult demands, but because there are in the original texts so few specific demands of any kind. Its directions authorize no discoveries by a curtain or any scene in the balcony. One textual allusion, it is true, has been held to hint at use of the latter. *Hamlet* (IV, iii, 39) says of Polonius's body, "you shall nose him as you go vp the staires into the Lobby." But to argue that the lobby thus referred to is the one in which II, ii and III, i were played, or that such a reference means the balcony, seems to confuse a 'dramatic' with a 'theatrical' allusion. The fact is that *Hamlet* could if necessary be given almost anywhere, even on an arena stage, with less distortion than most Elizabethan plays. Differences of opinion on the way it was presented come mostly from our own different assumptions and inferences.

These have changed considerably in recent years. Formerly students assumed that all scenes in rooms were played in the inner stage, since it was a room; that no properties of any size were admitted to the front stage (two or three stools were assumed enough to require the use of the inner stage); and that no pauses were permitted to allow the resetting of the inner stage. These assumptions were natural enough, but have been disproved by modern performances in the more or less Elizabethan manner. Thus at Stratford-upon-Avon, even on its proscenium stage, but with no lowering of the front curtain, the settings have been changed before the eyes of the audience, and properties—like the throne in *Henry VIII*—left on the stage throughout the play. The conventions of the Elizabethan platform stage were in many respects unlike those of a proscenium stage. The latter, as it is usually employed, attempts to create unified and consistent stage pictures. The platform stage was by its very structure only a stage as the medieval stage had been before it; it might be set with some of the necessary properties, to be used in the performance as they were required, but otherwise disregarded by the audience.

Perhaps the greatest change of opinion concerns the importance of the curtained space. Formerly emphasized and used on the slightest pretext, it seems today more and more avoided. The most emphatic statement I have seen in print about it is that of Bernard Miles and Miss Josephine Wilson, founded on their experience in the Mermaid Theatre and at the Royal Exchange, 1951–3: "We have learned that it is impossible to play scenes on the so-called 'inner stage', or even far upstage at all. When the expanse of platform is there to be used, you have to use it."[1] Some scenes were certainly played in the curtained space, and all directors will scarcely concur in so sweeping an opinion, but the position of it at the far end of the front stage makes action in it less easy to see, speech from it less easy to hear, and—a matter receiving increasing emphasis—rapport with the audience less easy to establish. We need to note also that the very existence of a permanent inner stage at the Globe at the time when *Hamlet* was produced is more and more in question. The Swan picture shows none in that theatre, and really few of the plays produced by Shakespeare's company before *Hamlet* precisely require such an arrangement of the stage. Discoveries in bed are specified, but beds had their own curtains and

49

could be thrust out. Other properties such as the tent or shop or tomb could also disclose persons. The three caskets of *The Merchant of Venice* were behind a curtain, but they would require no large space. Most of the plays, though some of their scenes could advantageously be discovered and perhaps were, do not even hint at such a presentation, and have been supposed to have been so staged mainly because of modern custom. It is possible, therefore, that up to the time of *Hamlet* and even later, discoveries were made not only in the special properties, but also by means of a curtain hung on a removable frame placed on the stage only for the plays which required it. Such a furnishing would have projected in front of the tiring-house wall instead of forming an alcove within it, and would presumably have been not very deep nor so wide that more supports would have been required than at the corners. To keep the possibility of such an arrangement in mind I refer to it here as the curtained space rather than as the rear stage, and never as the inner stage. In such circumstances many room scenes would have been played on the front stage, with the arras as their background. And this would have been especially true of the more intimate and quiet scenes, which to hold the attention of the spectators could often do so more easily if acted closer to them. Scenes with many characters or with much action, like those for instance before the gates of a city or castle, might well use the whole stage, the curtains being drawn back to an inconspicuous position, the framework serving as an architectural emphasis on the middle door.

Hamlet occasions another change of assumptions about the staging, necessary as soon as it is mentioned. Many modern productions have treated the play within the play as the centre of interest in that scene, but Allardyce Nicoll has rightly pointed out that our interest is really in the effect on Claudius of *The Mousetrap* and of Hamlet's comments. It is Claudius therefore who should be placed conspicuously, not the play within the play. But where on the Elizabethan stage is the most easily observed position? On this there are differences of opinion. Some have thought that it should be in the centre rear, that is in the curtained space, opened in this scene for the king's and queen's formal seats. Others, influenced by the opinions already expressed about the ineffectiveness of the curtained space, have put the royal seats at one side further to the front and slightly turned so that the king is so placed that he can at least seem to be watching the play, but also be easily observed by the audience. (This position for the throne is also likely in other plays.) Hamlet then sits across the stage by Ophelia where, without turning his back on the audience, he can watch the king continuously, and be himself a second centre of interest for the audience.

This scene, III, ii, is the most important in determining the staging schedule for the whole play. The two early quartos differ on what was done in it. If, as students seem generally to agree, the Second Quarto represents Shakespeare's manuscript, he expected the scene to be played with a bank of flowers on which the player king "dies", and from which, according to the explicit direction, he is removed at the end of the dumb-show by attendants on the treacherous "nephew". This removal may imply, but not necessarily, that the bank stood on the front stage. Claudius breaks off the performance of the play, and the "dead" king presumably went out in the resulting confusion along with the spectators. But in the First Quarto, the directions of which J. Dover Wilson accepts as what the piratical reporter saw at the Globe,[2] the player king enters to sit in an arbour, and at its end is left there "dead" with no one to remove him. This seems to call for a curtain, but perhaps, as acting only in a dumb-show and having to re-enter immediately in the play itself, he was expected to walk off by himself. I remember, however, no such loose end in any other dumb-show. Or perhaps the arbour was a free-standing structure with its own curtain, on the stage along with the royal seats, placed there before the play began, and left on till the end. If this was the way the play was given at the Globe, there would scarcely have been any other curtained space, speculation about other possibly discovered scenes becomes unnecessary, and the staging of the whole play was either simplicity itself or, if more completely furnished with properties, unmistakably medieval. Is it not more likely that this arbour was a device to substitute for the theatre's curtained space when the company was in the provinces or playing in a private house?

The staging of this scene is also conditioned by the other scenes, more or less formal, in which the king and queen are seated: I, ii; II, ii; and v, ii. In modern productions these seats may differ to suit the scenes. In III, ii and v, ii chairs elaborate enough to be called thrones and placed on a dais have often been used.[3] Dover Wilson specifies thrones in I, ii; even if it is a council and not a court scene, a similar council scene in *Henry VIII* (I, ii) has a direction, "the king riseth from his state". As for II, ii, Granville-Barker,[4] pointing out its generally informal atmosphere, thinks a throne would not be suitable, but A. C. Sprague,[5] noting what probably provoked this remark, says "I have often seen Hamlet, as he cries 'O Vengeance', lunge with his dagger at the empty throne". In I, ii the entrance and departure of the king and queen are announced by a flourish of trumpets, as is their entrance in II, ii and III, ii. So though these scenes do differ in formality and may be differently furnished in modern productions, is it not likely that, on the Elizabethan stage, the same formal seats would be used for all these scenes? Sometimes for brevity I shall refer to them as thrones, more or less elaborate seats raised on a dais, but not necessarily provided with a canopy.

Other properties raise few questions.[6] The pictures of Hamlet's father and Claudius (III, iv) could most effectively have been miniatures worn by Hamlet and the Queen respectively. Large portraits could have been hung only on the rear wall, as in the Rowe picture of the scene, an awkward arrangement since the Queen would have had to turn her back on the audience to see them. It is another situation like that of the play within the play; what matters to the audience is the effect on the Queen of Hamlet's speeches, not the pictures themselves. The only other large property is the table brought in or discovered in v, ii. The grave (v, i) could have been the trapdoor in the curtained space, but would perhaps have been more effective as the front stage trap nearer the audience.

In accordance with these considerations of bringing the action forward and keeping it immediately clear, the following schedule may be tentatively suggested. It supposes a curtained space of only moderate size, its curtain the arras of the text. The royal seats are on the front stage throughout the play. The curtained space is used for the bank of flowers and for the table of v, ii. The two or more seats of I, i could have been either in the curtained space or, better, because closer to the audience, ready on the front stage. So with the scene in the Queen's closet. Her chair might be in the curtained space, but the scene would presumably be more immediately effective if played on the front stage; moreover, if she did sit in the curtained space, Polonius must have been concealed behind a second curtain, perhaps a wall-hanging concealing part or all of the middle door.

This is not a very good place for his concealment, but such a wall-hanging might be useful as an aid to clarity. I can see no advantage in the use of sceneboards, "Denmark" or "Elsinore", in this play, though such boards were still being used when *Hamlet* was produced. But care in the employment of the doors, for instance use of the one on the right for entrance from away or for departures in that direction, might help in keeping the action clear. And this wall-hanging, when displayed, would show that the curtained space was a room, but when the hanging was not visible, the scene would at once be indicated as an exterior scene, suitable for the platform of the castle, or the scene with Fortinbras. I do not urge this at all, but I mention it because I think the problem of clarity on the Elizabethan stage has not received the attention it should.

The act divisions are retained in the schedule not as significant, but for ease of reference. Brief phrases are given as reminders of the contents of each scene.

Act I

Sc. 1. The platform; ghost appears; FULL STAGE.

The Ghost enters, perhaps by the trapdoor of the curtained space. Darkness is suggested by Bernardo's and Francisco's challenges, by allusions to the striking clock, "yond same star", and in the first eighty lines by ten mentions of "night".

Sc. 2. A court or council scene; embassy sent to Norway; front stage; throne used.

Sc. 3. Laertes, Ophelia, Polonius; front stage.

Sc. 4. The platform; second appearance of the Ghost; FULL STAGE. In contrast to scene 1, there are only two references to "night" in all the scene. The Ghost leads Hamlet off right, his friends following a few lines later.

Sc. 5. Then, illustrating the convention that exit by one door and immediate or almost immediate entrance at another means change to an adjacent location, the Ghost leads Hamlet in, perhaps at the left door. The Ghost goes out, perhaps through the trap-door, and later speaks from under the stage. FULL STAGE.

Act II

Sc. 1. Polonius, Reynaldo, Ophelia; front stage.

Sc. 2. "Here in the lobby"; return of embassy from Norway; throne used; FULL STAGE, perhaps with wall-hangings.

Act III

Sc. 1. Ophelia at her orisons; the King and Polonius from behind the arras, spying on Hamlet and Ophelia; front stage.

Sc. 2. The play within the play; bank of flowers in the curtained space; throne used; FULL STAGE with wall-hangings. Torches as indications of a night scene.

Sc. 3. The curtains may have been closed during the last 109 lines of scene 2 and the first 35 lines of this one to allow the removal of the bank of flowers. Then FULL STAGE with wall-hangings, and the King at prayer, lines 72–96, in the curtained space, while Hamlet observes him from the front stage.

Sc. 4. Hamlet with the Queen. The Queen sits; Polonius killed behind the arras; Ghost appears, then goes out, according to a direction, "at the portall", thus not by the trapdoor; front stage.

Act IV

The seven short scenes arise from and are suited to only an open stage like the Elizabethan on which they can be presented without delay and with no necessarily precise statement of locality. Scene iv has already been suggested as a full stage scene without the wall-hangings. The door guarded in scene v would, in our suggested arrangement, be the one at the right.

Act v

    Sc. i. The graveyard. FULL STAGE; no wall-hangings.

    Sc. ii. The finale; throne used; perhaps front stage till l. 235, during which time the hangings are restored and the table prepared; then FULL STAGE and the table discovered or brought forward.

In this schedule there are eight full stage scenes, but in all of them most of the action is on the front stage. One can only guess how many lines should be spoken from the curtained space, but my highest estimate, because of placing the throne and Hamlet's scene with the Queen on the front stage, is less than 200. Whether these are desirable arrangements can be determined only by actual performances, and even then will depend on special circumstances: individual actors, the direction, the particular audience. Perhaps the clearest evidence which *Hamlet* offers concerning the Elizabethan stage is that in III, ii either the seats for the King and Queen or the bank of flowers must have been placed on the front stage, and that if these seats were placed there, they almost certainly would have remained there for use in the other scenes.

NOTES

1. 'Three Festivals at the Memorial Theatre' (*Shakespeare Quarterly*, v (1954), 307–10).
2. *Hamlet* (Cambridge, 1934), p. xxvi.
3. See R. Mander and J. Mitchenson, *Hamlet through the Ages*.
4. *Prefaces, Third Series, Hamlet* (1937), p. 66.
5. *Shakespeare and the Actors* (Cambridge, Mass., 1944), p. 149.
6. A faldstool has been suggested for Ophelia to kneel at, but A. C. Sprague (*op. cit.* pp. 151, 344) finds no record before 1847 of her kneeling.

HAMLET COSTUMES FROM GARRICK TO GIELGUD[1]

BY

D. A. RUSSELL

In the nearly two centuries that passed between Garrick's first performance as Hamlet and the emergence of Gielgud's interpretation of the Prince, much ink has covered myriads of manuscripts dealing with the textual criticism, production history and interpretation of the play, and more volumes pour from the presses yearly. At the present time considerable attention is being focused on its stage history, and a very comprehensive pictorial record from 1709 was published in 1952 entitled *Hamlet Through the Ages*. This excellent book by Mander and Mitchenson covers over one hundred and fifty 'Hamlets' and gives an excellent picture of the changes in the physical presentation of the tragedy since Betterton's day. Since this book covers so much material, however, it is but natural that it should give only a brief indication of the changes that have developed in the dress of the Prince of Denmark during several centuries; and it is, therefore, my purpose in this brief article to draw attention to some of these changes and to indicate if possible why they took place.

Garrick (Plate I, 1) first played Hamlet in 1742 and throughout his career he portrayed the Prince wearing a black velvet court dress of the eighteenth century. The effect he evidently wished to create was that of the dignified, fashionable gentleman-prince in no way removed from the manners and customs of his own day. Here is no rash and youthful romantic nor a brooding, melancholy intellectual, but the cultured, refined, sensitive Prince facing the events of the play with a temperament equally balanced between emotion and intellect, between action and thought.

The majority of the other eighteenth-century actors also presented Hamlet in black court dress, sometimes adding the Orders of the Garter and Elephant to give a more royal appearance. Henderson (Plate I, 3) usually wore such ornaments, though they do not appear in our print of him. Foote, however, seemed to be an exception; he presents the role (Plate I, 2) without a wig, wearing a ruffled lace collar, ballet-like slippers, loose trousers ending above the knee, a doublet and an outer coat that is eighteenth-century in cut but very loose-fitting. In general, the costume appears to be a theatrical attempt to place the Prince in a romantic era of the past—which in the eighteenth century usually meant the period of Vandyck, as evidenced by the "Blue Boy" of Gainsborough. For the most part the costume which Foote wears is a definite forerunner of the changes that were to take place in the dress of Hamlet at the end of the eighteenth century. In other words, Foote unconsciously ranged himself with the growing trend toward the coming romantic era, whereas Garrick remained within the neo-classic artistic ideal.

The tradition of presenting Hamlet in eighteenth-century court dress was brought to an end by John Philip Kemble, though at first he played the role in 1783 in the usual Georgian dress. In early performances he wore the Order of the Elephant, even the Order of the Garter, with his black velvet court dress and diamond-buckled shoes.[2] During his own management of Drury Lane, however, he substituted what we may loosely term the Vandyck costume and in adopting this made the first major change in the stage dress of Hamlets for more than a century. As may be seen from the print, the emphasis is much more toward the romantic, casually-dressed, emotional, young prince than in the past. His hair is dishevelled, the lace collar loosely open at the neck, the garments worn with marked negligence. The whole picture tells the story of the birth of the romantic period—the age of Byron and Kean.

The print showing H. E. Johnston in 1817 (Plate I, 5) illustrates what changes had come about in the few short years since the death of Garrick. The hose on one leg is carefully "down-gyved" and the short trousers are apparently an attempt to suggest trunk hose.

Master Betty, the celebrated infant Roscius, Young and Charles Kemble all show variants of this new romantic Hamlet (Plate I, 6, 8 and 7), a most poetic and romantic young prince. It is little wonder that Paris at the height of the romantic movement in the late 1820's chose Hamlet, as presented by Edmund Kean, as its hero. Edmund Kean (Plate I, 9) wears the by-now-traditional stage "Elizabethan" dress, and the very pose of the actor in the print gives an excellent idea of the turbulently emotional performance which he must have given.

In 1838, however, a second major change in the garb of Hamlet occurred with the adoption by Charles Kean, son of Edmund Kean, of the knee-length tunic. Charles, a friend of the archaeological costumer Planché and a keen student of history, felt the play demanded this change, since its basis was a Danish legend of the eleventh century. Kean's costume of 1838 was hardly eleventh-century in character, since it retained all of the romantic embellishments such as lace collar and puffed sleeves and merely substituted the skirted tunic for the usual stage version of trunk hose. Since our print of Kean (Plate I, 12) shows him as Hamlet during his management of the Princess' Theatre in the 1850's, the print of Macready (Plate I, 10) from a performance in the early 1840's will be considered first. Note that here the lace collar has disappeared, the skirted tunic is not of a rich fabric and is bordered very simply at the edges; however, the puffed sleeves, white cuffs and order still remain.

That this new costume for Hamlet as worn by Macready was not accepted without adverse comment may be illustrated by Coleman's description of him: "He wore a dress, the waist of which reached to his armpits, and carried a hat with a sable plume big enough to cover a hearse. He was the only Hamlet whom I ever saw wear gloves, and being much too large, they were very conspicuous objects. His undershirt of amber coloured satin looked simply dirty, and what with his gaunt, angular figure, his grizzled hair, his blue black beard, close shaven to his square jaws...he looked positively grotesque."[3]

Certainly Macready made no determined attempt at such archaeological accuracy as had been suggested by Planché in his costume plates prepared for Covent Garden in 1825. It will be remembered that Planché in 1823 had been the first to design an archaeologically correct production when he supervised the costumes and settings for Charles Kemble's *King John*, but at that time his work received only laughter and ridicule from a majority of the critics. That Planché did not really understand the purpose of dramatic costume even though he knew all the details of fashion history is well demonstrated in his plates and suggestions for *Hamlet*, which he published in 1825. In these he deplores the fact that Hamlet should wear black, since ancient Danes never mourned for the dead and, as one of the blood royal, he would have worn scarlet.

Black should have been reserved for the soldiers, since the Welsh chronicles continually alluded to the Danes as the black army. It is unfortunate that so many mid-nineteenth century producers were champions of this mistaken approach to theatre costume, and Charles Kean was one of its leading exponents.

In our print dated 1844 Henry Betty (Plate I, 11), son of Master William Betty, wears a Hamlet costume of the period just before the close of the romantic era. The border trim is an attempt at a medieval effect, but the romantic lace collar, the order, the sleeve puffs, and the lace cuffs continue from the earlier romantic garb. It is interesting to compare this figure with the staid, sombre, and relatively heavy effect of the famous Victorian Hamlets, Phelps (Plate II, 13) and Kean (Plate I, 12), both prints dating from the late 1850's and early 1860's. The simple black costume with varying amounts of trim and usually showing a shirt ruffle at the neck was to be the traditional "suit of black" for the Prince down to the early 1920's.

Brooke (Plate II, 14) and Creswick (Plate II, 15) made their reputations as popular Hamlets and, therefore, in costume retain many of the romantic elements of richness and decoration which appealed to their popular audience and gave little thought to their appropriateness or archaeological correctness. Dillon (Plate II, 16), who played at the Surrey in the 1860's, being stodgy in appearance and scarcely suitable in stature for Hamlet, tried to make up for these deficiencies by his dress. The bell sleeves lined in satin, the ornamentation on the under-tunic, the decorative lapels of the outer-tunic were all designed to make a prince out of a rather unprincely figure. Edwin Forrest (Plate II, 17) also adopted this type of costume to elevate and dignify his rather mean stature.

Vezin's Hamlet (Plate II, 18) indicates the extent to which a preoccupation with archaeological accuracy could obscure the sense of costume for character. The bold borderings, the Phrygian cap and a tunic that projects rather than disguises Vezin's bulk combine to project a well-nigh comic figure. Fechter (Plate II, 19) had more taste, but he too insisted on archaeological accuracy to the extent of wearing a blond nordic wig as Hamlet.

In the midst of this emphasis on historical correctness, it is surprising to find a Hamlet such as Allerton's (Plate II, 20) dressed in the accepted stage 'Elizabethan' costume of the late nineteenth century. Although this costume lacks the flamboyance of the romantic dress of the early years of the nineteenth century, and although the pose of the actor emphasizes the staid and melancholy Prince whom the Victorians so much admired, it is interesting to find an actor playing in stage 'Elizabethan' costume in the face of the current tradition of dressing Hamlet as an eleventh-century Dane.

The famous Irving Hamlet (Plate II, 21), first played at the Lyceum in 1874 and later in 1878, was considered by many the perfect combination of the medieval Dane with the Renaissance Prince. His costume shows this dual quality admirably. It is medieval in essence yet suggests in cut the sophisticated outline of the Renaissance figure. Clement Scott describes Irving as appearing in "thick-robed silk and a jacket, or paletot, edged with fur; a tall, imposing figure, so well dressed that nothing distracts the eye from the wonderful face; a costume rich and simple, and relieved alone by a heavy chain of gold".[4]

Wilson Barrett (Plate II, 22) appeared on the scene to challenge Irving's interpretation by presenting an impulsive, youthful Hamlet dressed in what was declared to be an adaptation of German student dress of the early sixteenth century. *Punch* commented that Barrett's suit of sable was "cut very low in front to show his schoolboy's chest" above some "tumbled linen, which...suggests the idea of its being one of his mother's old *chemises de nuit*". He had also "neglected to brush his hair, and to tie up one or two mysterious strings connected with his nether garments" in his rush to reach the stage.[5] The print bears out these comments.

Edwin Booth (Plate II, 23), who arrived in London in 1880 to present an American challenge to Irving's interpretation, put Hamlet forward in decidedly medieval trappings, even to cross-gartered legs, disdained by actors interested in giving a romantic appearance. It is interesting to note the type of chain worn at his neck, presumably to hold the miniature of his father, and to compare it with the chains worn by other actors. A medieval Hamlet usually wore a simple, large linked, heavy chain; the Renaissance Hamlet wore a delicate and more decorative one.

Several important foreign Hamlets visited England in the late nineteenth century, and all displayed a complete break with the medieval tradition. In 1876 Signor Rossi (Plate II, 24) presented an Italianate Hamlet dressed in operatic finery. Mounet-Sully (Plate III, 25) introduced the puffs and slashes of the true German student's dress of the early sixteenth century; and Sarah Bernhardt (Plate III, 26) acted the part in a very rich garb suggestive of the late medieval or early Renaissance period.

Beerbohm Tree (Plate III, 27) as Hamlet (first performed in 1892 and annually from 1905–10) also wore rich garments rather like those worn by Bernhardt. Forbes-Robertson (Plate III, 28), on the other hand, in 1897 returned to a more severe medievalism to set off the pale and ascetic beauty of his face.

Benson's Hamlet (Plate III, 29) was very conventional in attire and our print showing him portraying the role in later years (*c.* 1910) indicates a simple costume in the medieval tradition. Our print of Sir John Martin-Harvey (Plate III, 30) as Hamlet in 1905 shows a strong interest in early medieval archaeological correctness with much attention given to the magnificent cross-garterings. When Martin-Harvey revived *Hamlet* in 1916 and 1919, however, he eschewed all this paraphernalia in favour of the stark simplicity of the then popular Max Reinhardt method.

In the mid-1920's an important change occurred. The tradition of the simple, black medieval tunic for Hamlet was frequently replaced by a late Renaissance or Elizabethan costume or, in some cases, by contemporary dress. These changes were probably due to the gradual acceptance of the ideas of William Poel and Granville-Barker, to the gradual decrease of interest in archaeological correctness in costume and setting, and to the strong attacks which were being made on Victorian stage methods. In our prints, George Hayes (Plate III, 33) appears as one of the last of the traditional Hamlets; Ernest Milton (Plate III, 34) and John Gielgud (Plate III, 36) indicate the more prevalent approach of the late 1920's. Within a decade the Elizabethan costume had become so firmly set that the publicity on Leslie Howard's production of *Hamlet* in New York in 1937 was able to emphasize the 'novel' fact that the Howard production was placing the play in medieval times, utilizing eleventh-century costume!

The idea of presenting *Hamlet* in modern dress, though revolutionary for audiences in 1925, was certainly not new, and Sir Barry Jackson was merely returning to the ways of Garrick and his predecessors when he produced Colin Keith-Johnston (Plate III, 35) as his modern dress Hamlet at the Kingsway Theatre in 1925. One major difference occurs, however, between the eighteenth-century and the twentieth-century approaches. Unlike Sir Barry Jackson and his successors in the modern dress tradition, Garrick was not interested in approximating the realities of the everyday scene. Garrick in eighteenth-century court dress remained the gentleman-prince to his audience, since court life and dress were still sharply divided from the daily life of those in the audience. Colin Keith-Johnston's Hamlet, on the other hand, in the Oxford bags and the dinner jacket of 1925 became identified with life as experienced by the audience, and though the immediacy of the play increased, the stature of the Prince was greatly diminished.

With the Sir Barry Jackson modern dress production our series of prints has come full circle from contemporary eighteenth-century dress to contemporary dress of the late 1920's. A most interesting observation after viewing these prints covering nearly two centuries is that the costumes they show partake more of the qualities of the actor's own day than of any particular period they are attempting to establish for their audience. This will always remain true of theatrical costume no matter how strong an attempt is made to recreate a period in the past. Even period costumes of a decade ago often appear to have more qualities of that decade than of the period they intend to illustrate. In this connexion it should not be forgotten that the particular engravers and photographers responsible for the prints here shown have unknowingly enhanced the particular elements in dress admired by people in their day. Stage illusion is ever relative, and what recalls a past era to one generation may not serve for the next.

NOTES

1. In assembling the reproductions of various Hamlets I wish to acknowledge a considerable debt to an interesting portfolio of prints and photographs prepared by Maurice Wigham Richardson. For permission to utilize some of its contents I thank the Shakespeare Memorial Theatre Library, Stratford-upon-Avon.

2. J. Doran, *Annals of the English Stage* (1888), III, 255.

3. John Coleman, *Fifty Years of an Actor's Life* (1904), pp. 343–4.

4. Clement Scott, *Some Notable Hamlets of the Present Time* (1900), p. 61.

5. 'Letter to some People', *Punch* (25 October 1884), p. 196.

HAMLET AT THE COMÉDIE FRANÇAISE:
1769–1896

BY

PAUL BENCHETTRIT

The fact that *Hamlet* is quite alien to the classical idea of tragedy need not be emphasized. Until recently the Comédie Française was the keep, the inner defence, of Aristotelian theory. It is not surprising, therefore, to find that whenever the play was performed there, it had to undergo many a change both in form and substance so as to be brought nearer the classical models. Between 1769 and 1932 the Comédie Française staged only two versions of the play—one by Ducis and the other by Dumas and Meurice—but as public taste evolved, these versions were gradually altered until they came to be not too unfaithful to the original. Unfortunately, progress was very slow and it was a good many years before it became evident which way the battle—waged both on and off the stage—was turning.

In 1745 was published the first partial translation of the play by P. A. de La Place. Because of Voltaire's numerous attacks on this drama, the French public was already acquainted with it but had had no opportunity as yet of reading it. Actually, La Place translated only those passages which he deemed acceptable to the French taste and gave a summary analysis of all scenes not directly concerned with the main action. After having thus been able to read the play the French theatre-goers had to wait for no less than twenty-four years before they could see it performed. The first stage adaptation was the work of J. F. Ducis, whose admiration for Shakespeare could be matched only by his ignorance of the English language: he read La Place's rendering and let his imagination fly. In a letter to Garrick he explained his purpose and accounted for his lack of audacity:

> I conceive, Sir, that you must have thought me exceedingly rash in placing such a tragedy as *Hamlet* on the French stage. Not to speak of the barbarous irregularities with which it abounds—the spectre in full armour and long speeches, the strolling actors, the fencing bout—all these appeared to me to be matters utterly inadmissible on the French stage. Nevertheless, I deeply regretted being unable to bring upon it that awful ghost who exposes crime and demands revenge. I was therefore obliged, in a certain sense, to create a new play. I simply tried to make an interesting part of a parricidal Queen, and above all to paint in the pure and melancholy soul of Hamlet a model of filial tenderness.[1]

Here in a nutshell were all the objections to the so-called irregularity of the play, together with a statement of Ducis's somewhat novel aim. Ducis went a stage further than the English playwrights who had rewritten Shakespeare after Dryden's manner: his was an entirely new play, scrupulously classical.

In this *Hamlet* of 1769, written in Alexandrines, everything takes place within twenty-four hours at the palace and only the courtly characters have been kept. It has become an ordinary court-intrigue, not unlike Corneille's *Cinna*. Hamlet is not Prince but King of Denmark because the legitimate order of succession has to be kept. Claudius is no longer Hamlet's uncle but the first Prince of the blood, and therefore his marriage to the Queen cannot be regarded as incestuous. Ophelia is Claudius's daughter, probably owing to the example of *Cid*. There are two Danish Lords: Norceste, Hamlet's confidant, and Polonius, Claudius's confidential friend. A new character, Elvire, is introduced, as Lady-in-waiting to the Queen.

The drama is thoroughly neo-classical, and patently imitates *Phèdre* in several scenes. Pressed by Elvire, Gertrude confesses that she had murdered her husband. The first time Hamlet appears on the stage he is seen fleeing before his father's ghost which he addresses behind the scenes: "Fly, dreadful spectre! Carry to the depths of the grave thy frightful aspect." The ghost seems to be more terrified than Hamlet for, obeying his order, he never presents himself again. Hamlet lets the audience know that the ghost has just disclosed to him the terrible secret with which they are already acquainted. He asks Norceste, who has recently returned from England, to tell Claudius and Gertrude the story of a regicide perpetrated in that country. The 'play within the play' is flattened into a conversation: Gertrude is troubled, but, unlike his namesake in Shakespeare, Claudius feels no pangs of remorse. Hamlet rejects Ophelia's love: what he hopes for is death and nothing else. He asks his mother to swear on the urn which contains the late King's ashes that she is innocent of his father's death. She refuses to do so and faints, thereby confessing her guilt. Hamlet discloses his secret to Ophelia, and as he remains firm in his determination to devote himself to the duty of revenge, she showers abuse on him. Shakespeare's delicate flower is turned into an energetic woman, almost a virago. With the help of his followers Claudius forces his way into the castle and kills Gertrude, and he in turn is stabbed by Hamlet. The play concludes with Hamlet's pompous words:

> Privé de tous les miens dans ce palais funeste,
> Mes malheurs sont comblés, ce poignard seul me reste;
> Mais je suis homme et Roi, réservé pour souffrir,
> Je saurai vivre encor, je fais plus que mourir.

Ducis's *Hamlet* was performed for the first time on 30 September 1769 and was quite favourably received. Incredible as it may seem, for eighty-two years it was the only *Hamlet* staged at the Comédie Française, and the only one in France for that matter. It had 203 performances before it was withdrawn in 1851: very few plays of the time have fared better. Between 1831 and 1840, at the peak of the Romantic movement, it was played on 65 nights, more than in any other decade. In the Comédie Française library there is a loose sheet of paper on which Ducis himself wrote in 1787 several alterations to the 1769 text. Feeling the awkwardness of Hamlet's position when fleeing before his father's ghost, Ducis makes him speak to the ghost instead of running away, which is undoubtedly more noble. At the end of the play, Hamlet's words "ce poignard seul me reste" are changed into "mon amour seul me reste". For the 1803 revival, Talma, who was to play Hamlet, asked Ducis to change the fifth act, which he did not find satisfactory from the actor's point of view. Ducis suppressed the whole act. The new fifth act, the result of the breaking up of the original fourth act, was mainly formed by the great scene between Hamlet and his mother. Instead of being killed by Claudius, Gertrude commits suicide on the stage, and once again Ducis changed Hamlet's last words, this time to "mais ma vertu me reste". Talma probably disliked Ducis's remodelling, for the Comédie Française possesses a completely new version in Talma's handwriting, and almost certainly of his own composition. It is original in so far as it outlines, in very poor verse indeed, a happy ending of the play: Hamlet has been the victim of his own imagination; Claudius is innocent; Ophelia is going to marry the one she loves and already calls Gertrude "mother"; everything ends in universal happiness.

Unfortunately, progress was very slow, and the second French stage version of *Hamlet* appeared seventy-eight years after Ducis's, which, to a certain extent, inspired it.

In 1818 Alexandre Dumas, who was then fifteen years old, saw Ducis's *Hamlet* performed by the students of the Comédie Française dramatic school. Writing many years later, Dumas still remembered his first reaction to the play, which was probably similar to that of many of his contemporaries:

I had not the slightest idea of what *Hamlet* was. I did not even know that there had ever existed a playwright named Shakespeare. Thus, as Ducis's *Hamlet* could not suffer from any comparison, since I had never heard of Shakespeare's, its hero, with his fantastic entrances, his apparition visible only to himself, his struggle with his mother, his urn, his soliloquy, the sombre questions put by Doubt to Death, made *Hamlet* seem a masterpiece and made a prodigious impression on me.[2]

In 1827–8 the Companies of Covent Garden, Drury Lane and Dublin came to Paris, and Charles Kemble, Macready and Kean played Hamlet. By that time Dumas had been able to read the original play:

I knew my *Hamlet* so well that there was no need for me to buy the text. I could understand what the actors said, translating the words as they were speaking them. I must confess that the impression made on me went beyond all my expectations. The platform scene, the fan scene, the portraits scene, the madness scene, the graveyard scene, excited me greatly. Only from that moment did I have an idea of what the theatre really is.[3]

Although Dumas had the immense advantage over Ducis of having been able not only to read Shakespeare's own text but also to see the play performed by an English company, the adaptation which, with Paul Meurice's help, he wrote in Florence in 1840–1 was not very faithful to the original: public taste was slow in evolving and the time was not ripe for a French version without any alterations.

The new *Hamlet* is written entirely in verse and is divided into five acts and eight parts. At the beginning of each of these parts a change of scenery occurs, while various scenes have been transported so as to avoid any other changes of scenery. For instance, the curtain does not rise on the platform but on the Council Chamber. Hamlet declares his love to Ophelia in a new scene, entirely of Dumas's composition, and in his declaration of love "jolie" of course rhymes with "Ophélie". He writes a note which he leaves in her hands. She exclaims: "He loves me! He loves me! O how happy I am!" Shakespeare's sweet and coy Ophelia is turned into an exuberant young French lady. On the platform Hamlet does not follow the ghost, and his request that Horatio and Marcellus leave him alone with the ghost has its comic side. There is no dumb-show and in the play within the play Lucianus pours poison on Gonzago's lips, not into his ears. Hamlet does not go to his mother's closet but she, at his request, has to come to him in the Council Chamber. After the murder of Polonius, Hamlet conceals himself on the sea-shore; he is not sent to England, just as Laertes does not go to France. No mention is made of Fortinbras and Norway. During the fencing bout Hamlet is not once hit by Laertes, but succeeds in wrenching his rapier from him, and out of politeness presents him with his own. Hamlet therefore gets the poisoned weapon into his hands and mortally wounds Laertes and then the King, whereupon the ghost appears and pronounces judgement on the perpetrators of the crime. Laertes and Gertrude, who pray for mercy, are forgiven—but not so Claudius. Laertes is told to "pray and die", Gertrude to "hope and die" and Claudius to "despair and die". Hamlet then asks the ghost what he is to do:

Am I, am I to remain on earth, a disconsolate orphan, breathing this air saturated with misery?... Will God stretch forth His arm against me, Father? And what chastisement then awaits me?

The ghost replies: "Thou shalt live!" and on this the curtain falls.

When writing his play Dumas intended it for the Comédie Française but, because of a breach with F. Buloz who was then at its head, it was performed on 15 December 1847 at the Théâtre Historique which Dumas had just founded. The play had 135 performances there and was a great financial success. Rouvière was the protagonist on the opening night and for the next twenty years, so that Dumas wrote: "Hamlet et Rouvière pendant vingt ans ne firent qu'un." Rouvière was rather small and unattractive but displayed extraordinary force. When Th. Gauthier went home after the first performance he wrote: "This is the first time that I have really seen Hamlet." Rollé, a critic who was famous in his time, wrote: "He has given life to the Hamlet drawn by Delacroix. He has taken him from the canvas on which he stood motionless and made him live." Rouvière was dressed entirely in black, as in the well-known painting. His clothes were cut after the fashion of the sixteenth century, a cloak hanging from his shoulders. His hair was rolled up and his thin beard ended in a point. Talma had been against wearing a beard: "The Prince of Denmark is a young man and therefore the actor who plays the part must try to look as young as possible."

The play was magnificently revived at the Comédie Française on 28 September 1886, with the great Mounet-Sully as Hamlet and Madame Reichenberg as Ophelia, but this time it was more like Shakespeare's. Dumas had died in 1870 and even before his death, Meurice had, in 1864, revised their collaborative version; this was the text used in 1886. Here Francisco, Bernardo and Osric find their place with the other characters, although Fortinbras is still absent. The opening scene with the allusion to the mouse is restored. The second apparition of the ghost takes place on two different parts of the platform so that Hamlet need not ask his friends to leave him alone with the ghost. Hamlet and the Queen meet in her closet and not in the Council Chamber. Finally, Hamlet dies at the end of the play. Chatelain had written that Hamlet's survival was "une idée burlesque" and Meurice agreed with him although he felt that Shakespeare's dénouement was not a "dénouement à la française".

Jules Claretie was then Director of the Comédie Française, having been appointed on 20 October 1885. He was both playwright and critic, and it was his life-long desire to see Hamlet acted under his direction. Claretie has left a few notes on this revival in his Diary and as we turn the pages, we find the everyday story of the fight waged within the walls of that fortress of tradition.[4] As early as 29 October he decided to have Hamlet staged at the same time as Octave Feuillet's Chamillac. On 17 December he was paid a visit by Emile Augier, who had one of his own plays to offer. "I give way to Feuillet", said Augier, "he is in a difficult financial position, but why be encumbered by this Englishman?" This Englishman, of course, was Shakespeare!

On 25 January 1886 Meurice read the play to the Selection Committee. Augustine Brohan laughed at the passage when Hamlet speaks of a pin: "Ma vie, une épingle vaut mieux!" Meurice defended himself: "Madame, ce n'est pas de moi, c'est de Shakespeare." As Peter Alexander recently remarked:

> When a French man of letters can silence a distinguished *sociétaire*, as she protests against the presence of vulgar expressions in a tragedy, with "c'est de Shakespeare", we may conclude that we are reaching the end of an epoch.[5]

All that Reichenberg wanted to know about Ophelia was how she would be dressed. This lack of interest in the character itself can be explained partly by Reichenberg's own superficial personality, and partly by the indifference shown by the French critics towards Ophelia. That is presumably why the French actresses preferred to play Hamlet.[6]

1886 was to be a vintage year in the history of *Hamlet* in France, for at the time when rehearsals were about to begin at the Comédie Française another version was performed in Paris on 27 February at the Théâtre de la Porte St Martin. It was the work of Lucien Cressonois and Charles Samson, and bore evident traces of the influence of Dumas's and Meurice's adaptation: the opening scene is that in the Council Chamber; the characters address one another as "Monsieur"; during the fencing bout Laertes lets his rapier fall and Hamlet presents him with his own. The major difference is that Hamlet dies and the play ends with his words: "mon âme entre dans le silence". The reception of the play was rather mixed. In his article in the *Temps* of 8 March 1886, Francisque Sarcey tells us that Sarah Bernhardt, who played Ophelia, sang the ballad with incomparable charm, but her deliberately monotonous delivery of the part did not appeal to all. Ph. Garnier was an indifferent Hamlet. H. Luguet's rendering of the ghost is described as "superb". This, however, was not Hugues Le Roux's opinion, who wrote in the *Revue Bleue* of 6 March that in the scene in Gertrude's closet, where the ghost came out of a cupboard, Luguet's pantomime, his three mincing steps forward, and his quavering voice were tricks worthy of the *Conservatoire* but unknown to ghosts. This new production was the occasion for a whole series of articles in the press which made the public wait even more eagerly for the *Hamlet* the Comédie Française was to put on the stage seven months later.

On 16 August the first rehearsal took place. Two days later came the first of many controversies concerning the text. Mounet-Sully suggested an alteration to the passage in Act II, when Polonius tells the King and Queen that if love be not the cause of Hamlet's madness,

> Let me be no assistant for a state,
> But keep a farm and carters.

Instead of the translation: "J'irai gouverner une ferme", Mounet suggested: "Et moi, Garde des Sceaux, j'irai garder les oies!" Meurice went as far as proposing: "Et moi, Chambellan des vaches...." On 20 August Claretie noted that Got was turning Polonius into a pompous ass of the Middle-Ages, "un prudhomme du Moyen-Age". On the following day, he wrote that Mounet-Sully was making Hamlet a shrill-voiced tenor, a Ruy Blas. On 23 August was rehearsed the scene in which Ophelia is seen distracted for the first time: "They say the owl was a baker's daughter." When Reichenberg spoke her lines,

> Que le Seigneur vous garde! On dit que la Chouette
> Était fille d'un *boulanger*. Pauvrette!

Got immediately pointed out that this would bring laughter from the audience—1886 was the year in which the unpopular General Boulanger attempted his unsuccessful *coup d'état*. On 27 August Meurice wanted Mounet-Sully to be hit in the hand during the fencing bout, but the actor preferred to be hit in the chest so as to have an opportunity for unbuttoning his doublet and showing the blood. "But what about the author?" Meurice asked. "The author is Shake-speare, and he is dead!" replied the actor.

The rehearsal of 1 September went on throughout the whole day. Maubant, the ghost, expressed the wish not to appear in the opening scene. Reichenberg did not want to be on the stage when the curtain rose for the second part so as to make an entrance by herself: "Je voudrais faire ma Sarah." "She has been the ruin of all of them, this Sarah", Claretie put down in his diary. On 18 September Mounet-Sully meant to lie flat on his face over the grave during Ophelia's burial: "I want to bite the earth of the graveyard!" He even wanted Ophelia's coffin to be actually covered with earth.

The first performance was given on 28 September. Two days later Claretie recorded his impression on the opening night: "Mounet was superb." A few pieces of stage-business together with some information on the representation are afforded us by various newspaper articles.[7] Mounet-Sully's use of tablets was unprecedented. He always kept them with him. Early in Act I, he tore out a leaf to write his love verses, which he then gravely handed to Ophelia. He produced paper and pen on the dreadful summit of the cliff, in the first glimpse of dawn, and put into written words his opinion that a man may smile and be a villain. He also wrote at the end of Act II the scene he wanted the players to act. Just before the soliloquy "O, that this too too solid flesh..." he often looked at and sometimes kissed a picture-in-little of his father which was attached to a chain he wore around his neck. He sat for a long time motionless, wordless, his eyes closed as if he were asleep, his mouth partly open, and presently began his great soliloquy by touching arms and body on the word "flesh". Mounet watched the King's approach to the 'play' from behind the curtains of the mimic stage, and he realized that Polonius was within earshot at the very beginning of the great scene with Ophelia, thus making the meaning of that scene as simple as a child's primer. During the performance of the *Murder of Gonzago* he hid himself behind a fan so as to watch the King and Queen. As Lucianus spoke his lines, Mounet crawled up to Claudius and Gertrude and suddenly rose on his knees just in front of them. The scene in Gertrude's closet was regarded as by far the most striking, even although the device by which the ghost was brought on the stage meant it had to be performed in almost utter darkness: apparently, the actor playing the ghost was painted white and stood in a beam of light. Throughout the scene, Mounet was continually boisterous and tempestuous. The poor Queen was forced to sit in an armchair with castors, and Mounet rolled her about, to face now this portrait and now that, as he made his famous comparison! When the ghost appeared, he suddenly drew his dagger and held it menacingly over his mother's head. This was novel, but consistent with Mounet's idea of Hamlet. When the ghost vanished, he followed him out and screamed in the wings. His anger over, he took the Queen in his arms, kissed her and cried like a small child. During the fencing bout, Hamlet attacked in a straightforward manner, but Laertes lunged backwards wilily, after the Italian manner, then bent down and pointed his sword at Hamlet's body—thus making him spit himself. This brought to light perfectly the difference in character between the two men. It took more than a fortnight to get the action

PLATE I

1. DAVID GARRICK

2. SAMUEL FOOTE

3. JOHN HENDERSON

4. JOHN PHILIP KEMBLE

5. HENRY ERSKINE JOHNSTON

6. WILLIAM BETTY
'The Infant Roscius'

7. CHARLES KEMBLE

8. CHARLES MAYNE YOUNG

9. EDMUND KEAN

10. WILLIAM CHARLES
MACREADY

11. HENRY BETTY

12. CHARLES KEAN

Hamlets from Garrick to Gielgud (1)

PLATE II

13. SAMUEL PHELPS

14. GUSTAVUS VAUGHAN BROOKE

15. WILLIAM CRESWICK

16. CHARLES DILLON

17. EDWIN FORREST

18. HERMANN VEZIN

19. CHARLES FECHTER

20. CHARLES ALLERTON

21. SIR HENRY IRVING

22. WILSON BARRETT

23. EDWIN BOOTH

24. ERNESTO ROSSI

Hamlets from Garrick to Gielgud (2)

PLATE III

25. JOHN MOUNET-SULLY

26. SARAH BERNHARDT

27. SIR HERBERT BEERBOHM TREE

28. SIR JOHNSTON FORBES-
ROBERTSON

29. SIR FRANK BENSON

30. SIR JOHN MARTIN-HARVEY

31. MATHESON LANG

32. WALTER HAMPDEN

33. GEORGE HAYES

34. ERNEST MILTON

35. COLIN KEITH-JOHNSTON

36. SIR JOHN GIELGUD

Hamlets from Garrick to Gielgud (3)

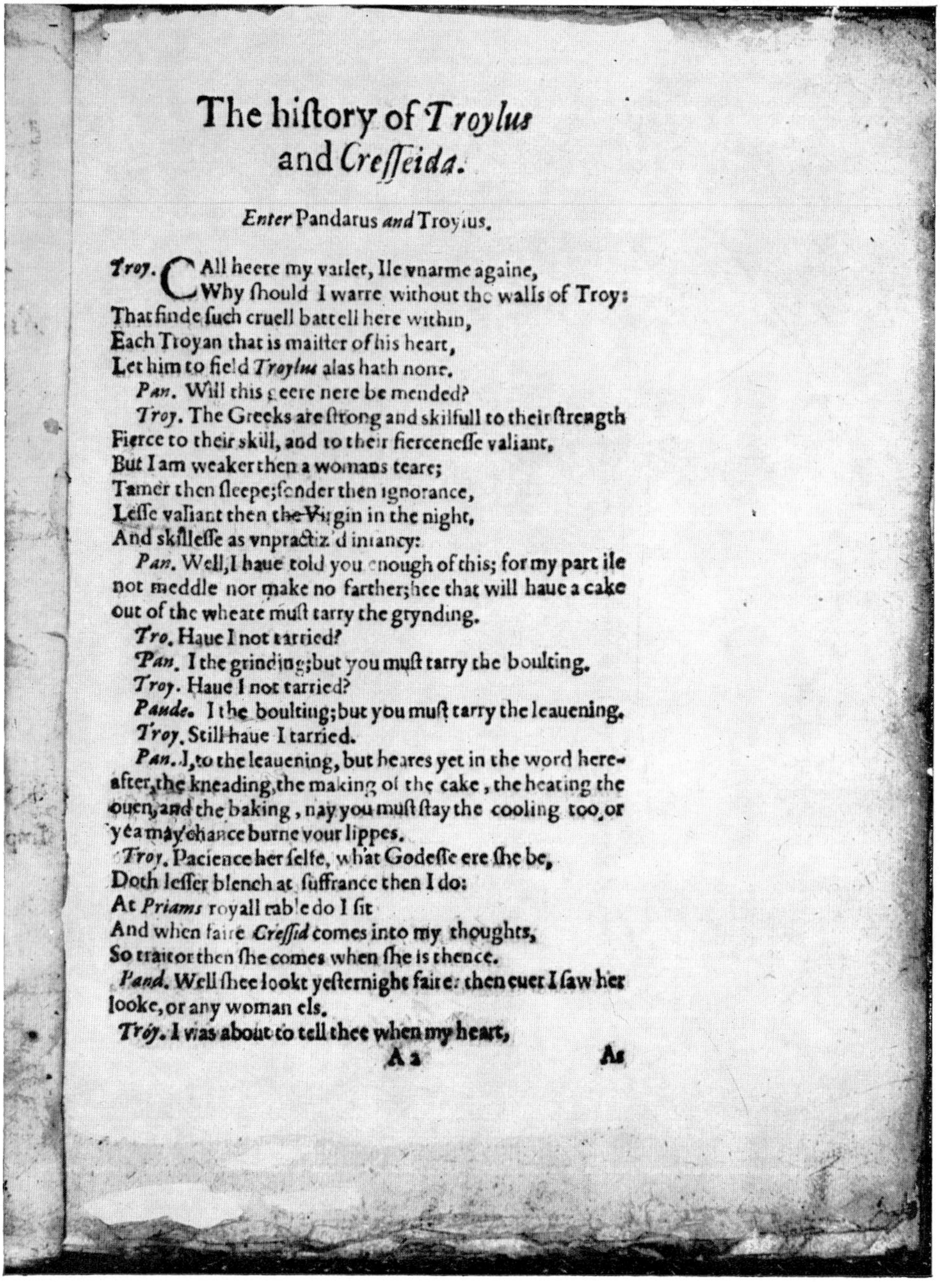

The hiſtory of *Troylus* and *Creſſeida.*

Enter Pandarus *and* Troylus.

Troy. CAll heere my varlet, Ile vnarme againe,
Why ſhould I warre without the walls of Troy:
That finde ſuch cruell battell here within,
Each Troyan that is maiſter of his heart,
Let him to field *Troylus* alas hath none.

Pan. Will this geere nere be mended?

Troy. The Greeks are ſtrong and skilfull to their ſtrength
Fierce to their skill, and to their fierceneſſe valiant,
But I am weaker then a womans teare;
Tamer then ſleepe; fonder then ignorance,
Leſſe valiant then the Virgin in the night,
And skilleſſe as vnpractiz'd infancy:

Pan. Well, I haue told you enough of this; for my part ile not meddle nor make no farther; hee that will haue a cake out of the wheate muſt tarry the gryndıng.

Tro. Haue I not tarried?

Pan. I the grinding; but you muſt tarry the boulting.

Troy. Haue I not tarried?

Pande. I the boulting; but you muſt tarry the leauening.

Troy. Still haue I tarried.

Pan. I, to the leauening, but heares yet in the word hereafter, the kneading, the making of the cake, the heating the ouen, and the baking, nay you muſt ſtay the cooling too, or ye may chance burne your lippes.

Troy. Pacience her ſelfe, what Godeſſe ere ſhe be,
Doth leſſer blench at ſuffrance then I do:
At *Priams* royall table do I ſit
And when faire *Creſſid* comes into my thoughts,
So traitor then ſhe comes when ſhe is thence.

Pand. Well ſhee lookt yeſternight faire: then euer I ſaw her looke, or any woman els.

Troy. I was about to tell thee when my heart,

A 2 As

Uncut copy of *Troilus and Cressida*, quarto, 1609 (Bibliotheca Bodmeriana) right. After the Queen died and Laertes warned Hamlet that the rapier was poisoned, Hamlet rushed up to the King. Some of the courtiers came forward to stop him, but recoiled before the poisoned rapier. This fear explained in an instant why Claudius found no one to defend him.

The play was lavishly produced. The dresses had been designed with exquisite taste by Bianchini. One single cloak which was worn for about five minutes cost 5000 francs—a large sum then. The whole production entailed the expenditure of 150,000 francs. A designer, indeed, had actually been despatched to Nuremberg just to take an exact copy of the spades used by grave-diggers there! Fortunately the play was a great success, and between 1886 and 1890 it had 110 performances.

The critics were, on the whole, favourable. On 4 October Sarcey wrote a lengthy article on the first representation. The Prince of Denmark puzzled him: "We neither know what Hamlet is nor what he wants." Recalling the various interpretations of the play, he added: "When a part is explained in so many different ways, apparently it is not very easy to understand." He thought that Mounet played the part as if Hamlet were a Brutus feigning madness and waiting for his time to come. The audience felt rather bored towards the end. The graveyard scene was too long and lugubrious: "It is sometimes omitted in England, but it would be difficult to omit it in France where some of its lines have become commonly used proverbs and are looked upon as being typical of the play," Sarcey remarked. It is surprising to find that what was possible for Garrick in London had become impossible on the stage of the Comédie Française. O, shades of Voltaire! Sarcey found the "slaughter" with which the play ended rather disgusting: "If the play was not from Shakespeare's pen, I would find all those deaths at the same time monstrous and childish." It must be remembered that this was the first time that the last act was acted in its original form. Mounet-Sully kept speaking in a very low voice, but was nevertheless convincing. Looking at him, Sarcey wrote, one would have thought Delacroix's Hamlet had come to life. (Rollé had already said that about Rouvière.) Mounet was a Prince "from top to toe": "If I read in to-morrow's newspapers that Mounet-Sully has been proclaimed King of Denmark, I should be only half surprised."

Also on 4 October 1886 Jules Lemaître gave his impression on the opening night. Some of his statements have a special interest for the modern reader: "I shall find nothing new to say regarding either Shakespeare's drama or its hero, for everything has been said already—everything, and more than everything." He explained that Mounet had to make a choice among all the Hamlets whom the critics had invented. He took for an ideal on which to model himself the incomplete but comprehensible Hamlet defined by Goethe in *Wilhelm Meister*. He diffused over his role an atmosphere of tenderness and melancholy, although perhaps, Lemaître added, the almost feminine gentleness of the youth was a trifle over-emphasized. In the earlier part of the play especially he had tears too continually in his voice and suggested too much the plaintive tones of a sick child or of a child suffering from a great sorrow. "But what an adorable Hamlet he has given us nevertheless!" Lemaître exclaimed.[8]

There can be little doubt that the success of the play was largely due to Mounet-Sully's acting, although there is some doubt as to what precisely was his attitude towards the role. Many years later, on 28 August 1911, he told Claretie that even as the opening night approached he was in doubt concerning the explanation of Hamlet's character. Then at his wife's suggestion, he read F. V. Hugo's translation, trying to imagine that he had never previously heard of the play. On the following day he made up his mind: Hamlet was a man in love, condemned to revenge and hatred, betrayed by his friends, by Ophelia who lied to him (she knew that her father was in the gallery). Interviewed by an American journalist at the time when he was touring the United States in 1894 and playing *Hamlet* in Meurice's version, his explanation of the character was somewhat different. He explained on this occasion that he did not believe that Hamlet was mad, even temporarily. On the contrary, he thought that his every action denoted a keen intelligence used for one purpose: that of avenging the death of his father. Hamlet, he said, was the victim of a fixed idea, a monomaniac. He was a being, bright and gay by temperament, condemned by inexorable fate to be sad and gloomy, a creature whose movement was one of expansion but whom circumstances forced to retire within his shell. He was simply a nervous, vacillating personality, tossed upon the waves of chance. Compelled to despise his mother, to doubt those by whom he was surrounded, to hate his uncle and to suspect Ophelia—whom Mounet did not think Shakespeare drew as the model of lovable womanhood his commentators had since made her out to be—all this made Hamlet a misanthrope, pessimist and cynic. The actor explained that as the action began to move rapidly, a state of intense cerebral excitement was noticeable in Hamlet; a nervous excitement, almost savagery, that had all the appearance of madness. But it was the semblance of it only. Hamlet thought of nothing but revenge at his father's command. There, according to Mounet, was the secret of the play and of the character.

The play was again revived at the Comédie Française on 26 May 1896, this time with the addition of Fortinbras. In his diary, Claretie wrote that after the scene between Hamlet and his mother, the Russian national anthem was played and was received with tremendous applause! It must be remembered that the Czar Nicholas II was then paying an official visit to France. Georges Berr, who played one of the grave-diggers made the audience laugh—a little too much, according to Claretie—by saying:

> Nos carcasses, Monsieur, sont parfois gangrenées.
> Un corps peut vous durer de trois à huit années!
> Par exemple, un tanneur se conserve *sept ans*.

The text reads "huit ans", but Berr wanted to refer to the fact that the Presidents of the French Republic are elected to office for seven years. Fortunately, Félix Faure, who had been elected President in 1895 and liked to recall that he had been a tanner in his earlier life, was not present in the theatre; and the following day, that violent pamphleteer, H. Rochefort, headed his editorial in the *Intransigeant*: "Félix Faure et Shakespeare."

Hamlet was performed forty-six times in 1896–7, and thanks again to Mounet-Sully, was very well received. It was the subject of lively discussion in the press. In 1886 Louis Ménard published a poetical version of the play dedicated to the Czar Alexander III, and in the *Revue Blanche* of 1 July 1896 he published an article in which he accused Meurice of having plagiarized his adaptation with the complicity of Claretie who, in 1886, had refused to stage it at the Comédie Française. In the article, L. Ménard asserted that Fortinbras was absolutely necessary to the play and that he was the first adapter to have felt the importance of the character. The play, he wrote, is built on a constant parallel between Fortinbras and Hamlet—two fathers killed, two uncles on the throne, two nephews deprived of their inheritance, two avenging sons—Hamlet who dreams, Fortinbras who acts. Many well-known writers such as Catulle Mendès, Octave Mirbeau, Mallarmé and actors like Lugné-Poë took part in the controversy.[9]

The *Hamlet* of Dumas and Meurice was played regularly at the Comédie Française until 1924, and was even played occasionally in various French theatres until the end of the last war. It was not until 25 April 1932 that it was replaced in the repertory by the version of Morand and Schwob which had first been played at the Théâtre Sarah Bernhardt on 20 May 1899 with Sarah Bernhardt herself as the Prince of Denmark. The new version contained a large number of omissions due both to the authors' wish to reduce the length of the play and to their desire to suppress all the more or less coarse allusions. Finally, the Comédie Française staged in 1942 an adaptation by Guy de Pourtalès, but the French lovers of Shakespeare are still waiting for their national theatre to present an adaptation worthy of its reputation and faithful to the letter and the spirit of the English text. Thanks to André Gide and Jean-Louis Barrault they can temper their impatience by going to the Théâtre Marigny.

Making a suggestive comparison, Karl Elze wrote:

It is said of the rattlesnake that it fascinates with its glance the birds which it has selected for its prey; in much the same manner *Hamlet* has fascinated the most eminent minds of the French nation, till, step by step, it has penetrated into wider and wider circles, and won them for itself.[10]

The French have indeed been fascinated, but not by Shakespeare's play, as the German critic thought. They were fascinated by the myth of Hamlet which they themselves had created through—or because of—the many distortions which the play suffered in the hands of its French commentators and adapters. The history of *Hamlet* at the Comédie Française exemplifies the curious phenomenon of a lasting attraction to Shakespeare's play blended with a constant repulsion. At the various periods, the French versions were more conservative than revolutionary: they were prone to follow the public taste rather than to break new ground. The road leading to a presentation of Shakespeare's actual text is a long and winding one, and the Comédie Française still has to travel part of the way.

NOTES

1. 14 April 1769, quoted in J. Doran, 'Shakespeare in France', *The Nineteenth Century* (January 1878). For a more detailed discussion of the translations, adaptations, stage history and criticism of *Hamlet*, see my own *A History of Hamlet in France*, a thesis submitted for the degree of Ph.D. of the University of Birmingham in October 1952.

2. *Mémoires*, II, 249–50.

3. *Mémoires*, IV, 280.

4. A few extracts from Claretie's Diary have been published in the *Revue de France* (May 1924), the *Oeuvres libres* (1934) and the *Revue des Deux Mondes* (1 December 1918, and eighteen issues between 1 December 1948 and 1 April 1951). Unfortunately, Claretie's text underwent many cuts and alterations each time it was published so that the same entry differs not inconsiderably from one publication to another. For permission to quote directly from the Diary, I wish to express my thanks to Madame Georges Claretie, the executrix.

5. *Hamlet, Father and Son* (Oxford, 1955), p. 16.

6. Madame Judith was the first actress to play Hamlet in France, in 1866, and Adeline Dudlay the second, in 1898, both in the version by Dumas and Meurice. Sarah Bernhardt, who had been Ophelia in the adaptation by Cressonois and Samson in 1886, was Hamlet in that by Morand and Schwob in 1899—and not as M. Fluchère wrote in *Shakespeare Survey* 2, p. 116, in Dumas and Meurice's.

7. Sarcey, article in the *Temps* of 4 October 1886. Lemaître, *Impressions de théâtre*, 1st series (Paris, 1890), pp. 126–39. There were various articles in the American press on the Paris production which Mounet-Sully took to the United States on a tour in 1894: cf. *New York Herald* (24 March 1894), *New York Times* (13 April 1894), *Boston Advertiser* (8 May 1894). Another article by H. A. Clapp is quoted in A. C. Sprague, *Shakespeare and the Actors*, p. 135. See also W. Winter, *Shakespeare on the Stage*, 1st series, p. 427, and a note in Sprague, p. 182.

8. Among the many articles published at the same time as Sarcey's and Lemaître's, see S. Mallarmé, 'Notes sur le théâtre', *Revue Indépendante* (November 1886); Hugues Le Roux, '*Hamlet* au Théâtre-Français', *Revue Bleue* (2 October 1886) and A. France, *La vie littéraire*, I, pp. 7–8.

9. Catulle Mendès in *Echo de Paris* (3 May 1896); Octave Mirbeau in *Le Journal* (7 June 1896); Mallarmé and Lugné-Poë in *Revue Blanche* (15 July 1896). See also André Brulé, 'Une page de Mallarmé sur Hamlet et Fortinbras', *Revue Anglo-Américaine* (December 1926).

10. *Essays on Shakespeare* (1874), p. 196.

THE NEW WAY WITH SHAKESPEARE'S TEXTS: AN INTRODUCTION FOR LAY READERS. III. IN SIGHT OF SHAKESPEARE'S MANUSCRIPTS

BY

J. DOVER WILSON

If these articles retain the interest of any reader, lay or learned, actor or 'customer', let him picture the writer wrapped in a white sheet and surrounded by the tapers of penitence as he sits at his desk to pick up the thread of his discourse after a break of two years. For a serial in an annual review is in any case absurd, and one that began in 1953 with a brief introduction and continued in 1954 with a lengthy digression has become an inexcusable contradiction in terms. The sinner can only plead that last year's article on *Romeo and Juliet* will at least have shown that the "new way" involves issues of real importance to actors and general readers.

The old way with Shakespeare's texts, as I pointed out in my introduction, was a purely eclectic one since editors knew little more than the editors of the ancient classics about the character of their authors' original manuscripts or about the intermediary links between those manuscripts and the earliest printed texts; and what they did know only weakened any confidence they might have had in the integrity of the latter. All this, I also pointed out, is now changed. Thanks to the rise of modern bibliography, together with an increase in our knowledge of the Elizabethan and Jacobean theatre and of the dramatic documents that have come down from that period, confidence has largely replaced perplexity or despair in regard to the quartos and First Folio; and editors today feel tolerably sure that a Shakespearian manuscript or at worst a theatrical prompt-book lies either immediately, or at only one or two removes, behind most of them. The change was revolutionary and, as I noted finally, it came suddenly. There was little opposition and within a decade most scholars had been converted. "The door of Shakespeare's workshop stands ajar"[1] I was emboldened to write in 1921.

It still does; but the hopes many entertained in those early days, of being able to push it open and walk in, have not been fulfilled. These hopes were much encouraged, too much encouraged, by the unexpected discovery (for it virtually amounted to that) in 1916, at the British Museum of all places, of three pages of dramatic manuscript, a whole scene in fact of a hundred and forty-seven lines, in what is probably Shakespeare's own handwriting. Pollard had taught us to think of Shakespeare's plays as composed of "sheets of paper with so much writing on them, by the aid of which actors had to say their words, and subsequently printers had to reproduce what the author wrote".[2] When he uttered these words neither he nor anyone else imagined we should soon be able to examine such sheets with our own eyes. Yet within a few months some of us felt we were doing so.

In the second volume of *Shakespeare Survey* R. C. Bald provided readers with a full scholarly account of the manuscript in question and of the evidence in favour of Shakespeare's authorship

69

of three pages of it. But the romantic story of its discovery, or rediscovery, by a venerable librarian, at the end of his life, on shelves formerly in his charge, and of the way in which, after a first chilly reception by the world, corroboration of his claim for Shakespeare seemed to keep turning up from different sources and in successive stages, will bear a re-telling. It is a story, I think, of some interest to actors today since it takes us behind the scenes of an Elizabethan theatre, shows us a prompt-book in the process of being reconstructed by four persons under the direction of another whom we should now call a producer, and illustrates in vivid fashion the drastic control which government censorship exercised on the stage in Shakespeare's day. Besides, I cannot deny myself the pleasure of a little anecdotage; for I played a small part in the story, being by good fortune in a position to supply some of the corroborative evidence. And looking back across a gap of forty years I now remember it all as one of the most exciting experiences of my life.

Shakespeare had been dead three hundred years in 1916, but the tercentenary passed almost unnoticed by a nation that was mourning more sons slaughtered in battle than at any other period of its history. Yet the heroic Alfred Pollard, who had lost his only two, celebrated it by delivering at Cambridge towards the end of 1915 a series of lectures, entitled *Shakespeare's Fight with the Pirates*, in which he developed the thesis of his earlier book. And an undaunted Oxford University Press did so by producing an elaborate tribute to the greatest of Englishmen in the shape of two volumes on *Shakespeare's England*, containing an ode by Robert Bridges and thirty chapters by different authorities upon various aspects of English life in the sixteenth and seventeenth centuries. The essay on Handwriting was entrusted to Sir Edward Maunde Thompson, at that date seventy-six years of age, who had formerly been Director of the British Museum and before that Keeper of its manuscript department. The most eminent palaeographer of the day, he was the obvious choice. Yet his chapter is, I believe, the earliest account of the handwriting of Elizabethan England published by him or any other recognized expert in this country. For palaeography, which he himself defined as "the study of ancient handwriting from surviving examples",[3] naturally concerns itself mainly with Greek, Latin and medieval scripts of which last Elizabethan handwritings are merely degenerate and dying variations.

One of them, however, is the hand that Shakespeare wrote, the hand that Pollard was teaching us to look for behind the quarto and folio texts. Thompson accordingly rounded off his chapter by subjecting the poet's six signatures, the only certain examples then known of his calligraphy, to a minute critical examination. And by so doing he performed a service of capital importance to Shakespearian scholars, quite apart from the startling sequel. He proved in the first place, beyond all possibility of doubt, that Shakespeare wrote the "English" or "Secretary" hand. In Shakespeare's day it was still the commonest variety of Elizabethan calligraphy, but one, however, beginning to go out of fashion, and superseded towards the end of the seventeenth century by the "Italian" or "Roman" hand. This, a product of the renaissance, which Elizabeth, her lords, and ladies—Malvolio, you remember, fancies that he recognizes the Countess Olivia's "sweet Roman hand"—as well as scholars like Ben Jonson, had already adopted a century earlier, is the hand we all write today, though we do so in a form that has become degenerate in its turn. Those of us, however, who learned at school to read and write the script current in Germany until quite recent times will have mastered an alphabet not very different from that which little William learnt at the Stratford Grammar School or more probably at a "petty school" earlier. Incidentally, Thompson pointed out, the signatures on the will which have puzzled many thousand pairs of eyes are clearly those of a sick man trying to form the "secretary" letters but without full control of his pen, a disability not of course to be seen in the other three signatures. When therefore Baconians and adherents of other noble pretenders to Shakespeare's throne (since no one but a lord can be allowed his genius) point to these final signatures as evidence that "the man from Stratford" was an ignorant or semi-literate rustic, they merely demonstrate their own ignorance of Elizabethan letters.

In the second place, by "translating for us the six authentic signatures into the hand in which the plays were written" Thompson placed all editors and textual critics deeply in his debt. For, as Pollard pointed out,

We now know at least approximately the rules to which the emendation of Shakespeare must conform if it is to be anything better than a game of literary guess-work. Ninety-nine per cent. of the shots which overcrowd the notes of the Variorum editions are shown to be altogether off the target, and the way is prepared for a saner class of emendations, wholesomely limited by the condition that in an Elizabethan English hand they must look sufficiently like what appears in the printed texts for it to be conceivable that a scribe or printer should have mistaken them the one for the other.[4]

In a word, Thompson's work on the signatures is one of the foundations of the modern textual criticism of Shakespeare, a fact which is often overlooked.

The immediate effect, however, of this intense study of the signatures upon the great palaeographer himself was to make him feel so intimate with Shakespeare's hand that he was confident he could recognize it at once if he met it elsewhere. Accordingly he next turned to examine other signatures or pieces of writing that had been claimed at times as Shakespeare's. There were, for instance, copies of two books, one at the Bodleian and the other at the British Museum, both carrying on their fly-leaves signatures purporting to be his.[5] He dismissed them both out of hand as forgeries. Very different was the verdict on the next document he investigated.

As I mentioned in my first article, some forty-five manuscript plays have come down to us from before the Puritan Revolution, which closed the theatres and brought to an end the Elizabethan dramatic tradition. Most of these found their way in course of time to the Museum and one of the earliest in date is a disorderly, partially revised, badly preserved folio volume, consisting today of twenty-two leaves, and entitled *The Booke of Sir Thomas Moore* on its parchment wrapper.

The word "Booke" here is the normal technical term for prompt-book in the theatrical parlance of that age, and the title is engrossed in a hand found in other theatrical documents and probably that of a prompter or "book-holder", as the phrase then was. Moreover, a command in the margin of the first page of the *More* manuscript signed by Edmund Tilney, Master of the Revels and censor of plays from 1579 to 1610, proves that it was acting-copy, though the drastic character of the command suggests that it can never have got as far as performance. Inasmuch as the theme of the play was the career and death of Sir Thomas More, the great Chancellor executed by Henry VIII for denying his claim to be Supreme Head of the Church, a claim maintained by his daughter Elizabeth, forcible action on the part of the censor is not surprising. It was not, however, the final and, one might suppose, most dangerous scenes upon which the full weight of his displeasure fell, but upon those with which the play opens. The injunction, translated into modern spelling and punctuation, runs as follows:

Leave out the insurrection wholly and the cause thereof, and begin with Sir Tho. More at the Mayor's session, with a report afterwards of his good service done, being Sheriff of London, upon a mutiny against the Lombards; only by a short report and not otherwise: at your own perils. E. TILNEY

The scenes, thus sternly prohibited, deal with "Ill May Day" 1517, when the London apprentices rose in riot against the "strangers" in the city and would have burnt them in their houses had they not been brought to reason by an eloquent speech from More, at that time under-Sheriff. The drama exaggerates the part More actually played, but the riot was historical enough, and well remembered by the authorities as the most violent outbreak on record of a xenophobia which was endemic in Tudor England.[6]

In some way or other, not yet explained, the instructions of the censor must be related to the disorderly condition of the "booke". Had they been carried out, Bald estimates, they would have involved the omission of about a third of the material as we know it,[7] while other material would presumably have had to be composed to take its place. At first blush, indeed, it looks as if an attempt was made to obey them. For the play as it comes down to us was clearly in process of being drastically overhauled, inasmuch as it consists of a basic text of thirteen leaves in one hand, and additional matter in five different hands, the new matter being written on extra leaves, in the margin of the basic text, and on scraps of paper pasted or (as was discovered by British Museum officials when they attempted to remove them) *glued* over deleted portions of the basic text. In short, a team of dramatic writers have been turned on to revise the play. The revision was, however, incomplete: the manuscript shows that something happened, we do not know what, to prevent its being carried through. Yet even had the revisers finished the job, they would have gone no way at all to meet the censor. On the contrary, instead of being left out, the insurrection scene was brilliantly re-written. We cannot therefore explain the revision as undertaken in response to Tilney's orders. Yet I agree with Edmund Chambers in finding it very difficult to believe a "booke" can have been submitted to the Master of the Revels, that is to say the chief government official for the control of the stage, in this "most untidy and in places almost unintelligible condition".[8] As it stands, the play could not have been acted. Nor do I believe it could have been read—or rather would have been read—by a dictatorial person intent on probing every line to discover whether it concealed dangerous matters of state. We face the chief puzzle of the manuscript, but there we must leave it and pass on to the question of the identity of the six hands involved.

In this direction considerable progress has been made up to date, if I may run ahead a little in my story. The man who wrote on the original manuscript was a second-rate dramatist, chiefly famous for his composition of Lord Mayor's shows, called Anthony Mundy. Though possibly the principal author of the play, at one place he makes a curious error, obviously of transcription, which proves that there at least he was copying someone else's manuscript. As for the hands in the additions, one of them belongs to the prompter or "book-holder", referred to above as engrossing the title of the "booke". The other four are all pretty certainly dramatists. One is undoubtedly Henry Chettle, another Thomas Dekker, and a third has been conjecturally identified with Thomas Heywood, a conjecture admitted as a possibility by Greg,[9] while the fourth when Maunde Thompson published his article on Elizabethan Handwriting had for forty-five years been labelled by the few who took any interest in the manuscript as perhaps Shakespeare. The addition contributed by this particular writer was in fact the "insurrection" or riot scene which the censor dropped on so heavily, though whether he was condemning the revised scene as we have it or the lost original in Mundy's hand which it replaced we do not know. All we can say is that, had Tilney ordered the passage to be rewritten instead of omitted, it is difficult to imagine any rewriting more calculated to meet his wishes. In the other scenes concerned with the rising, the sympathies of the audience are clearly being asked both for the prentices and against the foreigners. In this one alone the crowd is humorously represented as absurdly wrong-headed, while the speech in which More brings them to order is not only an eloquent plea on behalf of the plight of those they are proposing to murder or drive out of London, but a stern reminder that in rising against authority they are rising against God. The tone of all this is very similar to that of the crowd-scenes in Shakespeare, and on that ground, but also because of the supposed similarity of the handwriting to that of the signatures, one Richard Simpson in 1871, supported next year by a better scholar, James Spedding, claimed the addition as Shakespeare's.[10] Since then little had been heard of the attribution. In 1911, however, the whole *Booke* was reproduced in typographical facsimile for the Malone Society by Greg, who furnished a masterly introduction; "an edition", as Pollard observed, "which must always rank among the best examples of English literary and palaeographical scholarship".[11] On the possibility of Shakespeare being concerned in it, however, Greg was non-commital and wrote as follows:

> The question is one of stylistic evidence, and each reader will have to judge for himself. I do not feel called upon to pronounce; but I will say this much, that it seems to me an eminently reasonable view that would assign the passage to the writer who, as I believe, foisted certain of the Jack Cade scenes into the second part of *Henry VI*.[12]

It will be noticed that there is nothing in this about Shakespeare's handwriting.

Such was the position when some time early in 1916 Maunde Thompson returned to his old Department of Manuscripts and taking down *The Booke of Sir Thomas Moore* from its shelf opened it at the scene which Simpson and Spedding had picked out as a holograph by the greatest of English poets. What his hopes were I do not know, but the effect, I have been told, I think by Pollard, was instantaneous: he threw up his hands and cried "Shakespeare!" The Three Pages had passed a test to which palaeographers attach considerable weight, that of being at once identified by an expert relying upon general impressions, themselves the result of an exhaustive investigation of the authentic handwriting of the identified author. Nor did Thompson later waver for a moment in his conviction. But he had to convince the world and that was not easy. Before the year was out a slim volume entitled *Shakespeare's Handwriting* appeared with full-sized photographs both of the six signatures and of the Three Pages, with an independent transcript of the latter so that those unfamiliar with Elizabethan calligraphy could see at a glance how the writer spelt and punctuated, and with an analytical study of the handwriting, which sought to demonstrate that it also passed the further test of exhibiting peculiarities of penmanship previously detected in the signatures.

The evidence was marshalled and analysed with great skill. But those qualified to assess its value were very few in number: palaeographers are scarce and those with a special acquaintance of Elizabethan hands are scarcer still. Indeed, at that date Greg was probably one of the two or three scholars in the country competent to judge, and he was at first inclined to reserve his verdict. As for scholars in general, a claim depending upon six signatures, five of them penned in somewhat abnormal circumstances, seemed slender indeed. And though of course Thompson was a great authority he was getting old! But Pollard, to the best of my recollection (and I was already intimate with him in 1916), from the first accepted the attribution.[13] And in the present writer he had a disciple, six years younger than Greg, no palaeographer and a very amateur bibliographer, who nevertheless embraced the cause with enthusiasm because he was in possession of a body of material which he thought might strengthen Maunde Thompson's argument. I cannot, to my annoyance, remember at this date when it was that I first began to study *Shakespeare's Handwriting*. Probably not at once, as I was an exceedingly busy government official in 1916 and 1917, the middle of the first Great War. But it was sometime before the end of 1917 and there followed almost immediately a long correspondence between Maunde Thompson and myself which was for me in the nature of a "correspondence course" with the greatest English palaeographer as instructor and the "secretary hand" as the subject of instruction. For the old man took an ardent believer to his heart, made me write my letters to him in "secretary" which he diligently corrected, wrote letters (beginning "Dear Shakespeare") in reply, also in "secretary", and so gave me a working acquaintance with the hand that "went together" with the mind which I was to spend my leisure hours for the rest of my life trying to follow through the plays—little as I dreamt of such a sequel at that time. It was a gift beyond price, for which I can never express gratitude enough. And he was a wonderful and formidable old man, irascible and impatient of contradiction or criticism, but intensely human and full of fun; and, if the fun was a little heavy at times,

> wearing all his weight
> Of learning lightly like a flower.

Happily I was privileged to repay the debt in a small measure and while he was still alive.

Some people collect postage stamps, bus tickets, the names of railway engines, or what not. Before I encountered Maunde Thompson I had begun to collect misprints and odd spellings in the original Shakespearian texts. It is quite an amusing mania and one not without its method. No doubt it served to some extent as dope for the anxieties of war time. But the reason I took to it was that as a disciple of Pollard's and sharing his belief that many of the good quarto and folio texts were printed direct from Shakespeare's manuscripts, I hoped to discover something about the way he wrote and the way he spelt by studying the aberrations of the compositors who had to set up those manuscripts in type. Accordingly I made lists of the obvious misprints (i.e. misprints which have been corrected in all modern editions), and of the abnormal spellings, to be found in the good quartos; beginning with these because they were the texts Pollard had suggested as likely to be close to the dramatist's drafts.

By "abnormal" spellings I meant spellings that I thought a reputable compositor of the time would not wittingly have introduced into the text himself. Many compositors' spellings which now seem to us archaic were of course then quite normal. Yet even these spellings were on the whole far more modern than those of the average author with whose manuscript they had to cope; and far more consistent too, since manuscript spelling at that time differed not only from author to author but often from page to page, even from line to line, in the same author. In short, it was a blessed age when every gentleman spelt as he liked! This wide variety of usage by authors forced compositors to be more or less systematic. In the first place, to set up a manuscript in type letter by letter would have been not only tedious but costly, since time was money and speed was, then as now, an important element in compositorial skill. In the second, speed meant the compositor carrying a number of words at a time in his head as he turned from the "copy" to set up the type in his "stick"; and the head-carrying process inevitably meant translating the spelling of the copy into his own spelling, the spelling, that is, which he has learnt from his master when a prentice.

Why then was it that abnormal spellings frequently crop up in the quartos, so that my list when completed numbered many hundreds of examples? The answer is that they came, a large proportion of them, from the manuscript; they are words which caught and arrested the compositor's eye. An unskilful compositor, i.e. one not yet able to carry more than one or two words at a time in his head, will of course cling close to his "copy" and so introduce a number of his author's spellings into print. And even an accomplished craftsman will at times let copy-spellings through—when he is tired, when the light is bad (as it often was in Elizabethan printing-houses) or when a difficult or unusual word confronts him which has to be spelt out. In this connexion, it is important to notice that the commoner the word the less likely was it to be given an abnormal copy-spelling in print, since, other things being equal, common words are the easiest for a compositor's eye to pick up. Such is the theory of the business which is given in much the same words I used in 1923[14] and which Greg confirmed in essentials shortly afterwards by reproducing one of the few specimens of sixteenth-century printers' copy side by side with what the printer made of it in print.[15]

Already, however, in 1917, feeling confident that my collection of spellings and misprints provided information more or less definite about Shakespearian "copy", no sooner did I hold Maunde Thompson's book in my hands than I turned to his transcript of the Three Pages to see how far their spellings tallied with those I had culled from the quartos. To my delight they fitted in like pieces of a jig-saw puzzle. Modern or normal spellings of the Addition were not countered by abnormal spellings in the quartos; spellings of the Addition which are common in sixteenth-century manuscripts but rare in print could all be paralleled in the quartos either directly or by implication through misprints;[16] and finally all the abnormal or old-fashioned spellings in the Addition, some of them very old-fashioned or unusual, had also their parallels in the quartos. One of these was striking enough to make a small name for itself with the general public, since Sir John Squire took it as a theme for one of his short stories.[17] It made a little stir among scholars, too, for two reasons: on the one hand, no other example of it has since been found in any book or manuscript of the period though a sharp look-out was kept for it; and, on the other hand, "silence", the word in question, being quite a common one, had by then acquired its modern spelling in all the London printing-houses, so that any but a modern spelling for it was most unlikely to appear in print. Yet it is spelt "scilens" on the second of the Three Pages, its only occurrence in them, and after the same odd fashion eighteen times in the first quarto of *2 Henry IV*, though it always wears its modern dress elsewhere in the quartos and, as far as I am aware, in the Folio also. Hair-raising as the notion may be to the modern school-teacher, it looks as if "scilens" was Shakespeare's spelling or at least one of his spellings.[18] Yet if so, why do we find it in only one of the quartos and there so often? The explanation illustrates the principle just enlarged on. Compositors normalized it or modernized it everywhere else, but in *2 Henry IV* they found it (probably with an initial capital) as the name of a character and so reproduced it literatim. For a wise compositor left the spellings of names alone. How was he to know that what his author wrote as "Master Scilens" was not intended to be pronounced "Master Skilens"? Taking it all round, "scilens" was quite a nice little nugget for a digger to turn up. Yet a single parallel, however unique or remarkable, carried less weight than the *general* agreement and the over-all absence of disagreement which I noted between the spelling of the Addition and that of the quartos.

And the evidence of spelling was borne out by that of misprints. My list of these consists of a large and heterogeneous assortment, many of which may of course be due to other causes than compositorial misreading. Yet the prevalence of specific types of misprint, in a dozen or more quarto texts produced by some seven or eight printing-houses over a period of some fifteen years, can be safely attributed to the one common factor behind them all—the pen of William Shakespeare. These common types fall into five classes according to their apparent derivation from a confusion between certain letters in the "secretary" handwriting. Now an examination of the Three Pages showed that the hand which wrote them was prone to just the sort of pen-slips as would naturally give rise to these five common misprints. The two hands, I felt sure, were the same. But how was I to convince others, unfamiliar with "secretary" script? Or how could I prove that a compositor faced with the Three Pages would have stumbled in the same way and as frequently as his brethren who set up the quartos? I could not prove it; but I was able to point to a rather persuasive and not unamusing piece of circumstantial evidence in its favour. Once again Greg came to my aid, though without meaning to this time. He and Maunde Thompson had recently and independently transcribed the Addition. And in these transcripts their readings of three words differed, while that of a fourth was wrong, as Greg later admitted. It so happened that these four readings illustrated four out of the five classes of misprint just described. That is to say, modern palaeographic experts with magnifying glasses had fallen into four of the five traps which most commonly led to the undoing of the compositors of the quartos. I could not have hoped for better evidence.

But I must apologize for spending thus much time over these spellings and misprints. My excuse is their relevance to the main theme of this series, namely a modern editor's attitude towards the texts of Shakespeare. For in dealing with any given passage, what he needs above all things is (*a*) some knowledge of how Shakespeare is likely to have, or might have, written or spelt the words, and (*b*) some knowledge of how those words are likely to have been or might have been misread and/or misprinted. And, in point of fact, the lists of spellings and misprints I made some time about 1916 have proved a constant help with individual cruxes during thirty years of editing. But cruxes, though important, are but one of an editor's problems. He wants to know also how Shakespeare punctuated, whether he was careful or consistent with his stage directions and speech-prefixes, and if the manuscripts his printers printed from were full of erasures or actually bore out, to some degree at least, the statement of Heminge and Condell, who know them well, that "his mind and hand went together: and what he thought, he uttered with that easiness that we have scarce received from him a blot in his papers". In a word an editor must, if he can, visualize Shakespearian copy in general, so as to be able at need to reconstruct in imagination particular portions of it that give rise to his problems. Maunde Thompson's claim that in *The Booke of Sir Thomas Moore* we had three whole pages of his copy would, therefore, if it could be established, place a tool of the utmost value in the hands of all future editors. And Pollard, believing that the bibliographical evidence of spellings and misprints, by supporting the evidence of palaeography, went some way towards establishing it, began planning a co-operative statement of the position in the form of a book with contributions from himself, Greg, Maunde Thompson and the present writer, to be called *Shakespeare's Hand in the play of Sir Thomas More*. This appeared in 1923, but when it was already at an advanced stage another contributor turned up who was to provide fresh evidence, and evidence of a kind far more likely to convince the world in general than any bibliographical or palaeographical argument could hope to be.

This was R. W. (not to be confused with Edmund) Chambers, who, already at work upon his own famous book about Sir Thomas More, was naturally interested in this play, and had been investigating the literary aspect of the claim that three pages of it were Shakespeare's. And so the "little company of upholders of Shakespeare's authorship of the three pages" secured an unexpected but most welcome associate, who contributed to their book a final and crowning essay on 'The expression of ideas—particularly political ideas—in the Three Pages, and in Shakespeare'. Concentrating "on Shakespeare's concept of political order", which has since then become a commonplace of Shakespearian criticism, and his attitude towards the common people as expressed in the Jack Cade scenes of *Henry VI*, in *Richard II*, *Julius Caesar*, *Troilus and Cressida* and *Coriolanus*, he found "not merely striking parallels of expression and imagery with the Addition, but complete consistency of attitude and thought as well".

The little volume by Pollard's team of essayists on *Shakespeare's Hand in the play of Sir Thomas More* provoked a good deal of discussion among scholars and even attracted some notice in the daily press. Imagine for instance my astonishment one October morning to find London plastered with this poster from the *Daily Express*:

GREAT SHAKESPEARE FIND

Most valuable manuscript in the world

147 lines

Written by his own hand.

Imagine also my disappointment later at learning from the publishers that to the best of their knowledge the gratuitous advertisement had not sold a single extra copy.

Scholarly, or perhaps I should say pseudo-scholarly, criticism concentrated its attention upon the palaeographical aspect of the case. And even Greg felt that Maunde Thompson's presentation might with advantage be strengthened at certain points. Accordingly four years later he published a final summing up of the evidence on that side in which, after ridding Thompson's argument of certain disputable elements, he noted that the strength of the case for the identity of the two writers rested not so much on the fact that they both formed this or that letter in a peculiar way, undiscovered so far in other contemporary documents, as on their agreement in the formation of other letters also, inasmuch as "multiple agreement acquires considerable significance even though the individual forms may be common".[19] The same formula applies, as we have seen, to the bibliographical evidence, while in a second essay, delivered as a lecture in Manchester fourteen years after his first was printed, and later appearing in his volume entitled *Man's Unconquerable Mind*, Chambers reiterated it time and again. The true significance of his literary parallels, he insisted, lay not in the occurrence of this or that political idea, striking image or unusual turn of phrase in the plays of the Canon and in the Addition, but in the fact that similar combinations of similar units are found in both, the similarities of which if taken independently would prove nothing. And, as some persons found this line of argument a little difficult to follow, he illustrated it by telling the following story:

A Jew, obviously in a state of some distress, was met by his Rabbi, who enquired the cause. "I was called as a witness", was the reply, "and I was fined £10." "No, no! Abe. You mean you were called as a defendant, and were fined £10." "No, I was called as a witness; the Judge said, 'What is your name?' And I said (as you know) 'Abraham Isaac Jacob Solomon.' And the Judge said, 'Are you a Jew?' And I said, 'Now, don't be a silly ass.' And I was fined £10."

None of these names was conclusive, Chambers observes. "Think of Abraham Lincoln, Isaak Walton, Jacob Tonson, Solomon Grundy. But most of us would agree that the *combination* suggests Jewish origin with sufficient certainty to render the retort upon the Judge eminently justifiable.[20] It would mar the beauty of the story to give the Judge the further question "What is your address?" and Abe the reply "At Dree-ondert-dree Commercial Road". Yet that would make it still more apt. For, if Shakespeare and the writer of the Addition did not come from the same district, they belonged to the same very small circle of persons who were writing for the stage between 1590 and 1600, and if they did not mispronounce English in the same way they miswrote it and mis-spelt it alike. And yet, of course, a Gentile with an east German accent might very well be living in Commercial Road. We shall probably never be able to prove that Shakespeare wrote the Three Pages in *Sir Thomas More*. But a case, which in Greg's words rests on "the convergence of a number of independent lines of argument—palaeographical, orthographic, linguistic, stylistic, psychological—and not on any one alone",[21] can never be *dis*proved and is bound to win acceptance from an ever-widening circle of scholars. Indeed, two recent editors have actually included it in *The Complete Works*. We may say then that it has now been canonized.

As the sole surviving example of Shakespearian copy the Three Pages possess, as I said, a unique value for textual students. But it clearly cannot be regarded as a typical piece of copy. And Greg saw from the first that it could only be safely used when studied in the light of other surviving and more normal manuscript play-books of the period. The Malone Society, which he founded in 1906, for the exact reproduction in typographical facsimile of sixteenth-century plays, began at an early date to print those in manuscript and getting on for half of them have now been made available to scholars in this form. Meanwhile in 1931 he laid one of those "great bases for eternity" which at intervals he bestows upon the world of scholarship. This was a monograph entitled *Elizabethan Dramatic Documents* in two sumptuously produced volumes. One consists of full-sized facsimiles (with transcripts) of specimen pages of promptbooks, together with those of the more important theatrical papers which Alleyn left at Dulwich. Among these, by the way, was the only sixteenth-century "player's part" that has come down to us, that of Orlando in Greene's *Orlando Furioso*, which with the cues originally covered fourteen strips of paper, ten of these still surviving though four are imperfect. And the other volume gives us a full account of these papers followed by an analytical and descriptive list of all the forty-five extant play-books of the period.

Of even greater immediate importance, though in the nature of the case less enduring, was another two-volume monograph, called *William Shakespeare: a study of facts and problems*, published a year earlier by Edmund Chambers. With this, a great public official who rose to become Second Secretary of the Board (now the Ministry) of Education, crowned the parergon of a life-time by completing in a seventh and eighth volume his history of the stage that Shakespeare worked for, a history begun in 1903 with two volumes on *The Medieval Stage* and continued twenty years later with four others on *The Elizabethan Stage*. The publication of 1930 contained not only the facts of Shakespeare's life, set forth with a fulness and in a fashion superseding all previous biographies; not only a reprint of all the documents relating to his life, profession and contemporary reputation; not only a critical summary, play by play, of the facts known about each; but lengthy chapters dealing with practically every problem that confronts an editor; those headed The Book of the Play, The Quartos and the First Folio, and Plays in the Printing House being the most relevant. To all these matters the author brought unrivalled knowledge, refreshing common sense and a mordant scepticism in regard to the theories of previous writers among whom the man responsible for this article found himself uncomfortably but wholesomely prominent. In fact with those two masterpieces of scholarship, Chambers and Greg opened a fresh chapter in the study and understanding of Shakespeare's texts and the theatrical environment that conditioned them, and so virtually rendered out of date everything published on those subjects before 1930–1. And when it is observed that by then Quiller Couch and his colleague had been editing *The New Shakespeare* for ten years and had actually completed the comedies, to each of which was attached an elaborate "note on the copy", it will be seen how hazardous was, and still is, the life of an editor in these times of rapidly advancing knowledge. It was hazardous even for an Edmund Chambers, since in one important respect his account of the Book of the Play became obsolete almost before *William Shakespeare* appeared.

NOTES

1. *The Tempest* ('New Shakespeare'), Textual Introduction, p. xxx.

2. *Shakespeare's Fight with the Pirates* (second ed.), p. 54. This book was delivered as lectures at Cambridge in November 1915.

3. *Encyclopaedia Britannica* (tenth ed.).

4. *Shakespeare's Fight with the Pirates* (second ed.), pp. xxiii–xxiv.

5. See the article on 'Shakespeare's Hand in the play of "Sir Thomas More"' in the *Times Literary Supplement*, 24 April 1919, by Alfred Pollard, though unsigned.

6. In a letter to Burghley on 6 September 1586, the City Recorder relates how apprentices had been arrested for "conspiring an insurrection in this cittie against the Frenche and Dutche, but speciallie against the Frenche, all things as lyke unto Yll May Daye as could be devised..." (cited on p. 37 of *Shakespeare's Hand in the play of Sir Thomas More*).

7. *Shakespeare Survey*, 2, p. 50.

8. Chambers, *William Shakespeare*, I, 511.

9. See his article in the *Times Literary Supplement*, 24 November 1927.

10. Simpson's claim covered other additions as well; Spedding confined it to the scene before us. See *Notes & Queries*, 1 July 1871; 21 September 1872.

11. *Shakespeare's Hand*, p. 7.

12. *Sir Thomas More*, Malone Society Reprint, p. xiii.

13. Indeed he was already in November 1915 describing the Three Pages as "almost certainly" in the hand of Shakespeare (see *Shakespeare's Fight with the Pirates*, second ed., p. 57).

14. See *Shakespeare's Hand*, pp. 114–15.

15. See his article 'An Elizabethan Printer and his copy', *Transactions of the Bibliographical Society* (September 1923).

16. A good example is "deale" twice printed for "devil" in *Hamlet* (Q2) at II, ii, 628. This appears to be an *a:u* misprint of the spelling "deule", which actually occurs in the same text at III, ii, 136 and was not a very unusual manuscript spelling in the sixteenth century. Many other examples could be given.

17. *The Golden Scilens.*

18. E.g. the spelling "sylenct" (=silenced) also appears in the 'Shakespearian' Addition.

19. *Times Literary Supplement*, 24 November, 1 December 1927. It is to be hoped that these valuable articles may some day find a more permanent home. In his recently published monograph on *The Shakespeare First Folio: its bibliographical and textual history* (1955) Greg writes (p. 99): "In the present discussion it will be assumed that the three pages are in Shakespeare's autograph."

20. *Man's Unconquerable Mind*, p. 208.

21. *Times Literary Supplement*, 1 December 1927.

SHAKESPEARE IN THE BIBLIOTHECA BODMERIANA

BY

GEORGES A. BONNARD

Though, in the following notes, no attempt is made to give an adequate idea of the wealth of the Bibliotheca Bodmeriana, it is no doubt advisable, by way of introduction, to give some information on the origin of the library and explain what has inspired and is still inspiring its development.[1]

The Bibliotheca Bodmeriana is a private collection originating in the passionate interest felt by its founder and present owner, Martin Bodmer, for the greatest literary masterpieces of the world. He has built it up for now nearly forty years with rare devotion and a wholly admirable single-mindedness.

In the sixteenth century, at the time of the Reformation, a Bodmer left his native village in the upper Rhone valley and settled at Zurich, where his descendants soon played a not inconspicuous part in the life of the small republic. In the latter part of the eighteenth century they turned their talents to the already flourishing textile industry, gave it a new impetus and henceforth counted among those citizens who, in the course of the last hundred and fifty years, made of Zurich the important business centre it now is. From his forebears, Martin Bodmer inherited, besides a large fortune, a tradition of wide and deep culture, a genuine love of the arts. An early enthusiasm for Goethe gave him a vivid awareness of the supreme importance in the life of mankind of the great writers, the poets in particular. And he soon formed the resolution, not only of getting to know their works thoroughly, but of surrounding himself with what could best bring home to him the sense of their actual presence and all they had meant and mean for man, by collecting manuscripts, early editions, translations, and adding to these the necessary helps to study in the guise of bibliographies, modern scholarly editions and bibliographical studies.

Such an ambitious scheme could only be realized if it was strictly limited and Martin Bodmer determined to concentrate on the five literary monuments which he rightly regards as the pillars of Western civilization, the poems of Homer, the Bible, the *Divina Commedia*, the plays of Shakespeare and the works of Goethe. The collections he has formed round them are the main departments of his library. But the vital value of these supreme masterpieces is best illustrated and made sensible by placing near them some at least of the writers who without their influence would never have been what they were. To the Bible and Homer, to Dante, Shakespeare and Goethe he felt he must add the great classics of antiquity, of German, French, Italian, English and Spanish literature. And so, in his library we find, for instance, an early fifteenth-century manuscript and Caxton's second illustrated edition (1484) of the *Canterbury Tales*, Thynne's edition of *The Works of Geffray Chaucer* (1532), Stow's of 1561, Speght's of 1602 and 1687; the 1518 *Utopia* and More's collected Latin works published at Basle in 1563; the first editions (1590, 1596) of *The Faerie Queene*, *Arcadia* (1590), Raleigh's *History of the World* (1614), *The*

Anatomy of Melancholy (1621), Milton's *Poems* (1645); the 1667, 1668 and 1669 issues of the first edition of *Paradise Lost*, and the first edition of *Paradise Regained* and *Samson Agonistes* (1671), besides original editions and a large number of manuscripts and autographs of the more important eighteenth- and nineteenth-century English writers.

To give his growing collections a home worthy of their value, a fine old house at Zurich had been turned into a convenient library equipped with the necessary offices, show and reading rooms. But, in 1940, anxious to take an active share in the charitable work of the International Red Cross, Martin Bodmer came to Geneva to work under the central committee of which he eventually became a member and on which he is sitting still. Related through his marriage to influential Genevese families, he soon felt quite at home in a city that, owing to a long tradition, is a centre of international culture, and decided to make it his permanent residence and bring over his library there. A fairly large estate was acquired on the Cologny heights, and there, in a magnificent situation, a new library was built, two discreetly elegant pavilions in eighteenth-century style facing each other across a terrace whence one enjoys a wide prospect over the lake, the city at its end, and the steep Jura range beyond. In the northern pavilion there is a spacious reading-room, a beautiful show-room in the southern one; a wide underground passage, used as one more store-room, connects the two pavilions.

When the new library was inaugurated on 6 October 1951, Shakespeare was already represented in it by a set of the four Folios, the first edition of the *Sonnets* (1609), the *Poems* of 1640, and two of the plays reprinted for Thomas Pavier in 1619, *The Merchant of Venice* and *The Merry Wives of Windsor*, not to mention original editions of many of the translations of the plays into various languages. The small collection was already the best to be found on the continent. But Martin Bodmer—whose love for Shakespeare had been aroused, when he was but a boy of sixteen, by *The Tempest* illustrated by Dulac bought at a Zurich bookshop, the very first book he collected—could not rest content with it. He had long been on the lookout for more, especially for some of the early quartos which he knew had not yet found their way into public libraries. But the occasions of acquiring such treasures are rare and it was not until the Rosenbach company, in 1951, offered for sale all that was left of the Shakespeare early editions they had bought in 1919 from Marsden J. Perry, that the possibility of adding to the small collection a certain number of quartos presented itself. Martin Bodmer at once availed himself of it. He entered into negotiations with the American firm, succeeded in outbidding his competitors, and in February 1953 had the satisfaction of receiving, in two suitcases flown over the Atlantic by a representative of the Rosenbach company, the whole invaluable collection.[2]

In the description of the Shakespeare books in the Bibliotheca Bodmeriana, to which we can now proceed, we shall confine ourselves to publications up to 1700.

Let us begin with the plays printed before 1623. Of these the library possesses six in first editions, *Loves Labors Lost* (1598), *Henry IV*, Part 2 (1600), *Much Ado* (1600), *King Lear* (1608), *Troilus and Cressida* (1609), *Othello* (1622)—and one, *Romeo and Juliet*, in the second edition (1599), which, as everyone knows, is the first authoritative text of the tragedy, the first quarto (1597) being quite definitely one of the 'bad' ones. The *2 Henry IV* quarto is a copy of the first issue, the E gathering having but four leaves, and so is the *Troilus and Cressida* quarto.

Eight of the nine plays printed by Jaggard for Thomas Pavier in 1619 and all ascribed to Shakespeare are present. Five are unquestionably Shakespeare's: *Henry V* (dated 1608), *King*

Lear (dated 1608), *The Merchant of Venice* (dated 1600), *The Merry Wives of Windsor* (dated 1619), *A Midsummer Night's Dream* (dated 1600). One is the spurious *Sir John Oldcastle* (dated 1600). The other two are *Pericles* (dated 1619), a play of doubtful authorship, and *The Whole Contention between...Lancaster and Yorke* (undated) which brings together *The True Tragedy* and *The First Part of the Contention*, the actual nature of which, whether 'bad' quartos or source-plays, is still in dispute.

Then there are single copies of several quartos other than the first: the third, fifth, sixth and seventh of *Hamlet* (1611, 1637, 1676, 1676), the sixth and eighth of *Henry IV, Part 1* (1622, 1639), the second of *Loves Labors Lost* (1631), the third of the *Merchant of Venice* (1637), the second and third of *Othello* (1630, 1655), the sixth of *Pericles* (1635), the fourth and sixth of *Richard II* (1608, 1634), the fourth of *Romeo and Juliet* (1637), the third of *Titus Andronicus* (1611).

Lastly we find copies of the two plays which were published in separate quarto form only late in the seventeenth century, the 1673 *Macbeth*, of which there was no subsequent edition, and the 1684 *Julius Caesar*, a first edition, too, which was followed by many more.

Altogether the Bibliotheca Bodmeriana now possesses 32 of the 1222 quartos listed by Miss Bartlett in the second (1939) edition of her *Census*. This gives it the tenth rank among other collections of Shakespeare quartos, after the Folger which has more than two hundred, the Huntington with its eighty-four, the Bodleian (sixty-nine), the Harvard (fifty-seven), the Trinity College Cambridge (fifty), the Boston Public Library (forty-seven), and the New York Public Library (thirty-three). But most of those libraries collect duplicates whilst Martin Bodmer has made it a rule never to have more than one copy of the same edition or issue. If we eliminate the duplicates from Miss Bartlett's lists, the relative importance of the Bodmer collection is seen to be greater than appears on the first computation. Of the eighty-five different editions and issues no library has the whole. The Huntington has seventy-five, the Folger seventy-two, the British Museum sixty-eight, the Bodleian fifty-eight, the Harvard fifty-three, the Trinity College Cambridge fifty, the Boston forty and the New York twenty-seven. The Bodmer collection has the ninth place in this list. It can therefore hold comparison with some of the most famous Shakespeare collections and is the only one of its importance in private hands.

Another rule always observed by Martin Bodmer is to secure of every book the best copy available, and whereas many of the quartos listed by Miss Bartlett are in poor condition, more or less damaged and repaired, all those in the possession of the Bibliotheca Bodmeriana are in excellent and many in really perfect condition. Of the twelve copies extant of *Loves Labors Lost* (1598), for instance, four only seem to be in really good condition; the Bodmer copy is one of the four. *Much Ado* (1600) exists in seventeen copies; six of these only are quite good; the Bodmer copy is among them. Most of the twelve copies of *King Lear* (1608) are damaged and repaired; the Bodmer one is almost perfect. The *Troilus and Cressida* (1609) is not only the best of the four known copies, it appears to be the only copy of any of the quartos which was left by the binder entirely uncut. Turning its leaves is, for a lover of Shakespeare, a strangely moving experience. It makes one realize, as nothing else can, what sort of unpretentious little books those quartos really were, obviously printed on sheets of paper slightly unequal in size, so that the leaves differ from one another.

From the quartos, let us turn now to the Folios, of which the library boasts a magnificent set. Its First Folio is the Holford copy, one of the fourteen which are in perfect or almost perfect state of preservation. Its only defects are about half an inch of the lower outer corner of one leaf torn away, and even less of the same corner of another slightly crumpled. Though apparently unwashed, it is wonderfully clean throughout. Bound in calf, most probably quite soon after publication, by a binder who took care to leave wide margins, it is one of the largest copies to be found, though the British Museum Grenville copy is still larger by half an inch in height and three-eighths in breadth. The Bodmer copy of the Second Folio belonged at one time to William Lord Craven, whose book-plate it bears. It is also in excellent condition and bound in seventeenth-century calf. It has the Allot title No. 5, to use R. M. Smith's terminology: in the fifth line 'copies' is spelt with a single p. The fourth line of Milton's *Epitaph* reads "Under a starre-ypointing pyramid" and not "ypointed" as in other copies. The Third Folio is represented by a very fine copy which combines the two issues of 1663 and 1664. In this it does not stand alone. In similar volumes the additional plays, first published in 1664, sometimes stand at the beginning. In the case of the present volume we have a copy of the 1663 issue with the place in the title for Shakespeare's portrait left blank, to which have been added, in front, the first two leaves of the 1664 issue, the first so turned as to have the portrait facing the title on the second—and, at the end, the additional plays. As to the copy of the Fourth Folio, which has the Kerr book-plate and is like the others bound in seventeenth-century calf, it really looks as though it had never been in use, so magnificent is its condition throughout. It is one of the copies with the "H. Herringman, C. Brewster, R. Chiswell and R. Bentley" imprint.

Besides its Folios and Quartos, the Bibliotheca Bodmeriana has early editions of plays ascribed to Shakespeare, of three of his source-books and quite a number of Restoration adaptations and abridgments. In his *Apocrypha*, Tucker Brooke included thirteen suppositious plays. Five of them are at Geneva in their first edition, *Locrine* (1595),[3] *Sir John Oldcastle* (1600), *The London Prodigal* (1605), *The Puritan* (1607) and *The Two Noble Kinsmen* (1634). *Fair Em* is represented by a copy of the second edition (1631), *Arden of Feversham* by one of the third (1633). The Jaggard-Pavier reprint of *Sir John Oldcastle* has already been mentioned. The three source-plays are a first quarto of *King Leir* (1605), a second of *The Famous Victories of Henry the Fifth* (1617), and a third of *The Troublesome Raigne of John King of England* (1622). Of Restoration plays based on Shakespeare's there are eighteen in their first and two in their second editions.[4] Of little or no literary value in themselves, most of these adaptations are interesting as documents in the history of late seventeenth-century taste, of the Restoration attitude to Shakespeare's works. But an excellent copy of the first edition of *All for Love* is a book which any library would be happy to possess, and there is one in Martin Bodmer's library.

We must now consider its early editions of Shakespeare's non-dramatic works, not the least valuable among its many treasures. Years before he secured the Rosenbach collection, Martin Bodmer had acquired one of the four copies of the 1609 *Sonnets* with the "John Wright" imprint. It was bound in old brown calf and the binder had unfortunately cut the margins so as to give the little book a size convenient for the pocket, doing, however, no harm whatever to the text. Apart from that cropping and two holes, honestly filled in, in the leaf of the dedication—one of them affecting two letters of its first line and the other the blank space in the lower part of the page—the copy is in very good condition. One of its eighteenth-century owners wrote in ink just below the last line of the last sonnet a one-line remark: "What a heap of wretched Infidel Stuff". Who may have been this scandalized reader? Was he perhaps the third duke of Grafton (1735–1811), who was a man of strong principles? At any rate, the copy bears both on the title and on the last page a dry stamp with the words "Grafton heirloom" round a coat of arms surmounted by a ducal coronet. So it must have been for some time in the possession of the dukes of Grafton. Of John Benson's 1640 edition of the *Poems*, there is a copy which, despite some slight repairs to the first two and the last leaves, may be said to be perfect. There is no *Venus and Adonis*, no *Passionate Pilgrim*, but a *Lucrece* in a truly wonderful copy of its first edition (1594), and in one of the eighth published in 1655 with the addition of J. Quarles's *The Banishment of Tarquin*.

Thanks to the Bibliotheca Bodmeriana, our little country in the centre of Europe has now the great privilege of sheltering the largest collection of early editions of Shakespeare, not only on the continent, but outside England and America. May it prove not unworthy of that privilege!5

NOTES

1. Cf. Martin Bodmer, *Eine Bibliothek der Weltliteratur*, and 'Über die Bibliotheca Bodmeriana' (*Atlantis* (Zurich), March 1955, pp. 121–8); also Martin Bodmer's speech at the opening ceremony of 6 October 1951 in Fritz Ernst, *Von Zürich nach Weimar*, Bibliotheca Bodmeriana, I, s.d. (1953).

2. In his article on 'The Rosenbach-Bodmer Shakespeare Folios and Quartos', *Shakespeare Quarterly*, III (July 1952), J. Fleming described it as "the largest and most important transaction since 1914" in the book world.

3. This is the copy referred to by Sir E. K. Chambers, *William Shakespeare*, II, 392. A note on the title-page, by Sir George Buck, Master of the Revels from 1610 to 1622, ascribes the authorship to Charles Tilney.

4. Dryden and Davenant's adaptation of *The Tempest* (1670), Shadwell's re-adaptation of that adaptation (1674), Davenant's adaptation of *Macbeth* (1674), Dryden's *All for Love* (1678), his adaptation of *Troilus and Cressida* (1679), Otway's adaptation of *Romeo and Juliet* (1680), that curious blend of the story of the Verona lovers with Plutarch's Life of Marius, Crowne's adaptation of *Henry VI*, Part 2 (1680) and Part 1 (1681), Tate's of *Richard II* (1681), *King Lear* (1681) and *Coriolanus* (1682), Dryden's abridgment of *Othello* (1681), Durfey's of *Cymbeline* (1682), Ravenscroft's of *Titus Andronicus* (1687), Settle's of *Midsummer Night's Dream* (1692), Lacy's of *The Taming of the Shrew* (1698), Betterton's of *Henry IV*, Part 1 (1700) and Gildon's of *Measure for Measure* (1700). Davenant's *Macbeth* and Lacy's *Sauny the Scott* are also present in second editions.

5. I wish to acknowledge with deep gratitude the help I received in the preparation of this article from Martin Bodmer himself. Not only did he place all the books at my disposal for free leisurely examination, but he generously gave me all the information I required.

AN UNPUBLISHED CONTEMPORARY SETTING
OF A SHAKESPEARE SONG

BY

JOHN P. CUTTS

In *The Winter's Tale* Autolycus, Mopsa and Dorcas sing a three-part song, beginning "Get you hence, for I must go". The original setting for this has hitherto remained unknown, but now it is possible not only to give the music to which it was sung but also to suggest the composer and to present the words of a second verse, not reproduced in the Folio text of the play.

The setting (see Plate V) occurs in a manuscript volume, 'Songs unto the violl and lute', which was once in the possession of Stafford Smith, author of *Musica Antiqua* (1812). The manuscript passed into the hands of Edward Francis Rimbault, a zealous musical historian, and subsequently to the Music Division of the New York Public Library, where it is now designated manuscript Dx. 4175.[1] How Stafford Smith came to miss the setting is a puzzle, for in his *Musica Antiqua* he printed no less than eight of the manuscript's songs,[2] and it is strange that he did not identify the words as those in *The Winter's Tale*. Probably the music was composed by Robert Johnson: the manuscript, although it presents no attribution to him, gives it in close proximity to several compositions certainly or almost certainly by him—"Come away Hecket" from Middleton's *The Witch*, c. 1610, "Deare doe not your faire bewty wronge" from May's *The Old Couple*, c. 1615, "O let us howle" (XLII) from Webster's *The Dutchesse of Malfy*, 1613, "Tell me dearest what is love" from Beaumont and Fletcher's *The Captaine*, c. 1611, and "Have you seene the bright lilly growe" (XLIX) from Jonson's *The Divell is an Asse*, 1616. The fact that all these plays were produced by the King's Men, for whom Robert Johnson was busily writing in the theatre and at court between 1608 and 1617—makes it not inconceivable that the setting is Robert Johnson's.[3]

In another seventeenth-century music manuscript which passed to the New York Public Library from Rimbault's collections[4] and is now classified as manuscript Dx. 4041, there is an incomplete musical setting of "Get you hence", which is scored dramatically for a bass and two trebles. Of considerable interest is the existence here of a second verse. Though one is naturally apprehensive about claiming that this second verse originally belonged to *The Winter's Tale*, there are certain indications tending to the belief that this may have been so. In the play the song is introduced by a short piece of dialogue (IV, iv, 298–317):

> *Mopsa.* We can both sing it; if thou'lt bear a part, thou shalt hear; 'tis in three parts.
> *Dorcas.* We had the tune on't a month ago.
> *Autolycus.* I can bear my part; you must know 'tis my occupation; have at it with you.

Song

> *Autolycus.* Get you hence, for I must go
> Where it fits not you to know.
> *Dorcas.* Whither?

86

AN UNPUBLISHED SETTING OF A SHAKESPEARE SONG

Get yee hence for I must goe, where it fitts not you to know, whether, o?

whether, whether it befitts thine oath full well, thou to mee thy sec-rets tell, and

mee to let mee goe thether, if thou goest to Grange or Mill, If to either, thou dost ill.

Neither what neither, neither, thou hast vow'de thy loue to mee, thou hast

sworne my loue to bee: then whether goest say whither, whither.

Errors in M.S. tablature
2 line bar 3 originally read   o. ♩   dca in the 4th. string;
3 line bar 2 originally read   o   c   in the 6th. string;
3 line bar 5 originally read   o   c   in the 5th. string;
                                           ♩   in the 6th string:

Mopsa.	O, whither?
Dorcas.	Whither?
Mopsa.	It becomes thy oath full well,
	Thou to me thy secrets tell.
Dorcas.	Me too, let me go thither.
Mopsa.	Or thou goest to the grange or mill.
Dorcas.	If to either, thou dost ill.
Autolycus.	Neither.
Dorcas.	What, neither?
Autolycus.	Neither.
Dorcas.	Thou hast sworn my love to be.
Mopsa.	Thou hast sworn it more to me.
	Then whither goest? say, whither?[5]

There follows a short speech:

Clown. We'll have this song out anon by ourselves: my father and the gentlemen are in sad talk, and we'll not trouble them.

Obviously, from the Clown's last words, there was more to the song than is presented here and consequently there is great interest in finding what the missing words were. The manuscript is noticeably corrupt, and this is probably attributable to the copyist's difficulty in making out the writing of his original;[6] he himself writes a mixed italian and secretary hand *c.* 1640. In general, however, the sense of the passage is clear:

> neuer more for lasses sake
> will I dance at fare or wake
> Ah mee
> oh Ah me
> Ah mee
> who shall then weare a rated shooe
> or what shall ye bagpipe doe
> recant or elce you slay mee
> (recant or elce you slay me)[7]
> if thou leaue our Andorne greene
> where shall fill or frize be seene
> sleeping
> what sleeping
> sleeping
> no Ile warrant the sitting sadly
> or Idely wallking madly
> (in some darke
> (in some darke
> (in some darke darke Corner weeping
> (in some darke darke Corner weeping.

The setting[8] is of much beauty and is fully worthy of performance in any future production of *The Winter's Tale* which seeks to establish something of the original musical atmosphere. The transcript[9] given here adheres faithfully to the original except to correct obvious mistakes.

NOTES

1. Rimbault's library was sold on 3 July 1877 and following days. Fortunately it was well catalogued. Several of the music manuscripts were purchased for the Drexel collection, which is now incorporated in the Music Division of the New York Public Library. The auction catalogue refers to : "Lot 1389. 'Songs unto the violl and lute', written in the early part of the seventeenth century, autograph letter of Thomas Oliphant inserted in the original binding, 'Anne Twice her booke' written on the outside of the front cover." This is the manuscript under present consideration.

2. Smith referred to the manuscript itself in a variety of ways (references in brackets are to the *Musica Antiqua*):

(*a*) "Come away Hecket" (I. 48), is referred to as 'The original music in the Witches scene, in Middleton's comedy of the Witch. from a MS. of that age in the Editor's possession';

(*b*) "Though your strangnes frett my hart" (I. 52)—'Song from a M.S. of James the 1st's. time in the Editor's coll^n';

(*c*) "Deare doe not your faire bewty wronge" (I. 53)—'SONG. Taken from the above mentioned MS—Composed by Johnson';

(*d*) "Rest awile you cruell cares" (I. 54)—'Song from Manuscripts in James the 1st's time';

(*e*) "Tell me dearest what is love" (I. 55)—'SONG. from the same M.S."

(*f*) "Ist for a grace or ist for some mislike" (I. 62)—'From ANCIENT SONGS UNTO THE VIOLL AND LUTE. written about the year 1620';

(*g*) "You herralds of my M^rs hart" (I. 63)—'Taken from an ancient MS. written about the year 1620, in the Editor's possession';

(*h*) "When I sit as judge" (I. 64)—'SONG'.

These are numbers LIIII, XXV, XLI, violl (and XLI lute), XL, XLIIII, XX, LVIII, and XXVI, in the manuscript respectively. The viol version of "Deare doe not your faire bewty wronge" is ascribed in the manuscript to "Mr Johnson". There can be no doubt that Smith took the songs from this source.

3. See my article 'Robert Johnson: King's Musician in his Majesty's Public Entertainment', *Music & Letters*, April 1955, XXXVI, 110–25.

4. *Auction catalogue of the library of Edward Francis Rimbault 1877*, Lot 1388.

5. The following manuscript variants occur apart from spellings, capitalizations and abbreviations:

6 befitts 4175; 8 and mee 4175: & me 4041; 9 if thou 4175, 4041; 9 to Grange 4175, 4041; 14 vow'de thy loue to mee 4175; 15 my loue to be 4175; 16 then whether goest say whither, whither? 4175: then whether, then whether, whether goest thou whether, 4041.

6. I can suggest no emendation for "rated shooe" or "Andorne", but "fill or frize" seems to be "Phill or Frize". The former would be a contraction for "Phillida" and "Frize" occurs as a country woman's name along with "Maudline", "Luce" and "Nel" in *The Two Noble Kinsmen*. (*The Works of Beaumont and Fletcher*, Cambridge, 1910, IX, 332.)

7. Brackets indicate repetitions attributable to musical licence and chorus needs.

8. The setting in Dx. 4041 is intrinsically the same as in Dx. 4175, only in a different key; it ends after "if to either thou doest ill". From the Dx. 4175 version I have been able to realize the Dx. 4041 setting, but prefer to give here in transcript the setting in the earlier manuscript.

9. By kind permission of the Music Division of the New York Public Library to whom I am also indebted for permission to print a photograph of the original manuscript leaf.

GARRICK'S STRATFORD JUBILEE: REACTIONS IN FRANCE AND GERMANY

BY

MARTHA WINBURN ENGLAND

Garrick's Shakespeare Jubilee held at Stratford-upon-Avon in 1769 generated a series of reactions that gave testimony to its almost unique power as Shakespearian publicity. The terms in which it publicized Shakespeare were markedly romantic. The Jubilee was a clear prefiguration of characteristic romantic attitudes towards Shakespeare, and the varied reactions to it in England, France and Germany were premonitory of the varied courses romanticism would follow. By overt statement and by dramatic presentation the Jubilee announced and fostered the interest in the poet's biography and milieu, the connexion of his writings with medieval times, the emphasis on subjective, emotional reaction which resulted in widespread democratization of critical authority, and most specifically the concept of Shakespeare as almost literally a creator of living characters. In England these concepts were met and modified by the force of satire in the press and on the stage. Of the vast amount of writing elicited by the Jubilee, by far the greater portion was satiric; and Garrick himself was quickly forced into a compromise position by the power of public opinion. The stage productions based on the Jubilee as they appeared the following season display one by one an increasing element of ridicule. Garrick's own play *The Jubilee*, staged 91 nights at Drury Lane, satirized the event he referred to by that time as "that foolish hobby-horse of mine". The production represented a compromise, for within the satiric play Garrick retained the 'blasphemous' procession of Shakespearian characters that marched from the street through the audience to do obeisance to their 'creator's' image on the stage, with unprecedented demand for audience participation in the idolatry. The play had the record run of the century, in 1769–70, and another extended run in the year 1776. It was considered the most spectacular theatrical display of the century in an age that believed in theatrical display. All that stage technique could do was done to impress the doctrine of Shakespeare as creator of character, and the doctrine was more and more explicitly dramatized week by week. Garrick's play was indeed a satire on the Stratford Jubilee, but its rational elements only partially offset the irrational idolatry. It typified at popular level the "Romantic Compromise in England" charted by Walter Jackson Bate at the level of philosophical concept.[1] The compromise involved concessions on both sides. Those who opposed their rational satire to Jubilee idolatry modified the course of bardolatry, but they surrendered as a concession in the compromise their basis of rational criticism; not one questioned the major premise of the Jubilee, Shakespeare's absolute perfection. It was not so in France; the Romantic Compromise could not be peaceably effected there.

FRANCE

The French reaction to the Jubilee must be considered against the background of Garrick's triumphant conquest of France at the time of his visit in 1765,[2] for in France the Jubilee as a rule was not considered an iconoclastic event, but a continuation and intensification of attitudes already adopted in 1765. Garrick had been received in social and theatrical circles of France with adulation surpassing any English enthusiasm he ever knew; moreover, he had been welcomed with great seriousness into the growing controversies centred in the theatre. He encountered an almost insatiable curiosity as to his views on philosophical and practical problems of managing, staging, writing and acting. Subsequent writings of Grimm, Mercier, Diderot, Marmontel, Suard, Bonnet, Ducis, Morellet and Beaumarchais bear testimony to the earnest consideration with which they heard his opinions. Garrick long ago had made common cause with Shakespeare, and now in French salons the names were inextricably blended. "Mon cher Shakespeare" he was called, and he turned to good account every opportunity to make Shakespeare the ultimate authority in dramatic theory or practice, and Garrick the interpreter.

In 1769 France received with rejoicing the news of the Jubilee. Yet the many enthusiastic accounts of the event showed important variations from the English reports in contemporary diaries, books, newspapers and manuscript records. Most obvious differences were in the story of the origin of the Jubilee and the English reaction to it. Actually it was Garrick who suggested and accomplished the Jubilee in the face of much opposition and the unfavourable comments far outnumbered favourable writings in England. But on the continent no cognizance was taken of these facts at any time. The Jubilee was accepted as having been both instituted and endorsed by the entire English nation, a spontaneous folk movement, England rising as one man to honour this great Child of Nature—'Nature' now carrying strong overtones of Rousseau. For months the praises of the Jubilee increased. Because of the central position of France in the cultural world, minor reactions deriving from French influence were felt in Russia, Spain, Sweden, Denmark and Italy.[3]

Certain developments in France occurred chronologically after the Jubilee and took impetus from the fervid publicity attendant upon it.

On the professional stage an era of Shakespearian adaptations was ushered in by Ducis's *Hamlet* in 1769, first of many from his pen. Baculard D'Arnaud, Douin, Butine, Collot d'Herbois and others translated and adapted Shakespeare for the stage. The plays are important, not for their literary quality, but for their spreading of Shakespeare's fame and for the part they played in modifying French repertory acting. Class lines had been firmly fixed in the French theatre, comedy in one class, tragedy in another, and—so far as accepted critical theory admitted—the rising sentimental bourgeois drama, *déclassé*. Actors and acresses were strictly 'typed' in one class or another. Tragedy was represented by Mlle Dumesnil, Mlle Clairon, Mlle Gaussin, Lekain and Brizard. Mlle Dangeville and Préville played comedy. Molé played in the new dramas of Diderot, Saurin and de Falbaire, considered beneath the dignity of tragedians and foreign to the gifts of comedians. Some good actors, like Grandval and Bellecourt, could play *rôles à manteau*—courtiers, princes, financiers—in any production, but even these sedate roles were performed with different techniques in different types of drama. In the 1770's, however, the clear lines of demarcation of *genre* were melting. The general term *drame* was first used in 1769; 'nature' in Rousseau's definition began to absorb the old conventions of the stage and gradually every type of character became appropriate for stage representation. It was the Shakespearian productions that established this middle ground and overstepped the old conventions; Shakespeare represented an acknowledged meeting-place of the tragic, the comic, the sentimental. From 1769 on Molé, Préville and Lekain appeared side by side in Shakespearian productions.

Drama and dramatic theory pale in comparison with a living drama played in France as a result of Jubilee enthusiasm—the celebrated Voltaire-Le Tourneur controversy. Shortly after the Jubilee, frankly riding the wave of Jubilee publicity, the Comte du Catuelan, Malherbe and Pierre Le Tourneur announced that an integral translation of Shakespeare was in progress. The noble name by courtesy came first, but the work was organized and performed largely by Le Tourneur, a man of high character and considerable ability who made known in France many literary works of foreign countries, especially those of England. Voltaire's attack on the Le Tourneur Shakespeare was as ludicrous in some aspects as it was serious in its profound implications. Certainly his exaggerated rage and grief, his violent terminology and epithets indicate that offended senile vanity may have been a factor in the case. Voltaire's antics during this battle are justly famous; an especially spirited and amusing account is that of J.-J. Jusserand in *Shakespeare en France sous l'ancien régime*.[4] In justice to the lean old warrior, however, it should be remembered that at least he knew what he was fighting, and by his standards all was fair in that war.

Voltaire's name had figured largely in Jubilee controversy in England, both sides claiming to be his sworn enemies. Satirists of the Jubilee represented it to be an instrument in his hands to degrade Shakespeare and his authorized critics; Garrick and the Stratford bumpkins were puppets to his machinations. On the other hand, those who supported the Jubilee claimed it was to be the crushing blow to the arch-enemy of Shakespeare, that Voltaire would be led in chains with the procession of Shakespearian characters and burnt in effigy in the streets of Stratford. There had been no burning in effigy, but Garrick's introduction printed with his *Ode to Shakespeare* and the dramatic skit that led up to his oration both were direct challenges to Voltaire.[5] In France Voltaire's friends felt a Voltaire 'Jubilee' would be an appropriate consolatory gesture, but the plan was dropped for lack of popular support. It was suggested that a column be dedicated to Voltaire, but this plan was discarded for the same reason. In 1770 by popular subscription Pigalle was commissioned to make a statue of Voltaire—a commission carried out with some difficulty because the subject was too restless to pose—and there the matter rested until the Le Tourneur controversy reopened it. Although growing Shakespeare idolatry drew some contemptuous protests from Voltaire, he observed moderation until he saw France giving all-but-official sanction to the same idolatry seen at the Jubilee in England, in Le Tourneur's volumes that exalted the Jubilee as an "événement le plus mémorable dont il ait jamais été fait mention dans les Annales des Théâtres, depuis que le Poésie Dramatique fleurit en Europe".[6]

From Voltaire's point of view, the long list of distinguished subscribers was alarming, and every line of the introductory material represented a challenge to his beliefs. The dedicatory epistle to the king praises Shakespeare by standards that amount to a reversal of Voltaire's evaluations of the nature and purpose of drama. "Sentiment and realism in drama are means to the end of an increased recognition of the rights of man", is the message Le Tourneur has for the King, couched in flattering praise of a monarch who is both artistically sensitive and famed for his sympathies with the common man. Shakespeare's lowly birth is most significant. His historical plays are especially commended to the King's perusal; far from apologizing for the scenes of low life, Le Tourneur holds them up as things of particular beauty to the eyes of a democratic king.

The rhapsodic account of "Jubilée de Shakespeare" appears to be taken in part without acknowledgment from Benjamin Victor's *History of the Theatres of London* (1771) and in part from a biography of Shakespeare printed in *The London Magazine*.[7] Le Tourneur anticipates two objections to the Jubilee which might occur to his French readers, excess of enthusiasm and the extravagant expenditure of government funds. To the first he answers that Frenchmen have heretofore had no good translations and therefore no opportunity to judge the merits that prompted such a demonstration. To the second he answers that it is the duty of a government to encourage poetic genius. "Ce n'est plus la profusion, c'est l'avare & *mesquine* économie, que est alors à craindre & à blâmer."

Le Tourneur's biography of Shakespeare is an emotionalized version of Rowe's with added emphasis (from biographies published for the Jubilee) on such ideas as Le Tourneur wanted to underline—the lowly origin, the charm of rural life—and added philosophical comment. Four pages attack openly the critical position of Marmontel's *Chefs-d'œuvre dramatiques*, systematically quoted with page references, and bluntly refuted in paragraphs beginning "La vérité est...".

A summary of English criticism as interpreted by Le Tourneur is made an even more effective polemical weapon. The method of presentation was masterly for his purpose. He claims to be presenting extracts from the prefaces to English editions of Shakespeare, adding only the phrases necessary for providing continuity. He mentions "Rowe, Pope, Warburton, Theobald, Hanmer, Johnson, Sewell &c". The quotations are not specifically accredited to the various authors, but are cleverly 'slanted' and embedded in a background calculated to controvert the established canons of French criticism. It is an interesting commentary on English neo-classicism that so much material of this nature could be selected from the writers named, but actually it is difficult to isolate many passages. Aristotle is drawn over to Shakespeare's side in the controversy concerning dramatic rules by the same method Maurice Morgann used in his essay on Falstaff printed the following year, that of putting in Aristotle's mouth words he presumably would have spoken if he had ever seen Shakespeare's plays.[8] Of special interest is Le Tourneur's defence of Shakespeare's mingling of comedy and tragedy, "ces deux genres, regardés ordinairement comme incompatibles". As proof of their compatibility he cites the mystic union of the two spirits of comedy and tragedy as embodied in Garrick.

The entire tendentious quality of the long preface is epitomized in the fact that the word *Romantique* appeared here for the first time in the French language, with the author stressing the need for both the word and the concept in France.[9] Voltaire called the book "son abominable grimoire", and it verily was black magic in the eyes of a man who had dedicated his life to the proposition that man was a rational creature and freedom, toleration, justice must be founded on that proposition. To make a case for toleration founded on irrational concepts did violence to his views of the nature of man, just as a case for sentimentality and realism in drama did violence to his views of the nature of dramatic convention. Voltaire had criticized Shakespeare as a dramatist, but he had praised him as a poet, had borrowed from his plays, had done much to make his name known in Europe; but Voltaire was confronted with something new, an attitude toward Shakespeare he could only denounce as long as he lived. His private letters—often made public in the newspapers—adopted the terms of total war. They spoke of treachery, intrigue, betrayal of France.[10] Exponent of free speech as he was, he attempted to have the volumes suppressed. D'Alembert was his chosen lieutenant in the war, and agreed to read before the Academy Voltaire's letter of protest. D'Alembert insisted on deletion of some of the obscenity in the letter and Voltaire reluctantly acquiesced. He was loath to dilute the wine of his wrath, thinking the situation should be presented in all its vileness so the youth of the nation might be saved from the slough into which their elders had precipitated themselves. D'Alembert read the letter on St Louis Day in 1776, having assured Voltaire that his pride as a Frenchman was involved and he would rush into battle shouting *Vive Saint Denis-Voltaire et meure Georges-Shakespeare*. A few days later, however, he wrote to Ferney in shocked surprise that the letter had been placed under royal proscription as injurious to the cause of religion, and the Academy was made to feel the royal displeasure.

It is testimony to Voltaire's power that Le Tourneur did not mention his name once in open defiance, and further testimony that the letter to the Academy went unanswered. In a nation of newly-converted Shakespeare idolaters not one openly joined battle. Still the Le Tourneur volumes continued to appear with steadily growing lists of subscribers. A second edition appeared in 1777. Individual plays were translated from Le Tourneur's versions into other European languages. The books were popular in France until the time of the Napoleonic Wars, when all things English fell into disfavour, but were reissued in 1821, and from 1827 on were very popular.

GERMANY

While French enthusiasm for the Jubilee was palely reflected in the countries of Europe where French influence was strong, in Germany rebellion was brewing against French cultural domination and the news of the Jubilee gave pretext for open revolt. Lessing's theories of aesthetics, Gerstenberg's letters on literature and—unintentionally—Wieland's translation of Shakespeare[11] had already provided some basis for mutiny. In the Alsatian city of Strasbourg, where French and German influences met in sharp contrast, news of the Jubilee served to enforce a movement tangential to French cultural centrality. The writings on Shakespeare connected with the Jubilee celebrations in Germany form a composite manifesto of the movement later to be called *Sturm und Drang*.

Johann Gottfried Herder came to Strasbourg in September 1770 at the age of twenty-five. His precocious professional success and his scholarly attainments drew to him a group of young intellectuals connected with the university. Like satellites they revolved around him at varying distances, the nearest orbit being that of Goethe, a law student aged twenty-one. Other members of the group were students of theology or philosophy, but Herder's interests charted for them amazingly varied extra-curricular studies: Gothic architecture, Shaftesbury, Lessing, Diderot, Ossian, Kant, Swift, Young, Hume, Locke, George Lillo, Rousseau, the *Knittelvers* of Hans Sachs, German folk song, theories of language and of national education, primitive religion, even magic. Shakespeare was their idol, subject of their most serious study and companion in their recreation. They translated scenes, they modelled their smart university-student conversations on the quips and puns of Malvolio and Toby Belch. Shakespeare, as they interpreted him, strangely aligned all their diverse interests.

Accounts of the Jubilee came to them through France. 'Fête de Shakespeare' from the *Mercure de France* was copied in eight pages of manuscript and bound into Goethe's copy of the Wieland translation.[12] Members of the group refer familiarly to material not found in French periodicals—Garrick's comic songs and the Stratford oration—so it is evident they also read

English accounts of the Jubilee. Like the French, they overlooked any evidence of English disapproval and unanimously regarded the Jubilee as a spontaneous, nation-wide, outburst of English enthusiasm. Like the French enthusiasts, they regarded the Jubilee as a dramatization of their own ideals; but their interpretation of its significance is removed from the French interpretation by the distance between *Sturm und Drang* ideals and the principles then current in France. For the German idolaters, the Jubilee was a true folk movement with emphasis on medieval pageantry, honouring a primitive poet in a primitive setting, yet operating within the framework of that great institution for inculcation of national ideals—the theatre. Prompted by Goethe, they felt they could do no less than emulate an event corresponding so closely to their ideal for Germany.

In August 1771 Goethe returned to his father's home in Frankfurt. At his urging two festivals were held simultaneously on 14 October, the Protestant name-day for 'William', Goethe presiding and giving the oration at Frankfurt, the actor Friedrich Rudolph Salzmann presiding under his instructions at Strasbourg. A student of theology at the university, Franz Christian Lerse, gave the Shakespeare oration at Strasbourg. Two undated letters from Goethe to Herder indicate the mood of the preparations.

[Frankfurt, September 1771]

Meine Schwester macht mich noch einmal ansetzen. Ich soll Sie grüsen, und Sie auf den vierzehnten October invitiren, da Schäckesp. Nahmenstag mit grosem Pomp gefeuert werden wird. Wenigstens sollen Sie im Geiste gegenwärtig sein, und wenn es möglich ist Ihre Abhandlung auf den Tag einsenden, damit sie einen Teil unsrer Liturgie ausmache.[13]

Later he wrote again:

[Frankfurt, October 1771]

Eschenburg ist ein elender Kerl. Seine Übersetzung /: der Stellen Sch. versteht sich :/ verdient keine Nachsicht sie ist abscheulich. Die Abhandlung selbst hab ich nicht gelesen, werde auch schwerlich. Schicken sie nur Ihre auf den 14ten October. Die erste Gesundheit, nach dem 'Will of all Wills' soll auch Ihnen getrunken werden. Ich habe schon dem Warwickshirer ein schön Publikum zusammengepredigt, Und übersetze Stückgen aus dem Ossian damit ich auch den aus vollem Herzen verkündigen kann. Meine Schwester lässt Sie grüsen.[14]

Herder did not accept the invitation and his letters in reply are not preserved. Goethe omitted from his autobiographical writings any mention of the Jubilee—possibly he was not proud of his *Sturm und Drang* oration. Neither it nor Lerse's oration was printed during their lifetime, but both survived in manuscript, Goethe's in a manuscript which by its appearance caused Max Morris's conjecture that it had been sent as a round-robin letter to any of the group who were absent from the celebrations. A letter from Goethe to Johann Gottfried Röderer seems to indicate that the oration was known in Strasbourg and highly praised.[15] Lerse's oration was found among Röderer's literary remains and is printed in part with omitted sections summarized in August Stöber's *J. G. Röderer von Strassburg und seine Freunde* (Colmar, 1874). In addition to these records, there is a line of Latin in the daybook of Goethe's father concerning expenditures:

Dies Onomasticus Schacksp. fl. 6.24...
Musica in die onom. Schacksp. 3 fl.

This notation helps to define Goethe's phrase "mit grosem Pomp", but it raises more questions than it answers. The Imperial Rath of Frankfurt regarded Klopstock's unrimed verse as a vulgar innovation, and presumably would have agreed with his admired Voltaire on the subject of Jubilees for the "drunken barbarian". By some means his co-operation was secured. Either insensitive to the Zeitgeist or in resignation to it, neo-classical conservatism paid the bills for the first Shakespeare festival ever held on German soil. One could wish to have seen Garrick at Stratford wring praise from his enemies and reduce his friends to maudlin unintelligibility with his ode and oration in one of the greatest performances of his life. The vision of Goethe on the evening of Shakespeare Day equally fires the imagination. Genius paid tribute to genius in the brightly-lit rooms on the first floor of the Goethe home. With music and dancing, toasts and festive garments, the Great Pagan hailed Shakespeare as the Great Pagan and in impassioned words acknowledged him master.

Along with the orations known to have been read at the two celebrations, two other writings of dubious 'Jubilee' connexion should be considered, for the connexion by internal evidence is obvious. Herder's *Briefe an Gerstenberg*, the first of three drafts of his essay on Shakespeare published in *Von Deutsche Art und Kunst* in May 1773, was written before Goethe left Strasbourg. He probably hoped for some version of this letter to be sent as "einen Teil unsrer Liturgie".[16] The *Anmerkungen übers Theater* of J. M. R. Lenz was begun about September 1771, but it is impossible to know with certainty in what form it existed at that time, despite brilliant conjectural analysis by Theodor Friedrich and later by M. N. Rosanov.[17] For purposes of generalization the four works may be considered together, with more detailed study later of the two works known to have been *Festreden zum Shakespearstag*.

General similarities of style are at once apparent. The reader is constantly aware of the tone of intimate speech addressed to a small, discerning group in a crass and tasteless age; but the speakers have an air of hope that the group may serve as leaven for the lump. "Wir feiern heute *Shakespears* Tag", said Lerse, "des so unrecht verstanden, so oft verlaumdeten und nur wenig edlen richt bekandten Shakespears". It is their accepted duty to reinterpret him for social and political reasons as well as for artistic ends. The style is what they considered 'bardic', exclamatory, full of sudden ejaculations, "Ha!", "Natur!", "Freiheit!", inserted apparently at random. The verbal structure is prominent and many verbs have intensive prefixes. Many sections have heavy rhythmical stress. The syntax manifests deliberate revolt against Lessing's almost tabular clarity; in Lerse this is least apparent, more in Herder, with Goethe exaggerating Herder and Lenz, "Goethes Affe", exaggerating Goethe's bardic style into complete incomprehensibility at times. Garrick's bardic ecstasy appears, on paper at least, very neat and orderly by comparison. But disorder was considered appropriate to the festival spirit. Goethe spoke with youthful enthusiasm. "Erwarten Sie nicht, das ich viel und ordentlich schreibe; Ruhe der Seele ist kein Festtagskleid."[18]

They unite in wholehearted idolatry of the great 'primitive' genius, whose name is linked with Ossian and Homer, two other great primitives. The historical plays and their social message are emphasized; Lenz in a striking passage describes Shakespeare as an almost Christ-like figure unwinding the grave clothes from the noble dead, breathing his spirit into the mummified figures and bidding the heroes of history arise in transfigured beauty to bless the eyes that behold them.[19] Shakespeare's 'Germanic' nature is set in opposition to the spirit of France. "Unser Shakespeare" makes his first appearance, and is allied with medieval Germany and Greek simplicity against "Alle Franzosen und angesteckte Deutsche, sogar Wieland". Goethe's "Schäkespear" and his father's "Schaksp." in the very spelling lay claim to their Germanic genius. Aristotle's rules are attacked with varying violence. Voltaire is openly accused of plagiarizing and debasing Shakespeare. Drama is elevated above epic and lyric as a genre (although Lenz confuses the issue by insisting that Dante be classified as a dramatist) because it is best suited to the promulgation of social and political ideas.

The obvious literary sources of Goethe and Lerse present a segment of the reading list of the Strasbourg group: Wieland's translation of Pope's *Preface to Shakespeare* (which includes Rowe's biography), the biographies published in English periodicals for the Jubilee, Shaftesbury, Mandeville's *Fable of the Bees*, Young's paradox of the imitation of the ancients, Lessing, Greek legend, and predominantly Herder. The influence of the oration spoken by Garrick at Stratford is pervasive. Both orators condemn their own age, but with characteristic contrast. Lerse, drawing heavily on biographical material, converts his description of Shakespeare's times into a scathing condemnation of contemporary Germany, inimical to poetry in its very social structure. The social and political wellbeing of a country is tested by its poetry and its criticism. Although Lerse suggests no positive programme for the nation, he implies that there was hope in the "purified" and "unbiased" taste of the small group he was addressing; despairing of middle-class optimism and stupidity, Lerse pins his hope on the sensitive, imaginative, complex intellectual, and at the same time on a paradoxical demand for a return to simple, sturdy folk poetry, inspired by Shakespeare, "einfaltige Schüler der einfaltigen Natur".[20] Goethe condemns his day, also, but includes himself in the condemnation. This is less a social document, more a personal testimony. The oration, as Paul van Tieghem points out,[21] marks the emergence of the personal and autobiographical elements characteristic of Goethe's style during the course of his long career. He expresses his criticism of Shakespeare in terms of his own reaction to his first reading of a play: "...stunde ich wie ein Blindegebohrner, dem eine Wunderhand das Gesicht in einem Augenblicke schenckt". He knew his own potentialities then—first realized he had hands and feet. But before Shakespeare's creativity he was ashamed of his own 'soapbubble' characters and of living in an age that made great artistic creation all but impossible.

Ernst Beutler's essay on *Goethes Rede zum Schäkespeartag* demonstrates the relationship of this early writing to Goethe's later work and its importance as personal philosophy. Garrick's key word at Stratford had been 'Nature'; he used it wherever possible, often altering even his borrowings from Milton or the texts of Handel's oratorios to interpolate it in more emphatic position. Goethe uses the same key word, but when he wrote, "Und ich rufe Natur! Natur! nichts so Natur als Schäkespears Menschen", Goethe had come a long way from any definition of nature intended by Garrick. Garrick may have been playing with fire when he bowed gracefully to those who saw his mystic kinship with Shakespeare in the unique ability of both to excel in both comedy and tragedy, but it never occurred to him that this mysterious aptitude resolved or even commented on the paradox of man, a creature of free will, and man, a creature acting under necessity. Goethe's literary influences are apparent, but the *Rede* stands closer in spirit to *Faust* than to any of its 'sources'. It has been said that Garrick did not grasp the significance of his oration when he spoke it;[22] surely he did not consciously intend anything comparable to Goethe's statement to be drawn from it. Beutler writes:

Zum ersten Mal wieder ist die Welt, der hier ein Dichter ins Auge schaut—auf das Schicksal des einzelnen gesehen—, heillos. Es ist kein personenhafter Gott in dieser Welt und keine Hilfe von oben.

Zum ersten Mal wird die ausweglose Tragik der menschlichen Existenz erkannt und formuliert, wenn von Shakespeares Stücken gesagt wird: 'Seine Pläne sind nach dem gemeinen Stil zu reden keine Pläne, aber seine Stücke drehen sich alle um den geheimen Punkt, den noch kein Philosoph gesehen und bestimmt hat, in dem das Eigentümliche unseres Ichs, die prätendierte Freiheit unseres Wollens, mit dem notwendigen Gang des Ganzen zusammenstosst.'...Ein Weltbild wird von Goethe entrollt, in dem der Mensch nicht mehr Mittelpunkt der Schöpfung, sondern ihr Opfer ist, das in seinem durch keine Gottheit abwendbaren Schicksal Grösse zu zeigen hat....Und dieses neue Weltbild wird gerühmt als Natur...und sie ist keinesfalls das Rousseausche Stichwort, das in erlösendem Gegensatz zur Zivilisation steht...Von Strassburg kehrte er heim, durchdrungen von einem neuen Kraft- und Weltgefühl, und eine Feier und Rede verkündete den Anbruch einer neuen Morgenrote.[23]

An account of the Jubilee in England is incomplete without a statement of its aftermath in the theatres of London and a consideration of the total effect of popularizing the ideas implicit in the event. So in Germany the complete account should include reference to two books that gave news in Germany of this aftermath of the Jubilee in England, the writings of Georg Christoph Lichtenberg and Johann Wilhelm von Archenholz. Lichtenberg has left the most vivid of all descriptions of Garrick's acting. His letters from England were widely read in the *Deutsches Museum*. He tells of the pilgrimages to Stratford, and of paying a shilling for a piece of wood from Shakespeare's own chair to be set in a ring. He was amazed at the idolatry of Shakespeare in all levels of the populace; the children learned "To be or not to be" before they learned the creed or the ABC. The use made of Shakespeare in Parliamentary debate impressed him. He constantly linked the names of Shakespeare and Garrick in praise, drawing an analogy which might strike a foreigner more forcibly than a native of London: that both had gone to school to that great city, had learned from London herself of beauty and wonder and hope and fear.[24]

Johann Wilhelm von Archenholz's book, *England und Italien*, in the opinion of John Alexander Kelly, did more than any other book in the eighteenth century "to present a complete picture of England to the German public".[25] The book appeared in many editions, was expanded to five volumes and translated many times. The only copy available to me is a cut English version made from a French translation and published in Dublin in 1791 under the title *A Picture of England*. Von Archenholz turned a cosmopolitan eye on the London theatrical season of 1769–70, and pronounced it good. His highest praise was for Garrick's play *The Jubilee* which he saw twenty-eight times with undiminished enthusiasm. He ignored the ridicule expressed in the play itself and lauded the processions. His story is so accurate it can serve as a supplement even to the notes of James Messink, the stage manager of Drury Lane,[26] and so vivid that, better than any English reporter, he makes clear the reasons why *The Jubilee* had the two record runs of the century. Von Archenholz gave Germany, France and Italy a popular account of Jubilee idolatry in its most concentrated and dramatic form.

These two popular writers seized upon the dramatized metaphor of the poet as creator. Garrick in his oration at Stratford had powerfully presented this analogy. "Above all others" Shakespeare created living characters "not creatures of the imagination...but partakers of the same nature with ourselves". He did not "imitate" nature in products to be judged by their uniformity to nature as we see it, he did not "imitate" but "created" by a power "absolute not relative". "He is as another Nature." His eye penetrated the deepest secrets of the source of life, and his language is "strongly marked with the characteristics of nature...his terms, rather than his sentences are metaphorical...this is the language of both the prophet and the poet". Not dramatic rules imposed from without, but his own mystic power of order was "sufficient to rein his imagination and reduce to system the new worlds he had made". This is the metaphor dramatized in the Jubilee processions—denounced in England as blasphemous, yet packing the theatre night after night. The metaphor of poetry as heterocosm was a commonplace of English and German criticism with a long ancestry traceable to the Italian Renaissance.[27] Used simply as a metaphor, it carried no stigma of blasphemy at this date; it had attained the piety of a trite and well-worn critical phrase. But never in English before the Stratford oration, never in German before Herder had it been used with such conviction of truth. Shaftesbury's "creation" is rational selectivity by rule prescribed by higher law. Lessing applied the term to a similar process of selectivity.[28] Gerstenberg spoke of Shakespeare's "world", but he was comparing him to no higher being than Raphael.[29] For Herder—who had not used the analogue before—it became the controlling metaphor of his life. By it Friedrich Gundolph characterizes his criticisms of Shakespeare.[30] By it Alexander Gillies interprets not only his criticism, but also his philosophy of history. "Shakespeare led Herder to history", Gillies says, and Herder, having convinced himself that all Shakespeare's plays are history (the thesis of his letter to Gerstenberg), convinced himself in his *Ideen* that the equation was reversible. "Just as Shakespeare was a kind of miniature creator, so God could be looked upon as a kind of superdramatist and the world as a stage."[31] In the letter to Gerstenberg Herder had written:

Shakespear, der Sohn der Natur, [Diener] Vertrauter der Gottheit, Dollmetscher aller Sprachen und Leidenschaften und Charaktere, Führer und Verwickler des Fadens aller Begebenheiten, die Menschliche Herzen treffen können—was sehe ich, wenn ich dich lese! Kein Theater, keine Koulisse, kein Komödiant, Nachahmung ist verschwunden: ich sehe Welt, Menschen, Leidenschaften, Wahrheit! Ich, der in seinem Lebenslaufe noch keinen Garrik spielen gesehen; ich sehe in Lear und Macbeth, in Hamlet und Richard keinen Garrik: Lear und Macbeth, Hamlet und Richard [sehe ich] selbst, keine Nachahmer, keine Deklamateure, keine Künstler! Bis auf das Schlechteste deiner Geschöpfe Alle sind sie ganze, individuelle Wesen, jeder aus seinem Charakter und von seiner Seite historisch theilnehmend, mitwürkend, handelnd; jeder gleichsam für sich Absicht und Zweck, und nur durch die schöpferische Kraft des Dichters, als Zweck zugleich Mittel; als Absicht zugleich Mitwürker des Ganzen! So spielt im grossen Weltlauf vielleicht ein höheres, unsichtbares Wesen mit einer niedern Klasse von Geschöpfen: jeder läuft zu seinem Zweck und schafft und würket; und siehe! unwissend werden sie eben damit blinde Werkzeuge zu einem höhern Plan, zu dem Ganzen eines unsichtbaren Dichters![32]

Herder in 1771 was master and his disciples followed him. Goethe's *Rede* linked the metaphor with the myth of Prometheus as Shaftesbury had done—but Goethe's creator has little in common with "a just Prometheus under Jove". Lenz used the metaphor in refutation of Aristotle's theory of the source of poetry in a statement that shows striking likeness to the twentieth-century aesthetic theory of *Einfühlung*. In English the elevation of the poet to the level of creative divinity is associated with Coleridge and Carlyle, who looked to Germany for inspiration, where the idea had spread from Herder's influence. Garrick's Jubilee, whatever it was in actuality, played into the hands of *Sturm und Drang* vitalism. It gave substance to the vision of the Poet as creator, prophet and national hero.

NOTES

1. *From Classic to Romantic* (Cambridge, Mass., 1946).
2. Frank A. Hedgcock, *David Garrick and his French Friends* (1911), pp. 153–237, gives a detailed account of this visit.
3. Paul van Tieghem, *Le Préromantisme*, III (Paris, 1947), 153, 196–8.
4. See also T. L. Lounsbury, *Shakespeare and Voltaire* (1902), pp. 330–97 *et passim*; C. M. Haines, *Shakespeare in France: Criticism* (1925), pp. 55–71; Paul van Tieghem, *op. cit.* pp. 249–87.
5. Garrick at some time sent a copy of the *Ode* to Voltaire. The undated letter that accompanied the volume is in *The Private Correspondence of David Garrick with the Most Celebrated Persons of his Time*, ed. James Boaden, 2 vols. (1831–2), I, 365. Boaden dated the letter 1776, the year when Voltaire, in his letter to the Academy, publicly drew Garrick over to his side in the controversy. The late David Little, editor of the Garrick correspondence, suggested to me that the date might be 1769. The introductory material printed with the ode would have made clear the fact that Garrick and his Jubilee were not in sympathy with Voltaire. Boaden prints no reply.
6. *Shakespeare traduit de l'anglois*, I (Paris, 1776), xviii.
7. *The London Magazine*, XXXVIII (1769). Also in *The London Chronicle*, XXVI (1769), 221–2, *Lloyd's Evening Post*, XXV (1769), 207. This article was adapted to form the biography of Shakespeare given in the second edition (1778) of the *Encyclopaedia Britannica*. It was known to the German group discussed below.
8. The parallel passages are found in Le Tourneur I, xcvii–xcviii and Maurice Morgann, 'On the Dramatic Character of Sir John Falstaff' (1777) in *Eighteenth Century Essays on Shakespeare*, ed. David Nicol Smith (Glasgow, 1903), p. 251. Morgann's essay was written in 1774.
9. Le Tourneur I, cxxii.
10. Voltaire, *Oeuvres Complètes*, 52 vols. (Paris, 1877–85), L, 58, 64, 77, 83 *et passim*.
11. Friedrich Gundolf, *Shakespeare und der deutsche Geist* (Godesberg, 1947), pp. 155–64 discusses Wieland's part in providing a foundation for the *Shakespearomanie* and its intense nationalism.
12. *Mercure de France*, December 1769, pp. 180–6.
13. *Der junge Goethe*, ed. Max Morris, 6 vols. (Leipzig, 1909–12), II, III.   14. *Ibid.* p. 115.
15. The date of the letter is in doubt, however. Michael Bernhays dated it 21 September 177(2), August Stöber, 22 September 1772; Morris dates the letter without indication of doubt 21 September 1771.
16. See Franz Zinkernagel, *Herders Shakespeare-Aufsatz in dreifacher Gestalt* (Bonn, 1912), p. 2, and Hertha Isaacson, *Der junge Herder und Shakespeare* (Berlin, 1930), p. 22.
17. Theodor Friedrich, *Die 'Anmerkungen übers Theater' des Dichters J. M. R. Lenz* (Leipsig, 1908), pp. 14–18 *et passim*. M. N. Rosanov, *Jakob M. R. Lenz* (Leipzig, 1909), authorized translation from Russian into German by C. von Gütschow.   18. *Der junge Goethe*, II, 137.
19. J. M. R. Lenz, *Gesammelte Schriften*, ed. Franz Blei, 5 vols. (Munich, 1909), I, 253.
20. Stöber, *Röderer*, pp. 33–5.   21. van Tieghem, III, 176.
22. Charles Knight, *Studies in Shakespere* (1868), p. 555. Knight prints, with interesting comment, part of the text of the Stratford oration. The oration may also be found in Robert Bell Wheler's *History and Antiquities of Stratford-upon-Avon* (Stratford, 1806) and in *The Public Advertiser* for 5 September 1769, *Scots Magazine*, XXI (1769), 398–400, *Lloyd's Evening Post*, XXV (1769), 222.
23. Ernst Beutler, *Goethes Rede zum Schäkespears Tag* (Weimar, 1938), pp. 3–4.
24. *Lichtenbergs Briefe*, ed. Leitzmann and Schüddekopf, 3 vols. (Leipzig, 1901), I, 240; G. C. Lichtenberg, *Satiren, Fragmente, Briefe*, ed. Hertzog, 2 vols. (Jena, 1907), II, 72–135.
25. John Alexander Kelly, *German Visitors to English Theatres in the Eighteenth Century* (Princeton, 1936), p. 50. See pp. 50–6 for an account of the editions and translations of von Archenholz's book.
26. James Messink, 'The Pageant of Shakspear's Jubilee', Manuscript in Folger Library, Case II, Folder 12 (1770).
27. See M. H. Abrams, *The Mirror and the Lamp* (Oxford, 1953), pp. 272–85, for a history of this analogue. Erwin Panofsky, *Albrecht Dürer*, 2 vols. (Princeton, 1943), I, 280–4, discusses its religious and psychological elements.
28. Gottfried Ephraim Lessing, *Hamburgische Dramaturgie*, ed. Jules Petersen (Berlin, n.d.), Stücke 34, 153.
29. *Hermann Gerstenbergs vermischte Schriften*, 3 vols. (Altona, 1816), III, 269.
30. Gundolf, p. 286.   31. Alexander Gillies, *Herder* (Oxford, 1945), p. 57.   32. F. Zinkernagel, *op. cit.* p. 9.

SHAKESPEARE AND BOHEMIA

BY

OTAKAR VOČADLO

An enduring link between Shakespeare's work and "fair Bohemia" has been forged by the poet himself. His fanciful geography has for ever endeared him to the land-locked Bohemians, and *The Winter's Tale* has frequently been produced with elaborate splendour and appropriate local colour in Prague. In the magnificent tercentenary pageant of 1864, unique in the annals of the continental stage, it was sweet Perdita, symbolizing the long-lost and newly recovered arts of Bohemia, who played the most prominent part among the two hundred and thirty Shakespearian characters represented.

FIRST TRANSLATIONS

In tracing the successive stages of the cult of Shakespeare in Bohemia and of the invigorating impact of his genius on the revival of the Czech national spirit one has to bear in mind the complexities of the historical background. The collapse of Bohemian independence after 1620 left the German and Catholic minorities in possession of the country. As a result of a system of calculated oppression the Czech language, banished from polite use, gradually declined to the level of a peasant patois. With the upper classes exiled or alienated and the political centre shifted to Vienna, the social and intellectual life of the Bohemian cities was exposed to intense Germanization. By 1781, however, the year of the edicts guaranteeing partial religious toleration and emancipation of the enslaved peasantry, the long night was ending—and it is noteworthy that in the following year the first crude Czech paraphrases of *Macbeth* and *The Merchant of Venice* were printed in a provincial town of South Bohemia in the form of popular chapbooks.

The first national theatre of Bohemia—now the Tyl Theatre—erected opposite the ancient Caroline College in 1783 was predominantly German in character.[1] Czech performances were tolerated only as matinees on red-letter days. However, three years later, a band of Prague patriots, anxious to awaken the national consciousness, opened a wooden playhouse which had been built on what is now St Wenceslas Square. The earliest attempt at a stage rendering of any Shakespeare play was made by one of these enthusiasts—K. H. Thám. In the preface to his prose translation of *Macbeth* he informs his readers that this tragedy "was composed in the English tongue, by Shakespeare, an Englishman who excelled all authors in the composition of heroic tragedy and, having surpassed them, achieved immortal glory". This Patriotic Theatre, as it was officially called, was but a shortlived venture and was replaced by an improvised stage in the dissolved 'Hibernian' monastery (so called after its former inmates, Irish Franciscans). Here, too, some Shakespearian dramas appeared in the repertory, but, apart from Thám's *Macbeth*, none of the earliest translations has seen the light of print. A *King Lear* by P. Šedivý has come down to us in manuscript, dated 1792; J. Tandler's *Hamlet*, played in 1792, was lost.

These translations, modelled as they were on inferior German adaptations with their reckless alterations and substitutions, were necessarily of small artistic merit. The first Czech translation that comes reasonably close to the original is a prose version of the *Comedy of Errors* by A. Marek, a country dean, poet and philosopher; this appeared in 1823.[2] About the same time, edifying quotations from Shakespeare in prose and lame verse appeared in a patriotic periodical edited by J. Linda, the "Czech Macpherson". He was a romantic admirer of Ossian and one of the alleged forgers of the notorious 'Queen's Court Manuscript', from which he took the theme for his play, modelled on Shakespeare, about the Czech victory over the Tartars (1241). In those years an increasing interest among Prague playgoers in Shakespeare's tragedies is attested by Washington Irving's note-books.[3] He noted down in his travel diary an enthusiastic reception of *King Lear* and referred also to a performance of *Hamlet*.

By the beginning of the century, Shakespeare, now regarded by critics as worthy to be classed with Homer, became well known to the young poets, and not one of the leading writers of the romantic period escaped his influence. Mácha, the author of *May*, the short-lived but most promising of Czech romanticists, left behind some dramatic fragments and notes which bear the imprint of his Shakespearian studies. Sir John Bowring's adviser on Czech literature, F. L. Čelakovský, the inspired imitator of folk songs, who corresponded with Sir Walter Scott, was a devoted student of Shakespeare. In his youth he longed to put him into Czech, but lack of leisure, as well as of confidence in his own imperfect command of English, prevented him from realizing his ambitious plan.

The year 1835 is memorable for the first metrical translation of any Shakespeare play to be seen on the Czech stage: *King Lear* in J. K. Tyl's translation, acted in the theatre which now bears that poet's name. In spite of considerable cuts and some rearrangement of scenes—including a happy ending—the play was a conspicuous success.[4] The cast consisted of professional actors and of some amateurs who had been trained by Tyl in his little theatre in another dissolved monastery underneath Prague Castle. That nursery of Czech histrionic talent witnessed in June 1836 the gay tavern scenes from *1 Henry IV*, also translated by Tyl, who himself played young Hal. Two other translations with which the versatile founder of the modern Czech theatre is credited, *Macbeth* and *Romeo and Juliet*, are not extant. As translator of Shakespeare he was presently eclipsed by his pupil and antagonist J. J. Kolar. Kolar's *Macbeth*, produced on the same stage on 20 January 1839 and his *The Merchant of Venice*, produced the following December, were the first translations by the great actor who is the real founder of the Shakespearian tradition on the Prague stage.

THE BOHEMIAN MUSEUM EDITION

The Prague insurrection of 1848 and its fatal consequences marked another setback in Bohemia's struggle to attain political and cultural independence. In the fifties under the repressive regime of Alexander Bach, which stifled nearly all national life, there was, however, an insatiable appetite for Shakespeare. At a time when native plays about Bohemian history were banned, Shakespeare offered an outlet and release, taking the Czechs out of their difficult lives into the realm of highest poetry. F. B. Mikovec, the spirited editor of the only review that was not suppressed by the Austrian police, was a pitiless critic of the worthless trash of imported Viennese burlesque, which he strove to replace by serious drama. His warm appraisement of new translations and performances of Shakespeare's plays shows a truly missionary zeal. For years he conducted a vigorous campaign on behalf of more Shakespeare, and his chance came in 1853 with the memorable production of *Hamlet* by J. J. Kolar, who with his wife, a gifted actress, were his favourite performers. It was Mikovec who urged the Bohemian Museum to sponsor a standard version of all Shakespeare's works, and eventually plans were made for the carrying out of this task, designed to be completed in 1864. The first two plays (*Richard III* and *Hamlet*) appeared in 1855. Though the work of the translators went on at full speed, so that in three years some thirty plays were ready, the printing proved a slow business owing to financial and political difficulties. By 1864 only nineteen plays were issued, and the public had to wait until 1872 for the completion of the work. The nine volumes of dramas were concluded with a critical study by Malý, the man to whom had fallen the lion's share in the entire enterprise. Though a prolific journalist, grammarian and co-editor of the first Czech encyclopaedia, he managed to find time for translating eleven plays (besides three additional translations which appeared separately). The equally learned and versatile priest and children's poet, F. Doucha, and J. Čejka, the cultured and musical professor of medicine, contributed nine translations each, while the remaining eight plays were equally divided between another university professor, L. Čelakovský, the son of the poet and a prominent botanist, and J. J. Kolar, who prepared for print his theatrical versions of *Macbeth*, *Hamlet*, *The Merchant of Venice*, and *The Taming of the Shrew*. Kolar was a dramatist himself and his vigorous but somewhat rugged translations showed an actor's sense of the stage. Each translation was closely examined by two experts before it was approved and sent to the press. The result may now seem somewhat uneven, but it was certainly a considerable achievement. It may lack the literary finish and artistic skill of the later translations, but it is straightforward and fairly accurate. To the reader of today the Museum translation necessarily appears rather archaic, but at the time it was, no doubt, the supreme test of the flexibility of the Czech language. The fact that the Czechs now possessed a complete metrical version of the world's greatest dramatic poet helped them to regain national self-esteem. A sense of pride in their pioneering achievement was indeed legitimate: they had embarked on an arduous enterprise prior to other Slavs[5] and before any of their Eastern neighbours. The plays were still being re-issued in the eighties in cheap and school editions and they were produced with success at the first independent Czech theatre, which was erected in 1862 on the site of the present National Theatre. Doucha's poetic translation of *A Midsummer Night's Dream* was considered good enough even for that great national institution; in fact, had not Smetana provided his magnificent *Libuše* for the festive occasion it might have been chosen for the opening gala performance.

THE ACADEMY EDITION AND ITS CRITICS

However, by that time, with the advent of a new poetic school headed by Jaroslav Vrchlický, the limitations of the first complete Shakespeare in Czech dress were becoming increasingly manifest. Vrchlický's genius reshaped the diction and considerably enriched the prosodical resources of modern Czech poetry, both in his own fine lyrics and in his numerous translations of the world's poetic masterpieces. From Shakespeare he translated *Venus and Adonis* (1905, published 1922) and 122 sonnets (published 1954), leaving the dramatic work to his friend Josef Václav Sládek (1845–1912). None of his literary contemporaries was better fitted for this task than Sládek, the first lecturer in English at the Czech university and the most virile poet of his generation. Encouraged by Julius Zeyer, a fellow poet and a student of the early English drama, he decided to devote the remaining years of his poetic career to Shakespeare. The first volume of what was to become the standard Czech translation, *The Taming of the Shrew*, was published under the aegis of the Academy in 1894 (his first attempt, *1 Henry IV*, had already been produced at the National Theatre in 1888). His industry was truly heroic. Though the invalid poet had to contend with constant bodily suffering, when he died in 1912 his arduous enterprise was practically accomplished. Four less important and doubtful plays that remained to be done—part of *Henry VI*, *Henry VIII*, *Titus Andronicus* and *Pericles*—were translated by his disciple Antonín Klášterský who, in addition, put into Czech all the sonnets (1923), *The Rape of Lucrece* and the rest of the poems. By 1922 the last of the plays, *Pericles*, had been published and in 1925 the whole body of Shakespeare's poetry was in the hands of Czech readers.

As a single-handed artistic achievement Sládek's rendering of thirty-three plays stands unique. Its poetic value remains unchallenged and, in this respect, his work is not likely to be superseded. Not often does he go astray; in fact, sometimes he tends to be too accurate, so that some have complained that in his anxiety never to miss a telling word or a valuable shade of meaning he has been forced sometimes to expand the number of lines at the cost of terseness. Though this tendency may occasionally lead to diffuseness, it is often impossible in a highly inflected language to preserve the exact number of the original English lines except by merciless cuts. Another objection to the Academy Shakespeare was that it tried to tone down the grosser expressions and soften the 'bawdiness' of the Elizabethan poet. Undoubtedly the obscene has its legitimate place in Shakespeare as in the work of other great full-blooded classics provided it is properly understood. But the modern temper and taste have changed and many of the stock jests and puns are no longer amusing. They affect the modern audience in a way that was certainly not originally intended and they are dropped by producers without appreciable loss.

The dominant position of Sládek's translation was first seriously disputed in 1916 by J. Baudiš, the Celtic scholar and medievalist, who was anything but squeamish in his taste for the Elizabethan and Restoration outspokenness. While recognizing Sládek's poetic merits, he argued[6] that in some respects the Museum translators came nearer to Shakespeare's dramatic intentions. In the same jubilee year A. Fencl, a scholarly actor-manager, criticized Sládek on the ground that he had not studied stagecraft at close quarters, and O. Fischer, a learned critic and minor dramatist, pleaded for greater freedom in the translating of modern classics. From the point of view of dramatic efficiency they found fault especially with the uniform smoothness and regularity of Sládek's verse as well as his diffuseness. Each offered a sample of the particular method proposed. Fencl's *The Merchant of Venice*, though less poetic than Sládek's, is certainly a work of an experienced actor. Like Fischer's *Macbeth* it avoids the multiplication of lines which was considered Sládek's chief drawback. Fischer's doctrine of free translation, however, though justified to some extent by his own practice, proved a dangerous slogan when applied by his less scrupulous followers in the flurried years between the two wars. B. Štěpánek's daring efforts to replace Sládek by a more concise and up-to-date text can hardly be considered an improvement on his predecessor. Numerous passages strike one as mere paraphrases of the model which he and his advisers have belittled. The boldest attempt at a re-translation of Shakespeare in modern terms had been made by E. A. Saudek, Fischer's professed disciple, who claims to cater for a popular audience. But there is room for doubt whether Shakespeare's appeal is likely to be widened by the disfigurement of the dialogue by conversational and slangy expressions. This unconventional style, which is liable to interfere with aesthetic enjoyment at moments of intense emotion, shows that Saudek is somewhat lacking in that sensitive tact which J. Malý had declared to be an essential part of the translator's equipment. Saudek is, no doubt, a clever translator and his technical qualifications are generally recognized, but his two versions of *Hamlet* prove convincingly enough that, while his skill may suffice for a witty and uproarious comedy, for the magic and grandeur of the major tragedies it will not. The nobility and pathos of Shakespeare's tragic characters, the deeper metaphysical meaning of the playwright's mind, seem to elude him.

The eagerness on the part of each generation to recast Shakespeare afresh[7] in order to suit the changing linguistic habits of the age, thus making him, as it were, their contemporary, may well puzzle the Englishman who is content to enjoy the national poet in the archaic Elizabethan garb. But this strange obsession is, at any rate, a tribute to the vitality and perennial appeal of his genius. However, it is not shared by all. J. Vodák, the most stimulating among Prague dramatic critics for the past half century and one whose opinion on any question connected with Shakespeare and the Czech theatre must be listened to with respect, maintained that the poet's tongue should have a patina of age like an old jewel that is handed down as a treasured heirloom from generation to generation. Though thoroughly progressive, he did not approve of modernizing Shakespeare; indeed, he made it clear he would not have minded had even Sládek's version been less colloquial.

Apart from faithfulness the only valid test of any translation must ultimately be its own artistic importance. Sládek's work has become a classic because he was a genuine artist. Since it is unlikely that another poet of his magnitude will dedicate a quarter of a century to Shakespeare, the Academy edition is sure to remain the standard for a long time to come. In spite of his shortcomings, for reading purposes he has had so far no serious competitor. For the playgoer some sort of compromise will doubtless be devised between bookishness and vulgarity, in order to meet changing fashions and to keep abreast of the steady progress in Shakespeare criticism and research. Much could be gained here by an intelligent co-operation of competent critics and Shakespearian scholars.

SHAKESPEARE CRITICISM AND SCHOLARSHIP

In Shakespeare criticism the Czechs completely escaped the narrow conventions of French classicism, while their instinctive distrust of German sentiment made them equally immune to the more extravagant claims of romantic bardolatry. The first historical study of Shakespeare of any intrinsic worth was published in the learned organ of the Bohemian Museum by its editor V. B. Nebeský, an authority on classic and Spanish drama, in 1851–2. Twenty years later the first book on Shakespeare and his works was written by J. Malý, an admirer of Samuel Johnson. He pointed to the doctor's vigorous common sense as an effective safeguard in securing a balanced appreciation of the English poet. Doucha's learned notes to his translations proved him to be a well-informed scholar. The best qualified modern critic was Jindřich Vodák (1867–1940), who did much for the true appreciation of Shakespeare as a dramatic artist. His numerous articles, collected in a posthumous volume under the title *Shakespeare, a Critic's Breviary* (1950), provide an impressive record of all the notable Shakespearian productions between 1900 and 1940.

From the start, the study of English literature in Prague centred on Shakespeare. V. Mourek discussed the Baconian heresy in 1896, and in 1897 and 1898 Vrchlický, in his capacity of professor of modern literature, gave courses of lectures on Shakespeare's art illustrated with specimens of his own translations. In 1909 Mourek's successor in the chair of Germanic philology, J. Janko, who wrote also on Shakespeare's relation to Austria and Bohemia, published his university extension lectures on the poet. The scholarly study of Shakespeare's life and work came into its own when V. Mathesius was made the first professor of English in 1912 and F. Chudoba (1878–1941), who had been a student of Sir Walter Raleigh's at Oxford, started his lectures on English poetry. Mathesius, a sober and well-informed scholar, attempted a synthesis of contemporary Shakespearian research, and his periodical reviews of new publications were of outstanding merit. Of his Elizabethan studies the most popular was a little book on Shakespeare's life, stage and artistic methods. This was one of his contributions to the Shakespeare jubilee of 1916—for, although Bohemia was cut off from Shakespeare's country and was not even represented in the polyglot *Book of Homage*, in that darkest hour of the war, with the shadow of German hegemony over the land, when the leading Czech patriots were sentenced to death and the most distinguished Czech scholar, an outlaw, found refuge at King's College in London, the Czech academic world did not hesitate to recognize the immense debt their languishing country owed to Shakespeare. F. X. Šalda, the leading Czech critic, who carried on Vrchlický's work at the university, inaugurated the National Theatre Shakespeare Festival with a fine address on the poet's mind and art. His brilliant tribute to Shakespeare's genius was acclaimed by the packed house with thunders of applause. (The printed copy, however, shows traces of the censor's senseless pen.) The Czech Academy awarded a prize to Antonín Fencl for an essay on Shakespeare's plays on the Bohemian stage. A number of articles in his honour appeared in the press and a scheme was even launched to start a Shakespeare Society which was, however, not allowed to mature.

It was in another great war, while Bohemia and Moravia were subjected to even more savage repressive measures, that the standard work of Czech Shakespearian scholarship was published. Chudoba's *Book about Shakespeare* started appearing in instalments when the Battle of Britain was at its height, and English civilization was daily vilified in the Nazi press and radio. It was a challenge to German censorship, which prohibited serious books on England and proscribed all modern English literature but did not dare to include Shakespeare in its ban. The book is the outcome of a life's devotion to the study of Shakespeare and is indeed Chudoba's most notable achievement. The first part is a student's complete compendium of the poet's life and growth correlating in detail the poet's career with an imaginative reconstruction of the national background. In spite of the research which went into its making it makes easy reading on account of the lucidity and charm of the author's style. When the first volume appeared in 1941 it aroused a lively interest among the younger generation and became the season's best seller. The text is enlivened by reproductions from manuscripts and old books and by Wenceslas Hollar's engravings. There is nothing on that scale to be found in any Slavonic language. When Chudoba died on 7 January 1941, the greater part of his work was ready for press. The gaps were filled by his son, a professional historian, from his father's notes.

Both leading Shakespearian scholars died during the German occupation, but their work was carried on after the Czech universities reopened their gates in 1945.

SHAKESPEARE AND BOHEMIA

GREAT ACTING AND OTHER ARTS

Reading Shakespeare alone, still less reading about him, would never account for Shakespeare's popularity in Bohemia. It was the skill of a succession of gifted actors which awakened the public to the greatness and subtlety of his art. First, J. J. Kolar rose above a group of inexperienced amateurs owing to his impressive stage presence and fine rhetorical style fashionable about the middle of the last century. His overbearing and pugnacious spirit which had made him unpopular with his colleagues rendered him wonderfully suited to such domineering parts as *Richard III* and *Coriolanus*, probably his finest achievement. The greatest actor the Bohemian stage has seen and the foremost exponent of Shakespeare's heroes was Edward Vojan (1853–1920). There have been other actors of outstanding executive abilities since, but none of his successors has equalled him in his instinctive understanding of the leading Shakespearian roles. His voice had not the rolling sonority of some of his rivals, but his psychological insight and his power of expressing hidden emotions enabled him to give a superb interpretation of all the main Shakespearian characters. Among his many subtle creations his magnificent Othello, his wily Shylock and his modern, introspective Hamlet, for whom he was admirably equipped both physically and emotionally, were never surpassed. Lear's headlong primeval vehemence, however, did not seem to suit his complex personality. There he was probably eclipsed by V. Budil (director of the Plzeň Theatre). Vojan's worthy partner was the sensitive, fascinating Hana Kvapilová whose sudden death in 1907 at the time of her triumph as the high-spirited sparkling Beatrice removed from the Czech stage the most graceful interpreter of Shakespeare's heroines. Her acute intelligence enabled her to sink herself in her parts and give them her own intensely vibrating vitality. Those two set a high standard in the playing of Shakespeare and their joint example helped to develop the natural capacities of their fellow actors.

Music, the national art of Bohemia, has been notably enriched from Shakespeare's treasury. Since Benda's pioneering 'Singspiel' *Romeo and Juliet* (1776) all the leading Czech composers have fallen under his spell. Smetana was inspired by *Richard III* and *Macbeth* and contributed a special march for the apotheosis of 1864. It is not generally known that his last creative effort was an unfinished opera based on Krásnohorská's libretto of *Twelfth Night*. Vrchlický adapted *The Tempest* for Fibich (first produced at the National Theatre in 1895), and Foerster composed his *Jessica* with the help of the same librettist. Dvořák wrote an overture to *Othello* (Op. 93).

Among Czech painters of Shakespeare's characters the most important was Karel Purkyně, son of the famous physiologist, the art director and designer of the great pageant of 1864.

WARS AND FESTIVALS

While in most other countries the vitalizing stimulus of Shakespeare's art has been confined to the literary sphere, in Bohemia, as we may see from the foregoing, an unusual aspect of his worship deserves special attention: under alien domination the poet became a powerful ally in the struggle for cultural self-expression and emancipation. Fortunately none of the despotic misgovernments which have time after time blighted Czech national life dared to suppress Shakespeare. In the dark decade of Baron Bach's dictatorship as many as fourteen of his plays were put on. The spectacular Prague celebrations of the two tercentenaries were events of immense national importance. On both occasions Shakespeare received an apotheosis that could hardly be paralleled outside English-speaking countries.

In 1864 the Festival was arranged on a national scale by the Arts Club together with the conservatoire and other institutions. Permission was only reluctantly granted by the police shortly before the opening of the festivities at the leading Czech theatre. A week's Shakespearian programme under P. Švanda's capable management formed a prelude to an impressive ceremony for which the most spacious Prague stage was chosen. After Berlioz's dramatic symphony *Romeo and Juliet*, conducted by Smetana himself, F. Kolár, a gifted young actor, in Prospero's mask, introduced a series of *tableaux vivants* presenting various scenes from Shakespeare's plays, accompanied by Blodek's music. Those were followed by a long procession of Shakespearian characters from thirty plays paying homage to a huge bust of their creator under a shower of flowers. The apotheosis reached its climax in a moving address delivered by Otilie Malá in Perdita's costume. In a fiery peroration the rising star of the Shakespearian repertory called in her sweet contralto voice for cultural self-determination for her people. Literary historians agree that the Shakespeare Festival marked a turning point in the dramatic and artistic revival of Bohemia. Not the least striking feature of the celebration was its universal appeal. Choristers of all the Prague churches took part in it as well as members of the rationalist Sokol movement. J. Barák, a free-thinking journalist and the champion of labour interests, donning the mask of Othello, marched side by side with a bevy of Prague's fashionable debutantes, dressed as Shakespeare's heroines. Such a fraternal spirit was, indeed, needful in view of the troubles ahead. It was the year of the Danish war and the danger of Prussianism was looming large. Two years later Bohemia was invaded and a series of reverses followed which temporarily dashed Bohemian aspirations.

Fifty years after Sadowa, when the tercentenary of Shakespeare's death was approaching, England was an enemy and German Shakespearians were asking themselves the question if it was still permissible to honour "the poet whom an English mother bore". No such qualms troubled his steadfast Czech devotees. Since Bohemia was hermetically sealed against the West the Prague theatre men felt an even more urgent call to demonstrate their belief in the unity of European civilization by paying a tribute to England's towering genius. The problem was how to allay official opposition at a time when every sign of pro-Allied sympathies was considered a treasonable offence. Jaroslav Kvapil, the greatest Czech Shakespearian producer, attacked his task with his usual energy and gusto. His glorious cycle at the National Theatre, a feast of poetry, which started with the *Comedy of Errors* on 27 March and ended with *The Winter's Tale* on 4 May 1916 was an act of courage and faith which was fully justified by results. In artistic partnership with Vojan, his mainstay in the leading roles, he had prepared an ambitious programme of seventeen plays in Sládek's new translation. *King John*—with Austria's severed head—was, of course, ruled out, and the police at first took exception to *Henry IV*. However, this play was passed later in the year and added to the cycle, both parts being boldly compressed into one evening ($5\frac{1}{2}$ hours). Thus the Shakespeare year so splendidly inaugurated on 1 January with Vojan's wistful Hamlet was brought to a glorious end with the fooleries of Falstaff. This Festival still lingers in memory as the high-water-mark of Czech Shakespearian activities. Its resounding success, no doubt, strengthened Kvapil's hand for his next courageous move, which he had been planning together with A. Jirásek, the Nestor of Czech writers, another admirer of "the English giant": the memorable May manifesto of 1917 by Czech men of letters, a bold bid for Czecho-Slovak independence and an open challenge to the Dual Monarchy.

Kvapil was a creative producer and was also responsible for some attractive open-air performances of Shakespeare. Perhaps his greatest asset was his imaginative poetic vision. Himself a poet, dramatist and librettist, he penetrated deeply into every play he produced. Vojan and he had the same standards. After Vojan's death Kvapil continued his brilliant pioneering work for seven years (1921–8) at the Municipal Theatre where he produced eleven of Shakespeare's plays. At the same theatre popular appreciation of lesser known plays by Shakespeare was promoted also by the dynamic experimenter K. Hilar.[8]

RECEPTIVENESS TO SHAKESPEARE'S MESSAGE

In comparison with other countries, the Czech Shakespeare repertoire has been remarkably complete. Altogether thirty plays have been so far performed, all—with the exception of *All's Well that Ends Well*[9]—by first-rate professional players on Prague's most representative stages. Thus none of the plays which may whole-heartedly be accepted as Shakespeare's has been left out except the rhetorical *Henry V*, whose intense patriotism can hardly be expected to make much appeal to a popular public outside England. The film-version, however, has been much admired by connoisseurs and we may yet see the play on the stage as part of the great tetralogy on some future festive occasion.

If the number of versions of individual plays may be regarded as a test of their respective appeal, *Macbeth* is entitled to hold the first place with no less than nine translations, closely followed by *Hamlet* with eight and *King Lear* with seven. *Macbeth* was not only the first tragedy to be printed in Bohemia, but it also opened the long series of Shakespearian performances beginning in 1852. In 1916 Vojan's *Macbeth* was one of the outstanding events of the season. In the stormy period of the German occupation it was played at the National Theatre on the prohibited Independence Day (28 October 1939). The usurper's part was acted by Z. Štěpánek in a dark costume suggestive of the SS uniform. It was fortunate that the symbolic significance for once escaped the argus-eyed occupation authorities.

That Shakespeare's own fellow-countrymen should turn to their great heritage in times of danger and distress is natural enough. But for what did a storm-tossed country in the heart of Europe look to Shakespeare in the critical moments of her recent history? What sort of spiritual consolation did Bohemia derive from his grand panorama of human suffering when life was bitter and full of anguish? Did he offer courage and hope? Shakespeare is certainly not indifferent to injustice. He is on the side of moral laws against tyranny and violence. At the end of his darkest tragedies there is a sense of providential control and a prospect of a happier future. These plays teach us to accept without despair and rebellion the temporary triumph of evil. They strengthen our faith in the ultimate victory of eternal values. Far from generating defeatism they inspire a firm belief in the restoration of balance and in what has been aptly termed "the rejuvenation of defeat".[10]

NOTES

1. This was the theatre for which Mozart composed his *Don Giovanni* (1787). There was another Prague playhouse, opened in 1738, to which the origin of German 'bardolatry' has been traced. It was there that Schröder first saw *Hamlet* in Heufeld's adaptation in 1776 and resolved to start a Shakespeare season in Hamburg in the same year. See P. Genée, *Geschichte der Shakespearschen Dramen in Deutschland* (Leipsic, 1870), p. 137, and W. Widmann, *Hamlets Bühnenlaufbahn* (1931), p. 59. Heufeld's *Hamlet* appeared in Bratislava in 1773. F. J. Fischer started publishing his clumsy adaptations for the Prague stage, which influenced the first Czech prose versions, in 1777. Later he was of help to Goethe as producer of his Weimar theatre.

2. The honour of the first verse translation belongs, however, to Slovakia. Michal Bosý, a Protestant minister, whose pen-name was Bohuslav Křižák, started translating *Hamlet* from the original into Czech as early as 1810. A specimen of his *Macbeth* appeared in the Prague literary periodical *Květy* in 1841. Cf. J. Šimko in *Shakespeare Survey* 4, 1951, p. 109. The first complete play, Malý's *Othello*, was printed in Prague in 1843. It was followed by Doucha's *Romeo and Juliet* in 1847.

3. *The Journals of Washington Irving*, ed. W. P. Trent and G. S. Hellman (Boston, 1919), I, 123. The date of the entry about *King Lear* is 23 November 1822.

4. Tyl's translation was never published. An anonymous manuscript recently discovered in Count Kolowrat's library was identified by the present writer as the original prompt-book in Tyl's own hand. The playbills (13 December 1835 and 18 November 1838) are preserved in the theatrical section of the National Museum.

5. The first Russian metrical translation of all Shakespeare's plays appeared in 1865–8, Kraszewski's Polish edition in 1875.

6. In the Czech *Journal of Modern Philology* (*ČMF*, Prague, 1916). It was an abstract of an unpublished study written in 1906. Baudiš himself was then abroad having been surprised by war in Ireland, where he was investigating Celtic folklore.

7. B. Štěpánek translated twenty plays, E. Saudek ten, O. F. Babler three.

8. On Kvapil and Hilar see the present writer's 'The Theater and Drama of Czechoslovakia', *The Theater in a Changing Europe*, ed. T. H. Dickinson (New York, 1937), pp. 336–40. Among Kvapil's most interesting productions at the Municipal Theatre were *Troilus and Cressida* and *Love's Labour's Lost*, the most popular being, next to *A Midsummer Night's Dream*, again *The Winter's Tale*, of which he was particularly proud. In his youth (1888) Kvapil made of it also a libretto entitled *Perdita* for Josef Nešvera (National Theatre, 1897). Hilar produced *Antony and Cleopatra* (1917) and *The Tempest* (1920) for the first time in Prague, but in both he was forestalled by the Municipal Theatre of Plzeň. In this provincial theatre alone no less than twenty different plays by Shakespeare were put on between 1863 and 1918.

9. It is the latest addition to the Czech Shakespeare repertory. Though it is a "play which is of its age rather than for all time" (M. C. Bradbrook in her *Shakespeare and Elizabethan Poetry*, 1951, p. 162), it had a warm reception when it was produced in Prague in March 1932 in honour of the President's birthday by a group of amateurs led by V. K. Blahník, the theatrical historian. The event is not recorded in the survey of Shakespeare premières which was attempted by K. Engelmüller in his *Czech Theatrical Chronicle* (vol. I, Prague, 1946, in Czech). Nor does he note the first Czech performance of *Love's Labour's Lost* in Brno in 1922. A. Fencl also collected data of early performances of Shakespeare's plays in Bohemia, but of his long prize essay only a small extract was printed (in *ČMF*, 1938).

10. The cheerful paradox was coined by G. K. Chesterton in an English publication commemorating the five-hundredth anniversary of the fiery death of John Huss, the Bohemian martyr, which could not be properly observed in the hero's own country owing to the hostility of intolerant Austrian authorities in 1915.

INTERNATIONAL NOTES

A selection has been made from the reports received from our correspondents, those which present material of a particularly interesting kind being printed wholly or largely in their entirety. It should be emphasized that the choice of countries to be thus represented has depended on the nature of the information presented in the reports, not upon either the importance of the countries concerned or upon the character of the reports themselves.

Canada

Shakespearian activities are now dominated by the Canadian Stratford Festival held in a little town of 20,000 people on Canada's River Avon.

In its second season, the Festival, under the direction of Tyrone Guthrie and Cecil Clarke, presented *The Taming of the Shrew* and *Measure for Measure*. The Taming of the Shrew had much of pantomime in it, and included such extraneous things as a motor car and a stage horse. The production did not please purists, but was widely accepted by the Festival audiences.

With James Mason as Angelo and Frances Hyland as Isabella, *Measure for Measure* was a much more satisfying performance, especially since Lloyd Bochner, who played the Duke, provided the strong central character often missing in this play.

The fifth out-door Festival in Toronto by the Earle Grey players gave us a chance to see *Macbeth, As You Like It* and *Twelfth Night*. These plays were later taken on a tour of Ontario schools by the Earle Grey players; in its own way, this Company does as much for the education of Canadian children in live theatre as the Stratford Festival does for adults.

Amateur theatre, which is really the backbone of theatre in Canada, provided a number of Shakespearian productions in such places as Victoria, B.C. (*Romeo and Juliet*), Vancouver, B.C. (*The Merry Wives of Windsor*), Kingston, Ont. (*The Merchant of Venice*), Wolfville, N.S. (*King Henry IV*, Part I), Chatham, N.B. (*Othello*). The last four were all university productions, and in each case there is a tradition of a Shakespeare play being performed each year.

It is a long time since Canada had such a fruitful Shakespearian year to report.

ARNOLD EDINBOROUGH

Czechoslovakia

All theatres in Czechoslovakia are fond of Shakespeare. There are altogether six of his plays now running in Prague: *Romeo and Juliet, The Merchant of Venice, A Midsummer Night's Dream, Twelfth Night, The Merry Wives of Windsor* and *Much Ado About Nothing*. The *Merchant* in the National Theatre with its excellent cast headed by Zdeněk Štěpánek (Shylock) is somewhat disappointing. *Romeo and Juliet* on a renowned suburban stage is played by actors not versed in Shakespeare —but the youthful warmth of the two lovers has made up for their inexperience in this kind of drama. *A Midsummer Night's Dream*, with Mendelssohn's music, was received by less enthusiastic reviews in the press; though perhaps it deserved more praise.

Outside Prague, two plays deserve special mention, *Timon of Athens* in Hradec Králové and *Hamlet* in České Budějovice. I have not seen the former, but apparently the text was an adaptation. Because I collaborated in the staging of the latter I am unable to write about it without bias. The play was introduced by a prologue, spoken by Horatio, which combined Horatio's address in Act v and parts of Hamlet's soliloquy on the plain. Two other things may be found interesting: the Gonzago play was performed in dumb-show only, but the First Actor 'interpreted' it with verses selected from the lines of the Player King, the Player Queen and the Poisoner. Ophelia's second mad scene, full of pauses, was staged very slowly as a mock burial, with a black veil for a grave.

There is no sign that interest in Shakespeare is slackening. One of the foremost Prague theatres announces *All's Well That Ends Well*, another *Two Gentlemen of Verona*.

BŘETISLAV HODEK

East Africa

Shakespeare's Birthday was marked in East Africa by an early morning ceremony in the Kenya National Theatre. In the presence of some of the Festival actors, the founder placed a garland on the Brugiotti bust of the poet which stands in a niche in the National Theatre foyer. The stage production was *The Comedy of Errors*, with special matinées for English-speaking school-children of all races and for African adults. This rarely-performed play was presented in a permanent setting for rapid action. The house of Antipholus of Ephesus was given prominence at the right of the stage. A balcony jutted out above the door to conceal the men from the women when Antipholus tries to force his way into the house. The road to the Bay of Ephesus was above the house setting, with a small acting area beyond that, behind three archways, to represent 'The Mart'. This acting area was backed by cutouts of sails and masts of ships to indicate the coastal scene. To the left of the stage, facing the house of Antipholus, was a garden wall and the gate to the Priory. A stone judgment seat was set against this wall for the Duke. In the centre of the stage was a coping surrounding a tall, slender, palm tree. The pageant doors on either side of the permanent apron stage became entrances to 'The Tiger' and 'The Porpentine', from which scene-ending business developed. The presentation was gay and lively, divided into two parts with the interval coming at the end of Act III. A folk dance at the end of the first part was continued to open the second half, to indicate unbroken action. The lighting used was brilliant sunshine, fading to a rapid tropical sunset at the end of the play.

A. J. R. MASTER

Finland

Many foreign visitors to Helsinki have been struck by the remarkable Shakespeare tradition of the Finnish National Theatre, the leading theatre of the country. They have learnt that all of Shakespeare's plays are available in Finnish translation and that the National Theatre has had twenty-two of his plays in its repertory since 1872. The great tragedies and popular comedies are a regular feature in the repertories of most Finnish theatres. Of the less frequently produced plays, *Cymbeline*, *Measure for Measure*, and *Coriolanus* have proved considerable successes on the national stage. There is ample evidence that to the Finnish theatre-going public Shakespeare's plays have not only a classical value; they also have a peculiar attraction.

In the spring of 1955 the National Theatre presented *The Merchant of Venice*. It was produced by Wilho Ilmari, known for many earlier Shakespeare productions. Less interested in experimentation than in reproducing a full Renaissance atmosphere, Ilmari concentrated on richness of colour, vigour and subtle nuances of acting. Although the lighter tones and joy of life embodied in the younger characters of the comedy were predominant, full advantage was taken of the possibilities of character study provided by Shylock and Portia. Shylock was strong, human, suffering, but these features were not too much underlined, nor was there any attempt at caricature. The dominant character in the production was Portia. The setting, designed by Leo Lehto, a promising young artist, was both successful and original. A huge frame had been built round the stage, round tableaux of Venetian life. Some of the scenes in the streets, in Shylock's house, and in the court of justice were played partly on steps on the front stage.

RAFAEL KOSKIMIES

France

Théâtre de France hailed Shakespeare as the king of 1954 festivals. And it is true that, for the period under review, most Shakespearian productions took place outside Paris during the summer months. Open-air performances at night, in beautiful historical settings, lend themselves to exciting experiments.

Jean Renoir thought that nowhere could the atmosphere of imperial Rome be better recaptured than in Arles. As was to be expected from a film director, his production of *Julius Caesar* owed much to cinema technique and he made full use of the opportunity offered by the arenas for the introduction of crowds and armies, perhaps at the expense of the introspective aspects of the play. Yet the scene where Brutus and Cassius confront each other gained a new significance, with the swarming life of a camp as a background. The 'stereophonic' effects, which have now become an inevitable component of performances on such a large scale, were praised. These were considered the best feature of *Hamlet* as it was represented at the castle of Angers, and it became evident that the lesson of Olivier's picture had not been lost when the Ghost appeared on the battlements. Otherwise, Serge Reggiani's production and interpretation of the leading part were considered rather weak. Marcel Pagnol, the translator, had made a point of giving an unabridged version, but this was marred by prosiness and vulgarity.

The Dramatic Centres of the provinces have become a vital factor of French theatrical activities, which are no longer limited to the capital. Needless to say, the Centres often co-operate with festival organizers. One of the best companies, the Grenier de Toulouse, gave fine performances of *Romeo and Juliet* and *The Taming of the Shrew* in the little town of Sarlat, in Perigord, using the façade of the Présidial on account of its resemblance to the Elizabethan stage.

Hubert Gignoux is among those who believe in improving upon Shakespeare. He adapted and produced *The Merchant of Venice* for the Centre Dramatique de l'Ouest and it was given in Vitré, Rennes and Paris during the last winter season. Gignoux's principles were that Shylock's part should remain unaltered, that Portia's should be reduced as the text of the casket scenes was "un peu chargé, un peu fleuri pour le public actuel", that the comic scenes should be developed, with the addition of a female partner for Launcelot, and lastly, that full emphasis should be given to Act v, lest the actor playing Shylock should appear as the star of the cast.

The Comédiens de l'Est also gave a *Romeo and Juliet* in Strasburg, last February. They used the text due to the collaboration of an eminent poet, Pierre-Jean Jouve, and an eminent actor and producer, the late Georges Pitoeff. The production, by Michel Saint-Denis, the young actors' interpretation, and the translation, were described as particularly true to Shakespeare by Yves Florenne, the critic of *Le Monde*, who summed up his impressions by saying: "C'est sur les bords français du Rhin que j'aurai entendu pour la première fois l'alouette de Vérone chanter un chant vraiment matinal."

If we except the brief visit of the Comédiens de l'Ouest, the representations of *Macbeth* by the Théâtre National Populaire were the only Shakespearian feature of the winter season in Paris. Those who had an opportunity of comparing the Avignon performances, last summer, with those at the Théâtre de Chaillot, agree that in spite of some imperfections, the performances at the Palais des Papes were far more impressive. Judging by the Chaillot performances alone, I felt that the production had greatness and dignity. Jean Vilar, the producer, gave the right emphasis to the main tragic themes, and to the inner conflicts of the guilty couple. His interpretation of the main part showed what an intelligent actor he is, and it is a pity that the rhythm and tempo of his diction so often render the text obscure. One is conscious, with Maria Casarès, of a tragic fire which is lacking in Vilar. She was a Lady Macbeth of flesh and blood, and in the sleep-walking scene she really appeared like a defeated woman, shattered for having attempted to resist the voice of nature and conscience. The music was effective, the modal tune of the prelude, played on the bagpipes, immediately transporting the audience into a strange and distant world. But some of the sound effects were puerile (an actual croaking was heard when Lady Macbeth spoke of the raven). Black curtains and subdued lighting were meant to convey the idea of moral gloom, but they clashed with the highly sophisticated colours of the costumes. As for the translation of Jean Curtis, it is often inaccurate and the omission of such significant lines as iv, iii, 140–59 is to be deplored.

To sum up. Shakespeare enjoys at present a vast audience in Paris and the provinces, and remains, with the Greek and French classics, one of the main assets of enterprising companies whose directors feel that nothing but the very best is good enough to satisfy the spiritual needs of the people. JEAN JACQUOT

Germany

The year 1954 saw the ninetieth anniversary of the German Shakespeare Society, which was celebrated both at Bochum and Weimar. At Bochum, where the Shakespeare Festival lasted five days, *As You Like It* in Rudolf Alexander Schröder's translation was produced by Hans Schalla and *A Midsummer Night's Dream* was presented in Sellner's famous production. For the first time after the war a French company, the Théâtre National Populaire de Paris, took part in the Bochum Festival, performing *Richard II* with Jean Vilar in the title role.

On the German stage generally Shakespeare productions have been as frequent and as successful as ever. Of the histories *Henry IV* was produced by three different theatres, though each time in an abridged one-night version. *King John*, for the first time after the war, appeared on the stage at Schleswig. Of the performances of Shakespeare's tragedies, including *Othello*, *Macbeth*, *Lear*, *Hamlet*, *Romeo and Juliet*, a new production of *Hamlet* at Munich deserves special notice.

Of the problem comedies *Troilus and Cressida* in Rothe's translation produced by Sellner at the Schiller Theater, Berlin, attracted particular attention, while *Measure for Measure* was played in five different translations at five smaller theatres. Performances of *Twelfth Night* showed a wide difference of style and interpretation. While K. H. Stroux's production at the Schlosspark Theater, Berlin, using Flatter's translation, stressed the burlesque and comic element, Heinz Hilpert, at Göttingen, emphasized the melancholy mood of the play. All in all, more than twenty Shakespearian plays were produced in the period under review.

WOLFGANG CLEMEN
WOLFGANG STROEDEL

Israel

It may well be said that the year beginning with April 1954 will have been a real Shakespearian year for Israel.

In April 1954 the Habimah Players gave their grand performance of *Macbeth* with Aharon Meskin in the leading role and Hannah Rovina as Lady Macbeth, under the direction of Sando Malinquist, who also made the designs for the settings. The Hebrew version was E. Broida's. Although a trifle heavy, this production was grand in conception, beautiful in parts and generally very impressive.

In February 1955 the Chamber Theatre gave a very delightful performance of *As You Like It*, with Hanna Meron as Rosalind, Lea Knut as Celia, Salman Leviush as Touchstone and Joseph Milo, who in addition to directing the play, took the part of Jaques. The settings were designed by Theo Otto and the music, by Frank Peleg, was based on old English songs. The Hebrew version was Dan Gilad's. The performance was full of youthful freshness and can well be considered one of the finest Shakespearian presentations in our country.

The Habima Players are now preparing *King Lear* for presentation in April 1955.   REUBEN AVINOAM

Italy

The Shakespeare performance which has caused most discussion has been Castellani's film production of *Romeo and Juliet*; everybody agrees that the rendering of the text has been inadequate, with awkward insertions here and there, and that the alterations in the catastrophe have been unfortunate, but opinions are sharply divided as to: (1) the impersonation of Juliet (Susan Shentall); (2) the costume; (3) the setting. Most Italians find Susan Shentall too Northern as a type, and recall with nostalgia the old interpretation of dark Norma Shearer; only a few find her delightful in her Gothic naïveté and angularity, a figure out of a *livre d'heures*: not a professional actress, she is found very refreshing by these happy few. As to Leonor Fini's costumes, those who are acquainted with early Flemish art and Pisanello find the dance in Capulet's house fascinating, and the scene of Juliet with the wicker-manikin hung with her wedding dress (IV, iii) a brillant invention. The setting (devised by Gastone Simonetti), shifting from Verona to Siena, Montagnana and San Quirico d'Orcia, is found incongruous by most: the contrast between the ancient aspect of the buildings and the brand-new appearance of the costumes prevents, according to some, suspension of disbelief. But the final scene in San Zeno impresses all: a curious detail is provided by Escalus, impersonated

by a well-known Italian novelist, Elio Vittorini, under the pseudonym of Giovanni Rota. (In a previous report it was wrongly stated that he would appear in the role of Paris.)

Apart from this international performance, there is little of note to be said about Shakespeare performances in Italy this year. In September 1954 *Julius Caesar* was staged in the Taormina Greek-Roman Theatre by the Compagnia del Teatro Mediterraneo: the translation was due to the poet Eugenio Montale. The Compagnia Stabile del Teatro di Via Manzoni (Milan) has produced *Twelfth Night* in the translation of Gerardo Guerrieri, adapted by Renato Castellani, with a remarkable Malvolio (Memo Benassi) and Gianrico Tedeschi as a very spirited Feste. Roman Vlad has provided the music both for this drama and the film of *Romeo and Juliet*. C. V. Ludovici, continuing in his heroic task of rendering into Italian a complete Shakespeare, has translated now *Much Ado About Nothing*. Gabriele Baldini has given a new translation of *Henry IV* (published by Rizzoli) and of *Richard II* (Naples, R. Pironti publisher) with two appendices (*Cenno sulle fonti per la biografia e sulla trasmissione critica dei drammi di Shakespeare*; and *Note per servire a una interpretazione dello Shakespeare elisabettiano*) which are remarkable for lucidity of exposition and critical insight. Nicoletta Neri has translated for the UTET classics (Turin) *The Merchant of Venice* and *All's Well*.   MARIO PRAZ

Poland

In the ten years following the liberation of Poland in 1944 over 100,000 copies of Shakespeare's plays in Polish translations old and new appeared. Public interest in new translations is indicated by the figure of 60,000 copies of post-war Shakespeare translations, most of them by distinguished poets and men of letters, which came from the presses in these ten years.

The year 1954 is generally considered to be the most auspicious period in the post-war history of Shakespearian scholarship in Poland, as it was marked by the appearance of several new translations, all issued by one of the most enterprising publishing houses in Poland, the Państwowy Instytut Wydawniczy. The P.I.W. invited the best Polish translators to contribute to a special Shakespeare Series (Seria Szekspirowska), in which eight volumes appeared between 1950 and 1953. In 1954 in the same series two more plays were published: *Timon of Athens*, translated by Czesław Jastrzębiec-Kozłowski—well-known in Poland for his excellent translations of Byron and Poe—and *The Merry Wives of Windsor*, translated by the young playwright Krystyna Berwińska.

Of yet greater importance are special single-volume editions of selected plays in versions by distinguished Polish poets. In the Memorial Edition translations of *A Midsummer Night's Dream*, *Henry IV* and fragments of other plays by the late Konstanty Ildefons Gałczyński (1906–53) have appeared. His rendering of *Henry IV* closely follows the original and has been accepted as the best and most exact Polish version of the play.

Great scholarship, subtlety and an admirable grasp of Shakespeare's mood characterize a volume which contains *Romeo and Juliet* and *Hamlet*, both translated by the eminent Polish poet Jarosław Iwaszkiewicz. His artistic integrity and respect for the original text make his work a model for future translators of Shakespeare. His are by no means philological renderings of the original, nor does he aim at literal exactness, yet both his translations are a landmark by virtue of their beauty of language and form. His *Hamlet* was staged in 1939, and then for a second time in 1947, during the Shakespeare Festival held in Poland in that year.

In *Pamiętnik Teatralny* (*Theatre Journal*, 2, 1954) the present writer has published an extensive study on 'Przekłady szekspirowskie w Polsce wczoraj i dziś' ('Shakespeare translations in Poland, past and present'). He has endeavoured to present as complete a history as possible of the Polish translations destined both for theatre production and for the reading public. After an outline review of nineteenth-century achievements he analyses in fuller detail about twenty translations produced since the end of the war, with extensive quotations from the works in question.

STANISŁAW HELSZTYŃSKI

South Africa

Hamlet was produced in Johannesburg with considerable success by Miss Margaret Inglis in August 1954, the name part being in the hands of Siegfried Mynhardt, an accomplished actor of comedy roles in *Volpone* and *Twelfth Night* for the National Theatre. Opinions as to his reading of the Prince of Denmark were as diverse as modern interpretations of the character; but he added no new portrait to the gallery of Hamlet impersonators.

The universities in South Africa continue to present regular annual performances of Shakespeare's plays, and the standard of amateur acting among these players is generally high. Overseas producers are, however, needed to make possible the presentation of Shakespeare's lesser-known dramas, such as *Troilus and Cressida*, *Measure for Measure* and *The Winter's Tale*, for which South African theatre-goers are starved. A charming open-air performance of *The Tempest* was staged in Rhodes Park, Kensington, during September.

The most significant Shakespearian activity of the year, however, was that of a Zulu writer, K. E. Masenga, who is the S.A.B.C.'s senior announcer in that language at Durban. During 1953 and 1954 he translated into his native tongue *King Lear*, *Hamlet*, *The Merchant of Venice*, *The Tempest*, *A Comedy of Errors* and *Julius Caesar*, and gained an immense popularity for Shakespeare among the Zulu people. The plays were performed by a specially trained Zulu cast of over thirty players, including teachers, students, clerks and social workers; and they claim that the folklore of their people abounds in the moral virtues of courage and loyalty, and some of the evils, that are depicted in Shakespeare's plays. The last play, *Julius Caesar*, was presented serially in six 30-minute episodes—a total production time of three hours.

A. C. PARTRIDGE

In connexion with the note by A. C. Partridge in *Survey* 7, p. 114, Captain D. M. K. Marendaz writes: "The Marendaz portrait of Shakespeare has been for the past two and a half years the subject of exhaustive research and enquiry, all pointing to its authenticity.

"It will be recalled that in 1952 G. Wilson Knight announced that he had found in the collection of Captain D. M. K. Marendaz, of Somerset West, South Africa, what he believed to be a contemporary portrait of Shakespeare.

"Captain Marendaz at that time stated he considered the portrait was the work of the court painter of that period, Paulus van Somer. He has been supported in this by Raymond Henniker Heaton (an authority on Old Master paintings, well known both in Europe and America and for many years a director of leading art galleries in the United States) and by other experts.

"In the course of widespread research Captain Marendaz, in addition to securing further evidence that the portrait is contemporary, has also brought new facts to light on many incidents in Shakespeare's private life, all of which, with a reproduction of this portrait, will be embodied in a book entitled *The Marendaz Portrait of Shakespeare*, shortly to be published."

Spain

Luis Astrana Marín, *Shakespeare Survey* correspondent from Spain, has published the first volume of the collected works (*Shakespeare, Obras Completas*, Madrid,

'Biblioteca de Cultura Básica', Ediciones de la Universidad de Puerto Rico, 1955). This book, handsomely printed, contains a biographical and bibliographical introduction together with renderings of *Macbeth, Love's Labour's Lost* and *Much Ado About Nothing*, the English text of the plays appearing opposite Marín's translations. One of the most elaborate of recent continental editions of Shakespeare's plays, the new Spanish *Obras Completas* amply demonstrates both the up-to-date scholarship and the translating skill of the editor-author. Both he and the publishers are to be heartily congratulated on a large, important and beautifully produced addition to the Shakespeare library.

Sweden

The Swedish stage did not offer many striking productions of Shakespeare last year. *The Tempest* was acted at the Hälsingborgs stadsteater (director: Johan Falck). At the Malmö statsteater, where Shakespeare's comedies have found a real home recently, *Twelfth Night* was a notable event under the management of Lars-Levi Læstadius.

The need of new translations has been felt, especially by actors and stage-managers. A new rendering of *Macbeth* has been attempted by Sigvard Arbman. *Hamlet* was published in a slightly revised edition of the old Hagberg translation. An adaptation of Hagberg's text (not printed) was also used for the stage version of *Twelfth Night* above mentioned. NILS MOLIN

Switzerland

No performance of any of Shakespeare's plays was given in the French part of Switzerland, but there have been several productions in the German part. At Bern *Hamlet* was performed twice in the spring at popular prices with considerable success; *Twelfth Night* ran for the first two weeks of September in a hall where the conditions of the Elizabethan stage were realized, with a success that fully justified the attempt. At Lucerne, *Much Ado* was played twice in the early spring. For a production of *Macbeth* at St-Gall, there was new incidental music by Ernst Klug and rather daring light effects; for their production of *Midsummer Night's Dream*, the same theatre hit upon the happy idea of substituting for Mendelssohn's music a selection of the music of Purcell's opera, and the change was felt to be altogether refreshing. The Zurich Municipal Theatre gave *Othello* in March, *Twelfth Night* and *Henry IV* in the autumn. The last one was an abridgment of the two parts prepared by L. Lindtberg for a single performance. G. A. BONNARD

Turkey

Three plays of Shakespeare have been produced in three outstanding theatres of Turkey during this winter season of 1954–5.

The Istanbul Municipal Theatre opened with the *Two Gentlemen of Verona* on 1 October. This was the twenty-first Shakespearian play produced there since its inauguration in 1915. The Turkish text was by A. Givda, production by Suavi Tedü, who also played the part of Valentine. Settings and costumes were simple and effective, and the tempo unusually good.

Küçük Sahne of Istanbul, run by Muhsin Ertuğrul, opened on 30 September 1954 with a new production of *Hamlet*, the title role being played by Miss Nur Sabuncuoğlu. This version, by the late Orhan Burian, is the best Turkish translation of *Hamlet* so far produced.

The National Theatre of Ankara celebrated New Year's Eve with *Twelfth Night*. Cüneyt Gökçer, a very well-known actor of Ankara, produced the play and characterized Malvolio even better than his earlier performances in 1949. Miss Yildiz Akçan, the youthful star of the theatre, gave distinction to the part of Olivia. Salih Canar as Sir Toby, and Melek Gün as Maria were the two strong characters of the cellar scene. Miss Muazzez Lutas as a blonde Viola easily matched with Ziya Demirel's Sebastian, both in size and complexion. Unrealistic screen settings by Turgut Zaim were most effective.

The National Conservatoire is preparing, under my direction, to perform *Julius Caesar* at Aspendus, the ancient Roman Theatre of the second century at Antalya (Pamphylia district of the Roman Empire in Southern Turkey) with a cast of 200 in addition to the student-players of the Conservatoire. NUREDDIN SEVIN

U.S.A.

What of the 'Shakespeare Season' in New York this year? "A blank, my lord!" Not a single professional production of the works of the Bard has been seen during the winter of 1954–5. This must be something of a record; from now on the situation can only improve. A step toward that improvement is the steady progress of the plans of the American Shakespeare Festival and Academy which has started building its summer playhouse at Stratford-on-the-Housatonic in Connecticut. A 'birdcage of steel' is rearing its 90-foot trusses over a stage and auditorium destined to provide a permanent home in America for the Sweet Swan of Avon. Plans are already afoot for a late summer season as well as for the formation of an 'academy' under

John Burrell (formerly of the Old Vic), who is now gathering together a group of young professionals in preparation for an intensive course of training.

While Shakespeare languished on the professional stage, he flourished in college and university and in the professional and semi-professional community and summer theatres. Three major groups have been staging summer Shakespeare festivals with increasing success and competence during the last decade. In San Diego, the Old Globe Theatre offers a Shakespeare Festival with Elizabethan Folk Dances and May Day festivities thrown in. The building is a reconstruction of the Globe, and the plays are given with the vigour and freedom that such a setting makes possible. Frank McMullan of Yale University directed *Othello* there last summer and B. Iden Payne, *doyen* of Shakespearian directors, will stage *Measure for Measure* this summer. Three or four plays are given each season, as they are also in the Oregon Festival Theatre at Ashland. There, too, on a permanent stage along Elizabethan lines, built within the circling walls of an abandoned stadium, five major plays in repertory will be presented to celebrate Oregon's twentieth season. A younger but equally enthusiastic organization, the Antioch Area Theatre Shakespeare Festival, has embarked on no less of a project than the presentation of the complete canon on its out-door platform stage. This summer's formidable season includes *The Comedy of Errors, Love's Labour's Lost, Much Ado About Nothing, Hamlet, All's Well that Ends Well, Measure for Measure* and *King Lear*! All this and weather too! Did I say there was no Shakespeare in America?

These festival centres are of course only one manifestation of the college and community enthusiasm for the Bard. Universities, colleges and schools all over the country play him continually, the few professional theatre companies outside New York find him an ever-present help in times of a shortage of scripts. Robert Porterfield's Barter Theatre tours him into the remotest corners of the country, Margo Jones gives at least one of his plays a year in her Dallas '55 Theatre-in-the-Round. *Hamlet* has been played everywhere, from gymnasiums in Virginia to circus tents in Texas. Shakespeare is still good box-office west of Broadway.

ROSAMOND GILDER

U.S.S.R.

Shakespeare's plays are always on the billboards of the Soviet theatres; his productions are often included in broadcasting programmes. The collected works as well as texts of individual plays are rapidly sold out in the U.S.S.R. This applies also to Soviet editions of Shake-speare's works in the English language, which include a complete collection of Shakespeare (four volumes) and specific plays of the great dramatist.

Let us begin with the current Shakespearian repertory of the Soviet theatres. There have been one hundred and fifty-four productions of Shakespeare's plays in the last few years. *Othello* has been produced in forty-seven theatres, *Twelfth Night* in twenty-two and *The Taming of the Shrew* in twenty-seven.

More can be added to these eloquent figures. *Othello*, which is most popular among the Soviet public, figured on the billboards of twenty-six theatres in the thirties and fifty theatres in the forties. Productions of this play since 1950 have been almost as numerous as the total in the earlier ten years.

Besides the many bold and original interpretations of the play already mentioned, note may be taken of the rapidly growing interest of the Soviet theatre in *Hamlet*. *Hamlet*, of course, has had many Russian productions in the past. The late M. M. Morozov (1897–1952), who was a well-known authority on Shakespeare and a former Correspondent of *Shakespeare Survey*, in his book *Shakespeare on the Soviet Stage* has cited interesting information about the work of the Soviet theatre on this tragedy in the thirties and forties. But the latest productions of this tragedy represent a step forward: in all the theatres which have recently staged this play, the general interpretation has been more profound; the characters are made more significant and more realistic; they disclose better than ever the inexhaustible possibilities latent in the text of the Shakespearian tragedy.

This work of the Soviet theatres on *Hamlet* is at present just being analysed. As yet there is no fundamental treatise showing the merits and weaknesses of the various productions, drawing conclusions and summing up the experience of the Soviet producers, actors and scene designers. But the preliminary discussion in our newspapers and magazines demonstrates that these new productions are indicative of the great progress being made. In particular, the production of *Hamlet* at the Mayakovsky Drama Theatre in Moscow, under the direction of the well-known Soviet producer Nikolai Okhlopkov, has been hailed with enthusiasm. Reviews of this production spoke with full justification of a new reading of *Hamlet*. Yevgeni Samoilov, cast in the role of the Prince, has created the character of a youth who revolts courageously against the tyranny of Claudius, against the evil and oppression which had converted Denmark into a prison. Nikolai Okhlopkov has continued and deepened the finest traditions of the Russian classical theatre. In a review of the acting of the great

Russian actor of the nineteenth century, Mochalov, in the role of Hamlet, V. Belinsky noted with sympathy Mochalov's tendency to emphasize Hamlet's growing courage, to picture Hamlet as a man with strong emotions. Yevgeni Samoilov's Hamlet is a humanist who takes up arms against despotism. The settings designed by Ryndin are splendid (with the exception, perhaps, of the scene at the cemetery).

Of great value for the history of the production of *Hamlet* at the Mayakovsky Theatre—a production which unquestionably will be the subject of much study —is an article published by the producer, N. Okhlopkov, in *The Theatre* (No. 1, 1955), under the heading 'The Producer's Explanation of *Hamlet*'. In poetic language, as if giving an artistic recast of the play itself, Okhlopkov conveys the pathos of the tragedy as he understands it and describes the stages of his work on the production. His central idea is that Denmark is a prison: "Hamlet rebels against the cold embraces of this prison. A tragic fate awaits those prisoners who keep aloof from the struggle and bide their time, while the army of murderers is growing and growing. Tragic, too, is the fate of those who answer blow for blow too early or too late." Emphasizing his concept of Hamlet as a militant humanist, Okhlopkov declares that the clique of King Claudius raised the sword over Hamlet's head, taking recourse to such various means of terror as were used against Giordano Bruno, John Hus, and others. This comparison, which seems as it were a remark on the margin of the producer's copy, reveals his general perspective: the future belongs to Hamlet; he is aflame with the fire of great new ideas which could not be extinguished by the forces of reaction that were amassed against humanism at the junction of the sixteenth and seventeenth centuries. Speaking of his concept of the end of the play, of Hamlet's death, Okhlopkov further writes: "Beyond his death, beyond his personal defeat, lies the historic victory of humanism."

In the U.S.S.R. the Shakespearian student is closely connected with contemporary life, with the life of the Soviet theatre, with the requirements and interests of the Soviet people who know and love Shakespeare's plays. It is natural, therefore, that the development of Shakespearian interest is expressed not only in the publication of capital works about Shakespeare, but also in the heated and wide discussion of Shakespearian problems in the Soviet press. This characteristic feature was shown particularly in the work of the late M. M. Morozov, who was a translator, a literary scholar and an excellent theatrical critic. The wide range of his Shakespearian interests is made evident in a volume of his *Selected Articles and Translations*, issued in 1954, and containing, besides several essays previously published, important studies of 'Belinsky on Shakespeare' and 'The Dynamics of Shakespeare's characters'.

A comprehensive study of Shakespeare is included in the curricula of all the faculties of philology in the Soviet higher schools, whether the students in question are specially studying English literature, or whether they intend to become teachers of other languages. The traditional seminars and special Shakespearian courses in the Romano-Germanic Departments of the universities and at the schools which educate English language teachers are immensely popular among the students.

Students are encouraged to deliver lectures on Shakespeare's works before schoolchildren attending the literary circles. It is noteworthy that a second-year student of Moscow State University was appointed to deliver a report on 'Shakespeare on the Soviet Stage' at the students' 'scientific conference' dedicated to the 200th anniversary of the University.

Several old, pre-revolutionary editions of Shakespeare and many Soviet editions are available to readers in the U.S.S.R.; to meet the growing interest in Shakespeare, the Iskusstvo Publishing House is now preparing a new edition of his works for the press. The eight-volume edition of the collected works, publication of which was begun by the 'Akademia' and recently completed by the 'Goslitizdat' publishing house, has already become scarce.

Shakespeare is dear and understandable to the widest sections of the Soviet people; his heroes talk to them from the stage, and his works are published in many languages of the Soviet Union. This love for the great British writer is irrefutable evidence of the unbreakable cultural relations which promote mutual understanding and friendship between the peoples of the U.S.S.R. and Britain.

R. M. SAMARIN

SHAKESPEARE PRODUCTIONS IN THE
UNITED KINGDOM: 1954

A List compiled from its Records by the
Shakespeare Memorial Library, Birmingham

JANUARY

6   *Twelfth Night:* The Old Vic Company, at the Old Vic Theatre, London. *Producer:* DENIS CAREY.

11 *The Merchant of Venice:* Chesterfield Civic Theatre. *Producer:* GERARD GLAISTER.

25 *The Merchant of Venice:* The Elizabethan Theatre Company, London, on tour, opening at the Arts Theatre, Cambridge. *Producer:* PETER HALL.

FEBRUARY

15 *Twelfth Night:* The Century Mobile Theatre, on tour, opening at Hinckley, Leics. *Producer:* R. H. WARD.

17 *The Merchant of Venice:* Bradford Civic Playhouse. *Producer:* DAVID GILES.

20 *Henry IV*, Part II: at Eton College. *Producer:* RAEF PAYNE.

23 *Coriolanus:* The Old Vic Company, at the Old Vic Theatre, London. *Producer:* MICHAEL BENTHALL.

MARCH

1   *Twelfth Night:* Birmingham University Guild Theatre Group. *Producer:* ANTHONY WEIR.

    The Taming of the Shrew: Ipswich Theatre Company, at Ipswich Theatre. *Producer:* VAL MAY.

2   *King John:* Oxford University Dramatic Society, at Oxford Playhouse. *Producers:* MICHAEL ELLIOTT and JOHN POWELL.

8   *Julius Caesar:* Nottingham Playhouse. *Producer:* JOHN HARRISON.

    King Lear: The Marlowe Society, Cambridge University, at The Arts Theatre, Cambridge. (The Players and Producer are anonymous.)

16 *Othello:* The Shakespeare Memorial Theatre, Stratford-upon-Avon. *Producers:* ANTHONY QUAYLE and PATRICK DONNELL.

23 *Much Ado About Nothing:* Northampton Repertory Theatre. *Producer:* JOSEPH WRIGHT.

    A Midsummer Night's Dream: The Shakespeare Memorial Theatre, Stratford-upon-Avon. *Producer:* GEORGE DEVINE.

30 *Macbeth:* The Library Theatre, Manchester. *Producer:* PETER LAMBERT.

APRIL

13 *The Tempest:* The Old Vic Company, at the Old Vic Theatre, London. *Producer:* ROBERT HELPMANN.

27 *Romeo and Juliet:* The Shakespeare Memorial Theatre, Stratford-upon-Avon. *Producer:* GLEN BYAM SHAW.

    The Taming of the Shrew: The Piccolo Theatre Company, Chorlton, Manchester. *Producer:* FRANK DUNLOP.

MAY

3   *As You Like It:* The Taverners (Poetry and Plays in Pubs). *Producer:* HENRY McCARTHY. (On tour, opening at The Shirley Poppy Hotel, Croydon.)

24   *The Taming of the Shrew:* The Queen's Theatre, Hornchurch. *Producer:* STUART BURGE.

JUNE

1   *The Taming of the Shrew:* The Shakespeare Memorial Theatre, Stratford-upon-Avon. *Producer:* GEORGE DEVINE.

4   *Much Ado About Nothing:* Harrow School. *Producer:* RONALD WATKINS.

11   *As You Like It:* Tavistock Repertory Company at The Tower Theatre, Canonbury. *Producer:* MALCOLM HAYES.

15   *The Taming of the Shrew:* The Oxford University Dramatic Society, in the Gardens of Blackhall. *Producer:* JACK GOOD.

    Much Ado About Nothing: The Arena Theatre, on tour, opening at Cardiff Castle. *Producer:* JOHN ENGLISH.

22   *Sir Thomas More:* The Theatre Centre, London. (Sponsored by Donald Wolfit on behalf of Advance Players Association, Ltd.) *Producer:* BRIAN WAY.

29   *Pericles:* The Repertory Theatre, Birmingham. *Producer:* DOUGLAS SEALE.

JULY

13   *Troilus and Cressida:* The Shakespeare Memorial Theatre, Stratford-upon-Avon. *Producer:* GLEN BYAM SHAW.

AUGUST

23   *Macbeth:* The Old Vic Company, at the Edinburgh Festival. (Afterwards at the Old Vic Theatre, London, 9 September.) *Producer:* MICHAEL BENTHALL.

31   *A Midsummer Night's Dream:* The Old Vic Company, at the Edinburgh Festival. *Producer:* MICHAEL BENTHALL.

SEPTEMBER

9   *Macbeth:* The Old Vic Company, at The Old Vic Theatre, London. *Producer:* MICHAEL BENTHALL.

27   *Romeo and Juliet:* The Elizabethan Theatre Company, London, on tour, opening at The Arts Theatre, Cambridge. *Producer:* PETER WOOD.

28   *Twelfth Night:* Liverpool Repertory Company, at the Liverpool Playhouse. *Producer:* WILLARD STOKER.

OCTOBER

4   *Richard II:* The Elizabethan Theatre Company, London, on tour, opening at The Arts Theatre, Cambridge. *Producer:* JOHN BARTON.

    Richard II: The David Lewis Theatre, Liverpool. *Producer:* THOMAS G. READ.

11   *Richard II:* Salisbury Arts Theatre. *Producer:* RICHARD SCOTT.

18   *Much Ado About Nothing:* The Citizens' Theatre, Glasgow. *Producer:* RICHARD MATHEWS.

    Romeo and Juliet: The Repertory Theatre, High Wycombe. *Producer:* NEIL GIBSON.

SHAKESPEARE PRODUCTIONS IN UNITED KINGDOM: 1954

OCTOBER

19   *Much Ado About Nothing:* The Bristol Old Vic Company, at The Theatre Royal, Bristol. *Producer:* JOHN MOODY.

Love's Labour's Lost: The Old Vic Company, at the Old Vic Theatre, London. *Producer:* FRITH BANBURY.

NOVEMBER

1   *Romeo and Juliet:* Nottingham Playhouse. *Producer:* JOHN HARRISON.

The Merchant of Venice: Guildford Theatre. *Producer:* ROGER WINTON.

8   *The Merchant of Venice:* The Intimate Theatre, Palmer's Green, London. *Producer:* PETER COLEMAN.

The Merchant of Venice: The Perth Theatre Company. *Producer:* GRAHAM EVANS.

Othello: The Queen's Theatre, Hornchurch. *Producer:* STUART BURGE.

15   *Macbeth:* The Midland Theatre Company, Coventry. *Producer:* FRANK HAUSER.

30   *The Taming of the Shrew:* The Old Vic Company, at The Old Vic Theatre, London. *Producer:* DENIS CAREY.

THE TRAGIC CURVE

[*A review of two productions of* Macbeth: *at the Old Vic, winter 1954–5, and at the Shakespeare Memorial Theatre, Stratford-upon-Avon, summer 1955*]

BY

RICHARD DAVID

What *is* Tragedy? The two-thousand-three-hundred-year-old question, as evasive of answer as Pilate's, has recently been raised again. The latest to attempt the riddle, Peter Alexander in his Northcliffe lectures,[1] defines it (after Aristotle) as that which produces a certain special response in an audience; and he declares that what conditions the response is the nature of the chief character presented. Tragedy, then, is a demonstration of the virtue the Greeks called Arete, nobility of spirit triumphing over disaster and death. The argument is witty and exciting, and succeeds in determining more precisely the species of pleasure that Tragedy brings. But the tragic hero's cap, as cut by Alexander, fits his chosen mannequin Hamlet with difficulty, and only after some bodging of the prayer-scene. There is still much to explain.

I suggest that the one essential thing about a tragedy is its shape. It is a progress, a development, a course. The man who runs it (both the character and the actor who presents that character) must, it is true, be of such a nature that the audience is under compulsion not merely to follow his fortunes intently but to become emotionally engaged. The nature of the tragic hero, however, admits of much wider variation than does the nature of the tragic progress, which can be plotted with much the same mathematical accuracy as the fall of a wave or the flight of a shell. Of course there are waves of different wave-length and shells of varying trajectory, but each follows the same general pattern. Upon the plotting of the tragic curve, first by the playwright and then by producer and actors, depends the entire success of the play in the theatre.

It is not so with comedy, which is as often static as dynamic, relying on contrast, on the simultaneous presentation of incompatibilities, rather than on ordered progress to make its point. There certainly are "comedies of motion": Ben Jonson's *Alchemist* is one, though here the curve is not the parabola of Tragedy but rises with increasing steepness till it runs off the top of the page. They are, however, exceptional, and this is perhaps particularly true of Shakespeare's comedies. *As You Like It, Twelfth Night* meander. And if the late romances have a more direct progression, if the lush ornamentation of *Love's Labours Lost* embowers a streamlined structure, the total effect of even *Winter's Tale* or *Love's Labour* is not entirely lost if the producer foreshortens or distorts their shape. The least misplacing of emphasis will wreck any one of the tragedies.

During the season 1954–5 the Shakespeare theatres of both London and Stratford confined themselves to a single—and the same—tragedy: *Macbeth*. The two productions were diametrically opposed in intention and method. A comparison between the two is therefore interesting in itself. I hope it may also demonstrate the nature of the tragic curve, how it runs in *Macbeth*, and in what ways actors and producers may sustain or suppress it.

---

[1] Reviewed on pp. 137–8.

The producer's problem in *Macbeth* is a particularly hard one, for three reasons. In the first place the play, like so many of Shakespeare's tragedies but more so than most, exists on several levels at once. Like *Hamlet* it is a first-rate thriller as well as a tragedy; but whereas in *Hamlet* the tragic burden is so much wrought into the fabric that the work does not make sense when presented as a straight 'Revenge play', the Grand Guignol *Macbeth* can stand on its own legs. There are, then, the two equal and opposite errors, of playing the piece as melodrama without poetry and of sacrificing dramatic grip for the tragic overtones. Secondly, in taking the butcher Macbeth as his tragic hero Shakespeare was sailing as near the wind as it is possible to go; he risked alienating the sympathy and co-operation of the audience, which is essential if the tragic progress is to have significance. As Aristotle said, the fall of a plain bad man is plain uninteresting. Thirdly, the tragic curve in *Macbeth* is of a peculiar foreshortened variety. The hero is tempted in the third scene, falls in the seventh, and by the eighth is damned beyond redemption. Shakespeare uses some subtlety in making the process appear more extended than it is, and a corresponding subtlety is required of actor and producer.

Michael Benthall's production at the Old Vic, with Paul Rogers in the name part, leant very much towards the melodramatic. It must have been the noisiest *Macbeth* ever. The play opened with a wild and raucous cry, as a battle-casualty, leaving the field where Macbeth and the rebels could still be heard "memorizing another Golgotha", staggered on to the stage and fell, to be ghoulishly seized upon by the witches in the guise of ragged camp-scavengers. Every entry was clamorously accompanied by trumpet and drum, or by the pipes at full blow. At every opportunity the rough and eager thanes spurred on the action by their interjections of scorn or cheers of approval. The set (by Audrey Cruddas) was no more than a rough-hewn square arch, on either side of which appeared, as necessary for the indoor scenes, doorways, recesses, the lower treads of a sharply ramped and angled staircase. Through the opening of the arch was seen, dimly, the bleak heath or the dark inward of the castle and, suddenly, for the English scene, a dazzling rain-washed sky, pure and pitiful—the most moving visual effect in the play. In this spare setting the actors moved with exemplary speed and urgency. Such scenes as that of Duncan's murder gained enormously from all this; the racing terror of the interchange between murderer and accomplice—

> Did not you speak?
> When?
> Now.
> As I descended?
> Ay.

could hardly have been bettered. But there was seldom any variation in this hurdling pace, never a let-up or breather; even the English scene, after the initial effect of the heavens opening, was conducted at a brisk and worldly trot. This is not of course a matter just of words-per-second. The "Tomorrow" speech (of which more hereafter) was, by metronome, exceedingly slow; but because it was interpreted at plot-level, as an illustration of rather than as a comment upon the action, the audience's reaction-clock continued to tick brightly through it, keeping perfect time.

As Macbeth, Rogers accepted his part in the thriller. The play might as well have been called 'Manhunt' as 'Macbeth', for the audience was never called upon to agonize for a tragic hero but only to witness with excitement and approval the cornering of a dangerous killer by the forces of the law. This Macbeth, at his very first entry, was already clearly cut off from human help and human contact. He had that whickering look in the eye of a horse about to shy or a Faustus expecting the Devil at any moment to present his bill. He could not be drawn inexorably into the web of evil, for he was already in it and could only thresh about in the meshes. In other words the tragic curve had been cut down to its last, declining section, and this had then to be spun out over five acts. At this stage of his progress the hero is reduced to only two reactions, frenzy and exhaustion. These, exaggerated in the very conception of the production, became, by the usual debasing process of a long run, in the end almost ludicrous. At each performance the later speeches became more frothily unintelligible, the pauses between the "Tomorrows" were longer drawn out, the contrast between the black hair of Act one and the white of Act five was heightened, and the panting in the final duel sounded more like a wheezy steam-engine. It is only fair to add that these extravagances were as tumultuously clapped on the last night as on the first.

There could be little interaction between so dehumanized a hero and the other characters. Lady Macbeth's attack was necessarily reduced to the most blatant vamping, the crudest scorn, but even these could not penetrate impervious material. Ann Todd was never altogether happy in the part. At the beginning of the run she was defeated by the Shakespearian movement and idiom—to the end she insisted that Banquo "cannot come out on 'tis grave"; halfway through she had learnt where to put her feet and was delivering the lines with force and point; but by the last night they had hardened again into a conventional rhetoric that carried little conviction. The sleep-walking scene, being prose, was effective enough; but is it unkind to suggest that no competent actress can fail in this? The rest of the cast as representing Justice could afford to play out. Eric Porter gave us a powerful, shouldering Banquo, all bear-skin and decision; Paul Daneman an oddly smug and stolid Malcolm recalling the gum-chewing trilby-hatted station-sergeant in any gangster film. That it should be John Neville's young and amateurish Macduff who, over the heads of these two stalwarts, gets his man seemed all a part of the same tradition.

The Stratford production, directed by Glen Byam Shaw, was anything but gangsterly. David King's bloody sergeant and Geoffrey Bayldon's Duncan gave the play a rousing send-off, and the final battle-scenes, with the assailants tumbling up the battlements from the back of the stage, went with a swing; but with Macbeth's presence the movement became slow, quiet, withdrawn. The critics complained that Olivier seemed almost indifferent whether he killed Duncan or not. The effect, as we shall see, was deliberate, but in attaining it the producer was compelled to forgo precisely that kind of suspense and plot-tension that was the mainspring of the Benthall version. Against this loss must be set two overwhelming gains: a Macbeth who held the full sympathy of the audience to the bitter end, and a true conveying of that atmosphere of mystery that is peculiar to the play.

Here a digression is needed—a digression, because this mystery is not the essence of the tragedy, does not shape the tragic curve, but is an incidental colouring only, without which, it must be admitted, *Macbeth* would not be *Macbeth*. It is generated, in large part, by the witches. Can the witches, in this twentieth century, be presented as anything but figures of fun?

The tendency has been to make them human in the hope of making them credible, and to bring out in each a distinguishing "character" to give them solidity. Of the Stratford witches a gossip-writer objected: "Must they always be so *unanimous*, always give—like occult prototypes of the Beverley Sisters—an object-lesson in co-ordination and *esprit de corps*? Surely their scenes might gain from a suggestion of disharmony or at least variety between the three, from a little bumping and boring round the cauldron-mouth? They are unnatural enough in other ways without being, for old women, unnaturally co-operative." This surely is the most wrong-headed nonsense. The purpose, the effect of the witches are single. The three are collectively a manifestation of evil. There is more than one witch because antiphony is dramatically more effective than monologue; they are three, because that is a handy number and has magical associations.

The Old Vic followed the gossip-writer's recipe. There was one fishwife, one female impersonator haggish and falsetto, one ditto in *ottava bassa* and made up as the Ugly Duchess. Not for one moment did they suggest that they were to be feared, or create any atmosphere beyond that of the music-hall. The Stratford witches were all alike, in rags certainly, but rags of a silvery grey that seemed part of the early mist, and with lank grey locks unbound about their faces. Whereas the Old Vic witches kept up a perpetual hurly-burly, these were predominantly still (save for an unnecessary weaving of the hands), now in a huddle mid-stage, now, with a start, sliding three ways into its corners. Though their performance had not quite the concentration required to persuade us that evil was here personified, at least they never broke the mystery or fell out into the full daylight of ridicule.

The other ingredient of this mystery is of course provided by Macbeth himself in his more reflective speeches. Rogers, carried along post-haste by the action of the play, could never afford for a minute to relinquish the role of man of action and paint the scene. Such speeches as "Now o'er the one half-world Nature seems dead", or "Come, seeling night", were spurs to action, not reflections on the ghastly implications of action; each word was pressed to give, vehemently, its full and active meaning. Olivier, on the other hand, was able, without breaking the thread of the play, to step for a moment outside it and project an authentic spell over the auditorium. What a chill was in his rooky wood! The secret of his power was that the whole action was presented as, in a sense, outside time; it was not, as at the Vic, a crisp series of events, consequentially interlocked and reported by an outside observer, but Macbeth's nightmare vision of his own predicament. The hideous deeds presented to his will seemed, like the air-drawn dagger, unreal; his intellect rejects them, and yet he remains under a terrible and inescapable compulsion to do them. He is a man possessed, but by no petty devil capable of no more than fits and froth. It was Olivier's achievement to make the audience share this possession, to bring them under the same spell, so that they experienced Macbeth's progress from the inside and themselves travelled the tragic curve.

This sympathy, in the literal sense, was maintained until the very end of the play. Even when intellectually the audience has long changed sides and stands with the heaven-blest justicers from England, it could still be drawn to feel and to share the ache of the mind diseased, the rooted sorrow. Rogers, in this speech to the doctor, had been a Hitler rating an incompetent subordinate: there was no distinction between "Canst thou not minister" and "Throw physic to the dogs". Olivier's Macbeth, with a tender flexibility of phrasing, not only showed us the bond of affection between husband and wife but also (the hands gesturing dumbly and half-unconsciously towards his own breast) included himself in the plea for mercy. Or take the "Tomorrow" speech. In such set-pieces Olivier often appears to be unconventional, wilful even, for the sake of being different. There seemed no particular reason for any one of his intonations, pauses, emphases here. Paul Rogers had used the speech to portray utter spiritual exhaustion: the words issued one by one, with great silences between, as if from parched lips, in an almost monotonous whisper. Yet if you strained your ears through the pianissimo and the pauses you could detect that fundamentally every tone and stress was natural and logical. There was no obvious logic in Olivier's version; but as a whole—and with the mazed head-shake of the final "nothing"—it perfectly conveyed the hurt bewilderment of Fate's victim. Almost one said "a man more sinned against than sinning".

With the whole action of the play as it were absorbed into Macbeth the other characters and the accessories were automatically reduced in importance. Yet the meditative pace of the production allowed the designer, Roger Furse, to elaborate his scenery and devise some happy effects of atmosphere. The sets were for the most part realistic (except that the pointed arches were obstinately asymmetrical); the heath was authentically heathery, the castle had indeed a pleasant seat overlooking a loch-filled glen, and for the last scenes of the play we were on the very battlements with a distant view of snow-covered Grampians. Particularly effective was the narrow, cloister-like corridor at the far end of which suddenly appeared the spark of the sleep-walker's taper; while the only blunder was the setting of the English scene. Here what is needed is the strongest possible contrast to shag-haired Scotland, and this poor poster of Cumberland hills was not sufficiently distinct to become the rival symbol and to stand for sanity, piety and civilization. If we must have realism here, only Windsor Castle or the Tower of London will do. But for the most part the naturalism of the sets succeeded in underlining the supernatural strangeness of the scenes they framed. (The clothes were not so happy. Whereas Audrey Cruddas at the Vic dressed the characters in neat, dark kilts, workmanlike leather jerkins, and rough bear-skins, Furse chose the more treacherous kirtles and cloaks. Poor Banquo, in a carroty bob and knee-length greeny-blue nightie, was cruelly served.)

It was idle of the critics to object that the lesser parts at Stratford were weakly played, since it was a condition of the production that they should be played down. This Banquo was never the formidable antagonist of the Vic, but a forthright, bustling, unimaginative soldier with no inkling of the powers into whose orbit he had ventured. Malcolm was a mere boy, and unsure of himself; but this indeed was a virtue, for he attracted pity and sympathy without ever directly competing with Macbeth for the audience's favour. Macbeth had no *need* to fear such opposites. The killing of Banquo, the frantic fortifying of Dunsinane, were superfluous acts of savagery. Macbeth brings his end upon himself. Only the Macduff of Keith Michell, the fated instrument of heaven and by his birth himself outside normality, showed something of Macbeth's super-human stature.

Lady Macbeth, too, was a force to be reckoned with, and the scenes between husband and wife were always exciting in their give and take, in the dramatic modification of one character by another that was so lacking at the Vic. Vivien Leigh has superb attack: such an opening as "Come, you spirits That tend on mortal thoughts, unsex me here" was tremendous; but she lacks the gift of phrasing in verse necessary to carry her through a long speech. She was like a non-swimmer of great courage and determination attempting a passage out of her depth. There was a magnificent splash as she went in, and for a line or two she would manage to keep her head above water; but then her stroke would get faster and faster, her floundering more desperate, and it was touch and go whether she got over at all. This disability, however, hardly affected any but her first scene, and for the rest her force and drive whipped up the play and saved it from the courted risk of dragging. "Infirm of purpose—", "Are you a man?"—such explosions gave to their scenes the propulsion that the spell-stopped Macbeth could not provide. She, too, was a blood-curdling sleep-walker. But whereas the Lady Macbeth of the Vic, in contrast to her ever-ruthless husband, could sink to her knees and writhe herself from side to side in the abandonment of agony, at Stratford it was Macbeth who dissolved while his wife only momentarily let slip the hold she had upon herself, revealing her inward panic not in large gestures but in her secret, vicious wringing of the hands that would "ne'er be clean", not in the expected phrases ("Hell is murky" was firmly objective) but in the sudden high-pitched quaver of "The Thane of Fife had a wife; where is she now?".

It was Macbeth's play. And yet Sir Laurence's success was fed by the brilliant direction of Glen Byam Shaw. Scene after scene was lit by touches of genius: sometimes the merest details in aid of continuity and plausibility, as when the attendant, who is later to usher in Banquo's murderers, at Macbeth's state entry takes a step forward but checks at the look in the King's eye warning him not to broach the business at so public a moment; or Macbeth's overhearing of the young princes' plan to flee the country; or his threatening of Macduff, in the witches' cavern, interrupted by the sound of the galloping messengers who (we learn later) bring the news that Macduff has escaped him. Others added touches of vitality: the murderer, greeted by Macbeth with "There's blood upon thy face", claps a guilty hand to his cheek before resuming sufficient boldness to retort "'Tis Banquo's then". Others again, no less simple and direct, were of greater import. Let me take a few of the key scenes and, comparing them with the Old Vic versions, support my view that Byam Shaw gave us Shakespeare's tragedy in all its balanced perfection, Benthall another play of the same name.

The Old Vic opening has already been described. Stratford began with a conjuring trick. The witches were discovered, in a close group, apparently floating in mid air; as the scene proceeded they slowly came to earth. It was apparently because there was only one such stunt that the first-night reporters decided that on the whole the production was dull. At the risk of appearing merely contrary I say that this opening was Byam Shaw's one serious blunder. The audience was bound to be so curious as to how the trick was worked (was that a gauze sliding up to the flies?) that they could have no eyes or ears for the witches themselves, or for Shakespeare's purpose in bringing them on at all.

Skip to their meeting with Macbeth. At the Vic the day was more foul than fair. The witches, excited and garrulous, ranged over the whole stage before retreating right as Macbeth and Banquo entered from the left. The encounter was face to face across the width of the stage, factual, impartial. At Stratford there was a boulder mid-stage on which the witches huddled side by side to exchange their sinister confidences. At the sound of Macbeth's drum they shrank into the prompt corner, their greyness blending with the nondescript colour of wings and proscenium. Macbeth, entering up-stage right, advanced to the centre and stepped up onto the boulder, where he stood bathed in strong light as of the setting sun (here it was more fair than foul). Thus all attention was concentrated on the face of Macbeth as he stiffened at sight of the witches and as, guarded still, he listened to their prophecies. All the tension was gained by this device of focusing. Whereas at the Vic Banquo was made fiercely suspicious, Macbeth shaken to pieces by the apparition, at Stratford the commonsensical Banquo rather doubted his senses, while Macbeth, when he finally stepped forward to debate the "imperial theme", showed no more than head-shaking puzzlement till a sudden tremor on "unfix my hair and make my seated heart knock at my ribs" betrayed the hidden disturbance. Note also how Byam Shaw got the witches off the stage. At the Vic they had retired, under the persistent questioning, to the central arch, and thence slipped away together while the stage temporarily darkened. At Stratford the bland daylight remained undisturbed over all. As Macbeth fixed on the second witch the first slid like a lizard from the scene; when attention shifted to the third the second was gone; and as Macbeth and Banquo turned on each other in eager surmise the third too vanished. This was genuine producer's sleight of hand, worth all the flying-ballet apparatus in the theatre workshop.

Turn now to the long sequence leading up to Duncan's murder and its discovery. "If the assassination Could trammel up the consequence, and catch With his surcease success": again the opening speech, examined in isolation, did not convince. The hissing sibilants, the lines tumbling one into another, surely suggest breathless excitement, near hysteria, and so Paul Rogers rendered it, though perhaps with too much emphasis to catch the authentic note of panic. Olivier, on the other hand, was merely petulant—with the object maybe of avoiding a too early disintegration into hysteria. There could, however, be no doubts about the succeeding interchange with Lady Macbeth, a perfectly modulated 'movement', in which Macbeth's fate is sealed. To her first taunts he remained obstinately impervious, his back turned. She drew closer, and launched into the horrible boast of her own callousness that is to shock him into compliance. At this Macbeth swung round to her, his back now to the audience, and laid his hand on her elbow in a gesture at once deeply affectionate and protesting. As she persisted in her self-torture, he tore himself away and moved across the stage, but his rejoinder, over his shoulder, the last weak objection of "If we should fail", showed that his defences were shaken. Lady Macbeth again moved to him and seizing him by the shoulders from behind murmured in his ear the final temptation—how easy is it then. He turned to her with "Bring forth men children only", but it was said wryly, in almost mocking praise of her lack of scruple, and he still did not take her hand. There needed a further pause for reflection, the growing confidence of "Will it not be received...?", before with "I am settled" he was her own again.

Not long after came another imaginative stroke. Lady Macbeth has gone to drug the grooms, Macbeth is giving last instructions to the servant. The man is still beside him when he sees the spectral dagger and checks at it like a pointer. With a terrible effort he withdraws his gaze for a moment and dismisses the servant; then with a swift and horrid compulsion swings round again. The first part of the dagger speech was spoken with a sort of broken quiet, only the sudden shrillness of "Mine eyes are made the fools o' th' other senses" and "There's no such thing" revealing the intolerable tension that strains the speaker. Rogers at the Old Vic used more voice, and carried on in this more openly rhetorical style to the end of the speech. "Tarquin's ravishing strides" he illustrated by taking three paces, tramp, tramp, tramp, across the stage; and kneeling at the foot of the stone steps to Duncan's room he adjured them not to betray his further advance. Olivier dismissed the influence of evil in its physical manifestation only to be more strongly seized by it in his mind. The second part of the speech sank to a drugged whisper and, speaking, Macbeth moved, as in a dream, towards Duncan's room, but with his

PLATE V

Original setting of the song "Get you hence" in *The Winter's Tale*
(New York Public Library)

PLATE VI

Macbeth, Old Vic Theatre, 1954. Production by MICHAEL BENTHALL; costumes and décor by AUDREY CRUDDAS

PLATE VII

Macbeth, Shakespeare Memorial Theatre, 1955. Production by GLEN BYAM SHAW;
scenery and costumes by ROGER FURSE

PLATE VIII

Hamlet, Mayakovsky Drama Theatre, Moscow, 1954. Production by
Nikolai Okhlopkov. The Play Scene

face turned away from it. Tarquin's strides were only dimly reflected in the dragging pace, and it was the already trodden stones behind him that Macbeth, with deprecating hand, implored to silence. It was this scene above all that brought the audience under the enchantment.

About the murder itself little need be said. The Old Vic had the lead here, for Stratford allowed too much of the urgency to leak away. Yet there were great moments. Vivien Leigh was at her searing best, and I shall long remember the despairing, fumbling abhorrence with which Olivier sought to ward off the multitudinous seas of blood that seemed to be swirling about his very knees.

At the Old Vic the admirable thread of the scene was rudely broken by the most stupendous knocking—the same error that in *Lear* accompanies the King's distracted exit from Gloucester's castle with the father and mother of all thunderclaps. At Stratford the knocking was peremptory but distant—a summons, not instant execution. The flow of the scene was checked by it and diverted in a new direction, not permanently interrupted. Nor was the porter allowed to be more than an interlude. At the Vic the contrast between the racing murder-scene and Laurence Hardy's expansive jesting was too great, and the whole scene fell into incompatible sections of melodrama and farce. At Stratford Patrick Wymark, though funny, was briskly funny, with all the time a backward glance for the master and mistress whose stage he was conscious of usurping—an impression reinforced by the guilty speed with which he made himself scarce on Macbeth's re-entry.

Paul Rogers reappeared in a long ashen robe and, all the time that Macduff was in Duncan's room, remained leaning against the wall at the foot of the staircase, gazing up it as if almost fainting in anticipation. Small wonder that Lennox became immediately suspicious, or that suspicion grew by leaps and bounds at Lady Macbeth's patently false "What, in our house?", at her feigned swoon, and at Macbeth's extravagant rhetoric, so that at the end of the scene the murderer stood ringed by angry and accusing faces. Olivier, in a black monkish cassock, paced the stage uneasily, by fits and starts, during the conversation with Lennox, his guilty hands closely folded in his long sleeves except when, with a gesture at once furtive and half-automatic, he withdrew them for a moment and hurriedly inspected them front and back. The flurry of the alarm was well done, the stage filling confusedly and yet without confusion. In the hurly-burly "What, in our house?" was no more than faintly off-key, but Lady Macbeth, anxiously aware of the slip, was fain to feel her way to the support of the proscenium arch. Macbeth re-entered from Duncan's room at the opposite side and at the back, and began his act, glancing uneasily for support to his wife, now divided from him by the whole diagonal of the stage. She instinctively took a step forward to assist him and, as Macbeth's web of deception grew more and more tangled, slowly, inexorably, the two were drawn together by the compulsion of their common guilt to the centre of the stage. Just before she reached her husband Lady Macbeth fainted. Genuine? Feigned? No need even to ask the question. Her collapse was as inevitable a result of the dramatic process as is the spark when two charged wires are brought together. Here was first-rate theatre.

In these earlier scenes Benthall and Rogers, by speeding up the deterioration in the hero's character, had further foreshortened Shakespeare's already foreshortened process. Now even the action was concertina'd, for the scene of the murder led into a dumb-show of the coronation (the old man submerged) and this into the reception of Banquo. There was thus literally no time for the Macbeths to grow disillusioned with their gains and to realize that "Nought's had, all's spent". The duel between killer and cops was on, and nothing else mattered. Macbeth did not hide the malignancy of his questions about Banquo's ride, a scene played by Olivier in an enchantingly easy banter. The colloquy with the murderers, because it is long, because it is commonly considered dull, because it is not directly concerned with forwarding the plot, was heavily cut. After that it might be truly said of the Old Vic *Macbeth* that all was over bar the shouting.

At Stratford nothing was shirked. The scene of the old man, played with gentle pathos by John MacGregor, made a fitting end to the first movement of the play. His final couplet

> God's benison go with you; and with those
> That would make good of bad, and friends of foes!

has been denounced as a meaningless interpolation. Whatever its meaning, it is evidently authentic Shakespeare, for, like "All may yet be well", it conveys exactly the sense of uneasy pause that regularly occurs at this point in a Shakespearian tragedy. The interview with the murderers was given in full, and became one of the most dramatic and revealing scenes in the play. The murderers, half-scared, half-fascinated by the now evil magnetism of the King, shrank back each time he approached them in a swirl of robes, while he, pacing the stage between and around them, continuously spun a web of bewildering words about their understandings, about his own conscience, about the crime that between them they were to commit. Nor was there any loss of brilliance in the ghost scene; indeed it was here that Olivier's full power, wisely confined till now, was at last unleashed to range magnificently. It may be noted, too, that here again, and in the cauldron scene, the attention at Stratford was characteristically focused on the face of Macbeth, while at the Vic Rogers had his back to the audience, the "thing he looked on" taking the centre of the stage. The Vic incidentally used a vast cauldron from which speaking apparitions could emerge effectively. At Stratford the cauldron was small, and the witches, leaning over it, plucked horrible emblems from it—a severed head transfixed on a pike, a bloody foetus, a waxen crowned child—while the voices came, not altogether satisfactorily, from elsewhere. The severed head was a replica of Macbeth's. Having entered from up stage he stood behind it, echoing with his own head its agonized pose, and the message came as in a trance from his living lips.[1] I expected this severed head to reappear at the end of the play—a fine irony if it could have been brought off, but the producer did not risk it. Not only was Macbeth killed off stage (as in the text) but the "usurper's cursed head" was merely pointed at on an unseen battlement. This I feel is weak. *Macbeth* is the one tragedy of Shakespeare in which the hero does not die before the eyes of the audience, the author having deliberately substituted the more violent alternative of bringing on the head. No doubt the Elizabethans could take this better than we, and in addition were experts in such effects. Still, I should like to see it tried again.

One more scene requires analysis: the murder of Lady Macduff. This again is usually regarded as unimportant or unplayable or both, and is hurried over perfunctorily. The Old Vic made little of it, for Gwen Cherrell could not persuade us that the Lady was real (like the blinding of

---

[1] In later performances all three oracles appeared to come from the apparitions themselves—a safer, if tamer solution.

Gloucester in *Lear* this is essentially a realistic scene) and the killing of the boy was a dagger-of-lath affair. At Stratford Maxine Audley's noble bearing, her passionate resentment at her husband's flight, and her scarce-hidden pride in his honourableness established at once a great lady and a woman of character. The murderers entered to a startled hush; they paused, and then the boy made his ungainly run across the stage, a puny, unplanned, forlorn attempt at defence. A blow with the hilts, a thrust. The murderer hung back, as if himself aghast at what he had done, leaving the boy standing isolated in mid stage, with both hands huddled over his wound. For a long moment he hung, wavering, then crumpled slowly to the ground. There was still silence, a long, shocked silence, before the first animal scream broke from his mother.

This was hitting below the belt, but that is precisely what Shakespeare intended to do. It is not until this moment that the full horror of Macbeth's actions bursts upon the audience. Duncan's murder takes place off stage, and out of sight out of mind; Banquo's we see, but it is a huddled affair in the dark. The third murder is in broad daylight, cold, deliberate, wanton, without any shadow of disguise or palliation. And immediately we are switched from this savage, bestial, devil-possessed Scotland to England, humane, civilized England, the England of Edward the Confessor. Sanity is here to redress the balance; the audience changes sides, and the tragic curve begins to dip towards its setting.

THE YEAR'S CONTRIBUTIONS TO
SHAKESPEARIAN STUDY

1. CRITICAL STUDIES

reviewed by KENNETH MUIR

Allardyce Nicoll in his British Academy lecture[1] answers the complaint, with which those who survey the year's work must have a sneaking sympathy, that Shakespeare is being buried beneath his commentators. Although we may share Louis Wright's depression about the state of Shakespearian scholarship, "a great deal of energy...being wasted on minutiae that will add up to very little", Nicoll points out that "many things accomplished in the past urgently need to be done again" and "many productive areas await proper exploitation". He gives a number of examples—texts which demand proper editing, documents which await detailed examination, further investigation of Shakespeare's imagery, and, he might have added, the imagery of his contemporaries, "the imaginative consideration of Shakespeare's creative genius in the light of" his sources, the examination of Shakespeare's style, the publication of an adequate dictionary of Elizabethan English, the provision of an 'authorized' text. Nicoll concludes, not unnaturally, that such a programme can be carried out only by team-work. L. C. Knights, on the other hand, offers a warning[2] on the limitations of historical scholarship as exemplified by Virgil K. Whitaker's *Shakespeare's Use of Learning*. He emphasizes that in applying Elizabethan ideas to our study of Shakespeare

We should *not* approach them as Shakespearian scholars bent on reconstructing a merely historical background, but—paradoxically—that we should study them for themselves, responding to them as themselves actual and vivifying.

C. J. Sisson, meanwhile, gives the general reader a brief guide[3] to Shakespeare and his critics. He is well-balanced and catholic in his sympathies, though he seems to regard some admired modern criticism with suspicion. He implies that Wilson Knight was a disciple of Richards, Leavis, and Empson, though there is no evidence in his earlier work that he was acquainted with the writings of any of these three critics. There is a useful bibliography by J. R. Brown. Perhaps O. J. Campbell's *Shakespeare's Satire* might have been preferred to *Comicall Satyre* and Knight's *Imperial Theme* is certainly a better book than *The Shakespearian Tempest*. Kenneth Muir has written a short survey[4] of Shakespearian criticism, and Nils Molin a still briefer account[5] of recent scholarship and criticism.

Lorentz Eckhoff's book on Shakespeare appeared originally in 1938, the English translation having been made in honour of his distinguished services as a teacher.[6] He believes that it is

[1] *Co-operation in Shakespearian Scholarship* (London: Geoffrey Cumberlege, 1954).
[2] *Sewanee Review*, LXIII (Spring 1955), 223–40.
[3] *Shakespeare* (London: Longmans, Green and Co., 1955).
[4] *A Guide to English Literature. 2. The Age of Shakespeare*, ed. Boris Ford (Harmondsworth: Penguin Books, 1955), pp. 282–301.   [5] 'Modern Shakespeareforskning', *Göteborgsstudier i Litteraturhistoria*, pp. 10–25.
[6] *Shakespeare Spokesman of the Third Estate* (Oslo: Akademisk forlag; Oxford: Basil Blackwell, 1954).

possible to deduce Shakespeare's 'philosophy' from a study of the plays, but he does not always properly distinguish between the views of characters and those of their creator. "As flies to wanton boys are we to the Gods" is a natural sentiment in the mouth of a credulous old man who has been deceived about his sons and brutally blinded: there is no reason to believe that it expresses Shakespeare's outlook on life. In the most original part of the book Eckhoff argues that Shakespeare was a spokesman of the bourgeoisie, though he recognizes that the poet was fair to all his characters. The aristocrat, Eckhoff thinks, tends to be an optimist; Shakespeare, in spite of his comedies, is a pessimist—at least in big things. This book is clearly the fruit of a loving study of Shakespeare, though the portrait of the poet which emerges is probably more subjective than Eckhoff realizes. John Masefield has revised his famous little book[1] on Shakespeare which was in 1911 a challenge to orthodoxy, a manifesto for the renaissance of the theatre, and an interpretation which often threw more light on the author of *The Tragedy of Nan* than it did on Shakespeare. Now, forty years later, Masefield has modified some of his early opinions. As Poet Laureate, more conservative in his views, he omits the violent denigration of Prince Hal, derived largely from Yeats, though he still feels that *1 Henry IV* is not a success. He no longer believes that Angelo is the presiding genius of the English theatre or that *Measure for Measure* is one of the supreme plays. He still tends to read moral lessons, and not always the right ones, into the plays. He doubts the Shakespearian authorship of the scenes in *Sir Thomas More*, but he accepts the presence of Shakespeare's hand in *The Two Noble Kinsmen*, and possibly in *Edward III*. It is fair to say that Masefield has not kept up with recent scholarship on several matters—a poet has other things to do—but his criticism remains stimulating, if sometimes wayward.

John Garrett has made a selection of the lectures delivered at his popular Stratford Summer School during the past six years.[2] Good lectures seldom make good essays, but the contributors to this volume, though many of them are concerned with familiar topics, are lively and informative. Nevill Coghill writes sensibly on the action of *Hamlet*, Paul Dehn wittily on the filming of Shakespeare, Norman Marshall on acting the plays on the Continent (where people complain that English actors often sacrifice the music of the verse), Walter Oakeshott on the well-worn topic of Shakespeare's debt to Plutarch, Michael Redgrave on the problems confronting the Shakespearian actor, Glynne Wickham on the advantage Shakespeare possessed in having small Latin and less Greek, and L. A. G. Strong on the application of depth psychology to Shakespeare's characters. A. P. Rossiter contributes a lecture as brilliant in content as it is irritating in style on Ambivalence in the history plays. With this subject may be compared J. C. Maxwell's argument that Shakespeare is sometimes more subtle and ambiguous in his treatment of character than critics allow.[3] He shows this by an intelligent discussion of the Archbishop's support of Henry V's claims, of the killing of the prisoners later in the play, and of a passage in the quarrel-scene in *Julius Caesar*. Charles T. Prouty edits another series of lectures,[4] delivered at the Yale Shakespeare Festival, 1954. They include an important one by Helge Kökeritz, pleading for a

[1] *William Shakespeare* (London: William Heinemann, 1954).

[2] *Talking of Shakespeare* (London: Hodder and Stoughton with Max Reinhardt, 1954).

[3] 'Simple or Complex? Some Problems in the Interpretation of Shakespeare', *Durham University Journal*, XLVI (1954), 112–15.

[4] *Shakespeare of an Age and for all Time* (Hamden, Connecticut: The Shoe String Press, 1954).

detailed and up-to-date study of Shakespeare's language, Arleigh D. Richardson's defence of the actability of *Henry VI*, Eugene M. Waith's demonstration of the iniquities committed by adaptors of *Macbeth*, and Norman Holmes Pearson's apology for the love of Antony and Cleopatra, disfigured by a facetious misquotation from Wordsworth.

The main theme of *Shakespeare Survey* as of the *Jahrbuch* was Shakespeare's style and language. The contributions to the former may be mentioned briefly for the sake of completeness. Muriel C. Bradbrook gave[1] a valuable retrospect of the criticism of Shakespeare's style during the past fifty years; George Rylands wrote on Shakespeare as poet and actor;[2] Gladys D. Willcock discussed[3] 'Shakespeare and Elizabethan English'. Hilda Hume, it may be mentioned, contributed to Sisson's edition of Shakespeare a short essay on his language.[4] The essays in the *Shakespeare Jahrbuch* include Thomas Finkenstaedt's sensible and sensitive discussion of various approaches to an investigation of Shakespeare's use of rhyme and blank verse;[5] Hannelore Stahl's enquiry[6] into the question of how far stylistic criteria can support the assumption of Shakespeare's coinage of certain words; Alfred Schopf's analysis[7] of the function of certain dominant and reiterated words in the Histories; Una Ellis-Fermor's fruitful suggestion[8] that the verbal music of different plays may assist in our interpretation of them, her examples being taken from *Troilus and Cressida*, *All's Well*, and *Coriolanus*; R. A. Foakes's complementary notes[9] on style in the comedies and tragedies; Bogislav von Lindheim's analysis[10] of Shakespeare's verbal use of nouns in moments of heightened emotion; Kenneth Muir's more general discussion[11] of Shakespeare's use of rhetoric; and Kurt Schlüter's comparison[12] of Aegeon's narration of antecedent events with that of Prospero, to illustrate Shakespeare's advance from an essentially epic to a highly dramatic style of narration. F. E. Halliday has followed up his two mammoth works of reference with a shorter book[13] on the poetry of Shakespeare's plays. This is sound and intelligent, with many perceptive remarks, but it contains little which a responsive reader might not have discovered for himself. He does not, perhaps, recognize sufficiently the positive value of the study of rhetoric, but he has some valuable analysis of the poetic power of individual passages. He speaks of the "grotesque excesses" of the latinized diction of *Troilus and Cressida*, though Shakespeare may have been experimenting in 'epic' diction after reading Chapman's Homer. It is difficult to understand why Halliday should say that *Antony and Cleopatra*, "the most perfect of the tragedies", is "relatively little known". Percy Simpson includes a short essay on Shakespeare's versification in his recent collection of studies.[14] There have been brave

---

[1] 'Fifty Years of the Criticism of Shakespeare's Style', *Shakespeare Survey*, 7 (1954), 1–11.

[2] 'The Poet and the Player', *ibid.* 23–34.

[3] *Ibid.* 12–24.   [4] *Op. cit.* pp. xlii–xlvi.

[5] 'Zur Methodik der Versuntersuchung bei Shakespeare', *Shakespeare Jahrbuch*, xc (1954), 82–107.

[6] 'Schöpferische Wortbildung bei Shakespeare?', *ibid.* 252–78.

[7] 'Leitmotivische Thematik in Shakespeares Dramen', *ibid.* 124–66.

[8] 'Some Functions of Verbal Music in Drama', *ibid.* 37–48.

[9] 'Contrasts and Connections: Some Notes on Style in Shakespeare's Comedies and Tragedies', *ibid.* 69–81.

[10] 'Syntaktische Funktionsverschiebung als Mittel des barocken Stils bei Shakespeare', *ibid.* 229–51.

[11] 'Shakespeare and Rhetoric', *ibid.* 49–68.

[12] 'Die Erzählung der Vorgeschichte in Shakespeares Dramen', *ibid.* 108–23.

[13] *The Poetry of Shakespeare's Plays* (London: Duckworth, 1954).

[14] *Studies in Elizabethan Drama* (Oxford: Clarendon Press; London: Geoffrey Cumberlege, 1955).

attempts to translate some of the *Sonnets* into Italian[1] (by Alberto Rossi) and all of them into Spanish[2] (by Mariano de Vedia y Mitre); and David I. Masson has, with the help of phonetics, provided a subtle analysis[3] of the verbal music of several of the sonnets. G. Wilson Knight, hailed by John Jones as the best Shakespearian critic since Coleridge,[4] has written a full-length study[5] of the *Sonnets* and of 'The Phoenix and the Turtle'. He gives a brief summary of biographical problems connected with the *Sonnets* and agrees with Samuel Butler that the youth addressed was not of high birth. He argues that "the creative consciousness is bisexual" and suggests that the love-poetry in the plays is spoken by the female characters, the men, as lovers, being "presented objectively and critically". In the most valuable chapters Knight analyses the themes of the sonnets, especially time and eternity, and discusses Shakespeare's use of symbolism. Sometimes, we are tempted to think, Knight takes Shakespeare a bit too seriously, and he misses undertones of irony. The book would have been strengthened by more reference to the sonnet tradition. Some will feel that Nietzsche makes a superfluous appearance in these pages and that, so far as we know, Shakespeare regarded evil as an intruder. The second part of the book consists of a discussion of *Love's Martyr* and of 'The Phoenix and the Turtle', but few will agree with Knight's argument that Shakespeare revised Chester's poem. *The Mutual Flame*, eccentric as it sometimes is, is a valuable interpretative study, and a useful pendant to Knight's work on the plays. F. W. Bateson and Charles B. Wheeler debate[6] Empson's interpretation of "bare ruined choirs", the former arguing that the phrase probably did not refer to the dissolution of the monasteries, in spite of the latter's comparison of *Titus Andronicus*, V, i, 20–4. Two other interpretations of 'The Phoenix and the Turtle' may be mentioned, ingenious though not altogether satisfying. Walter J. Ong suggests[7] that the two birds

can be metaphorical terms for persons, for philosophical abstractions such as love and death, for mind and body, for Christ and the Church.

But he appears to incline to the view that the quest for unity, with which the birds are pre-occupied, is the purpose of metaphor "in its strange double focus". Ronald Bates, on the other hand,[8] is impressed by the contrast between the subject-matter and the associations of the verse form—"almost a tragedy", he remarks, "in the form of a posy of a ring". C. S. Lewis has a brief but revealing commentary on the same poem,[9] in which he makes the point that Shakespeare's "supreme invention was the introduction of Reason as the principal speaker". He adds that

We feel that we have been admitted to the *natura naturans* from which the *natura naturata* of the plays proceeded: as though we had reached the garden of Adonis and seen where Imogens and Cordelias are made.

[1] *William Shakespeare: Sonnetti* (Turin: Einaudi, 1954).
[2] *William Shakespeare: Los Sonetos* (Kraft: Beunos Aires, 1955).
[3] 'Free Phonetic Patterns in Shakespeare's Sonnets', *Neophilologus* (October 1954), pp. 277–89.
[4] 'Shakespeare and Mr Wilson Knight', *The Listener* (9 December 1954), pp. 1011–12.
[5] G. Wilson Knight, *The Mutual Flame* (London: Methuen, 1955).
[6] *Essays in Criticism*, IV (1954), 224–6.
[7] 'Metaphor and the Twinned Vision', *The Sewanee Review*, LXIII (Spring 1955), 193–201.
[8] 'Shakespeare's "The Phoenix and the Turtle"', *Shakespeare Quarterly*, VI (1955), 19–30.
[9] *English Literature in the Sixteenth Century excluding Drama* (Oxford: Clarendon Press, 1954), pp. 498–509.

Lewis also has some fine criticism of the poems and sonnets. He rates *Venus and Adonis* much lower than *Lucrece* and does not quite know how to take the earlier poem.

> If the poem is not meant to arouse disgust it was very foolishly written: if it is, then disgust...is not, either aesthetically or morally, the feeling on which a poet should rely in a moral poem.

There is, of course, an element of satirical realism in the poem, but it is wonderfully blended with other qualities, and it may be doubted whether any of it need arouse the reader's disgust. On the *Sonnets* Lewis observes sensibly that

> The love is, in the end, so simply and entirely love that our *cadres* are thrown away and we cease to ask what kind.

Several writers were entrusted with the subject of Shakespeare in the Pelican *Guide to Literature*. D. A. Traversi discusses the young dramatist and the last plays,[1] J. C. Maxwell the middle plays,[2] and L. C. Knights *King Lear* and the later tragedies.[3] These four essays together provide an admirable introduction and they are more stimulating than A. C. Ward's attempt[4] to cover the same ground.

The Comedies received little attention. Ernest Schanzer suggests[5] that since the reconciliation between the parents of Pyramus and Thisbe is not found in the sources, "the wall is down that parted their fathers" is due to the influence of *Romeo and Juliet*. K. B. Danks argues[6] that Antonio's melancholy is caused not by the fact that he is losing Bassanio to Portia but by his foreboding of his own misfortunes. P. A. Jorgensen has an interesting comment[7] on the quibbles on the different meanings of *nothing* and *noting* in the title of *Much Ado* and throughout the play. Sylvan Barnet demonstrates[8] that Lamb gave a misleading account of Bensley as Malvolio since other evidence shows that he played the part farcically. Milton Crane, criticizing[9] Coghill's views on Shakespearian comedy, shows that the Malvolio plot is classical satirical comedy and that deception is common to all three plots. John Shaw analyses with some subtlety the ideas of fortune and nature in *As You Like It* and their importance in the scheme of the play.[10] Rudolf A. Schröder discusses *Troilus and Cressida*[11] in relation to the *Iliad* and claims that it is essentially a penitential sermon, belonging in its content and purpose, if not in its form, to the genre of the Morality play. Winifred Nowottny has a more plausible thesis in her essay[12] on the play. She argues that Ulysses is attempting to preserve the stability of society, Troilus "the attitude of the man of creative imagination". This view was rightly questioned by Frank Kermode,[13] but her essay has the merit of defending the unity of the play. "The characters are formed with reference to the concept, the language is formed with reference to the characters and the concept, and the setting and the action manifest the concept." She adds that the formal genius shown by Shakespeare "in conceiving, stating and exploring such problems in dramatic terms, is the

---

[1] *Op. cit.* pp. 179–200, 257–81.   [2] *Op. cit.* pp. 201–27.

[3] *Op. cit.* pp. 228–56.

[4] *Illustrated History of English Literature*, vol. I (London: Longmans, 1954).

[5] *Notes and Queries* (January 1955), pp. 13–14.   [6] *Ibid.* (March 1954), p. III.

[7] *Shakespeare Quarterly*, V (1954), 287–96.   [8] *Philological Quarterly*, XXXIII (1954), 178–88.

[9] *Shakespeare Quarterly*, VI (1955), 1–8.   [10] *Ibid.* 45–50.

[11] *Shakespeare Jahrbuch*, XC (1954), 11–36.

[12] *Essays in Criticism*, IV (1954), 282–96.   [13] *Ibid.* V (1955), 181–7.

most staggering feature of his greatness". Aerol Arnold has a brief analysis[1] of the function of the Hector-Andromache scene.

There are a number of articles on the Histories. Alvin B. Kernan compares[2] the imagery of *3 Henry VI* with that of *The True Tragedie* and shows that an iterative image is absent from the latter. This is obviously relevant to a discussion of the relationship between the two plays. W. H. Clemen has a valuable article on *Richard III*, in which he argues[3] that Shakespeare obtained "new unity and coherence...without sacrificing the rich potentialities inherent in" the chronicle play. Aerol Arnold discusses[4] the dreams in *Richard III* and compares them with Lady Macbeth's. He shows that Clarence's dream prepares us for his murder, recalling events of *3 Henry VI* and his guilt therein. Richard's dream incorporates all the elements of Margaret's curse. E. C. Pettet analyses[5] sensitively some of the imagery of *King John* and suggests that the proposed blinding of Arthur and the fever of which the King died were the origin of the numerous images of fire and heat. I. B. Cauthen Jr. offers a brief addendum to Altick's study of the imagery of *Richard II*.[6] Travis Bogard has a more substantial article in which he shows[7] the importance of the play in Shakespeare's development since in the deposition scene he "first explored the ground leading to the achievement of tragedy". The lines towards the end of the scene (IV, i, 302–13) "project matured character with a reality that Shakespeare had not before been able to achieve". G. K. Hunter, by comparison with two-part plays by Chapman, Marlowe and Marston, maintains[8] that Shakespeare took pains to make a unity of *Henry IV*, though he may not have intended a sequel when he wrote the first part. C. A. Greer thinks[9] that the diminution of Falstaff's wit in the second part may be explained simply by the fact that he had there no opportunity of entertaining the Prince, and that his mind becomes sluggish. Johannes Kleinstück has a useful reminder[10] that Shakespeare was not a simple believer in the Tudor doctrine, a perfectly ordered state not being in itself desirable; and W. M. Merchant shows[11] that the distinction between status and function of Shakespeare's kings and the personal qualities of him who exercised them remained a permanent tension of potential tragic consequence.

The only book on the tragedies in the period under review is Peter Alexander's study of *Hamlet*.[12] Starting from the Olivier film, with its picture of an irresolute Hamlet, Alexander denies that the "dram of eale" passage should be regarded as an oblique reference to a tragic

---

[1] *Modern Language Quarterly*, XIV (1953), 335–40.

[2] 'A Comparison of the Imagery in *3 Henry VI* and the *True Tragedie of Richard Duke of York*', *Studies in Philology*, LI (July 1954), 431–41.

[3] 'Tradition and Originality in Shakespeare's *Richard III*', *Shakespeare Quarterly*, V (Summer 1954), 247–57.

[4] 'The Recapitulation Dream in *Richard III* and *Macbeth*', *Shakespeare Quarterly*, VI (Winter 1955), 51–62.

[5] 'Hot Irons and Fever: A Note on some of the Imagery of *King John*', *Essays in Criticism*, IV (April 1954), 128–44.

[6] '*Richard II* and the Image of the betrayed Christ', *Renaissance Papers*, ed. Allan H. Gilbert (University of South Carolina, 1954).　　　[7] 'Shakespeare's Second Richard', *PMLA*, LXX (March 1955), 192–209.

[8] '*Henry IV* and the Elizabethan Two-part Play', *Review of English Studies*, V (July 1954), 236–48.

[9] 'Falstaff's Diminution of Wit', *Notes and Queries* (November 1954), p. 468. Other short articles may be mentioned here: Henry Hitch Adams, 'Falstaff's Instinct', *Shakespeare Quarterly*, V (Spring 1954), 208–9; Warren D. Smith, 'The *Henry V* Choruses in the First Folio', *Journal of English and Germanic Philology*, LIII (1954), 38–57.

[10] 'The Problem of Order in Shakespeare's Histories', *Neophilologus* (1954), pp. 268–77.

[11] 'The Status and Person of Majesty', *Shakespeare Jahrbuch*, XC (1954), 285–9.

[12] *Hamlet Father and Son* (Oxford: Clarendon Press, 1955).

flaw in Hamlet's own character. He thinks, on the contrary, that the effect of tragedy depends not on the faults but on the virtues of men. He discusses the weaknesses of Bradley's theory of tragedy; he argues that Aristotle changed his mind and that he has been misunderstood; he examines *Oedipus* and *Philoctetes* in some detail in order to show that neither hero can be blamed; he brings in Keats and Wordsworth to describe the effect of tragedy, though few will agree that the experiences they describe can be equated with the Aristotelian catharsis; and then he returns to a consideration of *Hamlet*. He shows that the world of the play contains the juxtaposition of two ages—the heroic age of the father, the sceptical age of the son—and that Hamlet himself, both tough and sensitive, exhibits a union of opposites. The book is a valuable corrective to orthodox views on Hamlet's character, and it is written eloquently and persuasively. But it is significant that Alexander nowhere discusses the four great soliloquies. Hamlet's meditations on suicide, his reference to resolution "sicklied o'er with the pale cast of thought", his self-reproaches for his delay in carrying out his father's commands, his disgust with the "bestial oblivion or some craven scruple" cannot be brushed on one side. Presumably Alexander would argue that Hamlet's melancholy is the inevitable result of the situation in which he finds himself, and that his delay (if delay there was) should not lower him in our eyes. But the argument of the book is weakened by its failure to face these and other objections. Richard D. Altick has a convincing analysis[1] of the corruption imagery in *Hamlet*, and Adrien Bonjour wittily controverts[2] R. W. Battenhouse's view that Shakespeare wrote the play to demonstrate that humanism is not enough by showing that a thoroughly Christian Hamlet would have been unable to find a better solution. Abbie Findlay Potts, without suggesting that *The Faerie Queene* was a 'source' of *Hamlet*, offers some interesting parallels.[3]

A. José Axelrad develops[4] Donald C. Miller's view that Othello and Desdemona were united by a pre-contract in Venice some time before their marriage and that this fact explains how Othello could believe that Desdemona had committed adultery with Cassio. It would be a great satisfaction to dispense with the need for double-time; but although 'fruits' (II, ii, 9) may mean *offspring* rather than *consummation*, Iago's words to Cassio a few lines later seem to imply that the marriage had not yet been consummated. Otto Bergemann argues[5] that a consideration of the spiritual drama rather than the external action of *King Lear* leads to a recognition of its regular five-act structure, with the climax and turning-point coming precisely in the middle of the play. Thelma Greenfield shows[6] that in the clothing motif in the same play Shakespeare made use of "familiar traditional associations". Theodore C. Hoepfner shows[7] that the last speech must be given to Edgar. James L. Rosier shows[8] that *reason, custom, law* and *restraint* are

---

[1] 'Hamlet, and the Odor of Mortality', *Shakespeare Quarterly*, V (Spring 1954), 167–76.

[2] 'Hamlet and the Phantom Clue', *English Studies*, XXXV (December 1954), 253–9. John Waldron, 'Hamlet II, ii, 124', *Notes and Queries* (December 1954), pp. 515–16, argues that 'machine' is deliberately ambiguous.

[3] *Shakespeare Quarterly*, VI (1955), 31–43.

[4] 'Un Point de droit élizabéthain sur la scène dramatique', *Revue du Nord*, XXXVI (April–June 1954), 195–200.

[5] 'Zum Aufbau von *King Lear*', *Shakespeare Jahrbuch*, XC (1954), 191–209.

[6] 'The Clothing Motif in *King Lear*', *Shakespeare Quarterly*, V (Summer 1954), 281–6.

[7] '"We that are young"', *Notes and Queries* (March 1954), p. 110.

[8] 'The Lex Aeterna and *King Lear*', *Journal of English and Germanic Philology*, LIII (October 1954), 574–80. K. W. Salter, '*Lear* and the Morality Tradition', *Notes and Queries* (March 1954), pp. 109–10, connects "monsters of the deep" with *Everyman*, 47–50, but this has been pointed out before by F. P. Wilson and others.

significant terms in the play and that the Lear universe is implicitly Christian. Margaret D. Burrell, in a subtle examination[1] of oxymoron, chiasmus, equivocation, antithesis, irony, paradox and other rhetorical figures in *Macbeth*, comes to the conclusion that Shakespeare used them deliberately to emphasize the enigma of evil. Paul H. Kocher thinks[2] that the murdering ministers and spirits invoked by Lady Macbeth were the 'animal spirits' of the psychologist, since "she needs the callousness of melancholia and the courage of choler". Shorter notes on *Macbeth* include F. G. Schoff's argument[3] that the idea of "fair is foul" is to be found in the *Sonnets*, K. B. Danks's reference[4] to the iteration of the word 'strange', Paul N. Siegel's discussion[5] of biblical echoes in the play, and R. M. Frye's discussion[6] of analogues of "Out, out, brief candle". R. A. Foakes has a study[7] of the imagery of *Julius Caesar* in which he concludes that

The action of the play turns on the distance between the ideals and public symbols for which the names of Caesar, Brutus, and Cassius stand, and their true nature and actions.

Joan Rees discusses[8] the possible influence of Kyd's *Cornelia* on Shakespeare's play and suggests that the inconsistency of Kyd's Caesar, both boastful and heroic, stimulated Shakespeare to explore the deeper implications of the character. Norman Nathan argues[9] that in the first scene of the play the mechanicals are made to assert their right to take time off to see a play. Ernest Schanzer shows[10] that in depicting the divided mind, the self-deception, and the final tragic disillusion of Brutus, "Shakespeare received no hints from Plutarch", and that the play receives a unity from the adoption of the framework of an Elizabethan revenge tragedy and from the choice of Brutus as a tragic hero. In another article Schanzer points out[11] a repetition of some themes of the second act of *King John* in the third act of *Antony and Cleopatra*. Dolora G. Cunningham seeks[12] to show not merely that the change in Cleopatra's character at the end of the play is consistent with Elizabethan psychology and ethics, but also that it is in accordance with "the traditional Christian principles of repentance and preparation for death". We have it on good authority that the holy priests blessed Cleopatra when she was riggish, so we should not be surprised that Christians should claim her as a convert when she had immortal longings. Millar MacLure has an interesting article[13] on the conflict between the heroic figure (Coriolanus, Antony, Achilles) and the compromises demanded in the world. I. R. Browning, replying to Enright, argues[14] that *Coriolanus* is a tragedy, not a debate, and that the hero is tragically dependent on his mother. K. Muir puts in a word[15] in defence of the Tribunes in that play.

---

[1] '*Macbeth*: A Study in Paradox', *Shakespeare Jahrbuch*, XC (1954), 167–90.

[2] 'Lady Macbeth and the Doctor', *Shakespeare Quarterly*, V (Autumn 1954), 341–9.

[3] 'Shakespeare's Fair is Foul', *Notes and Queries* (June 1954), pp. 241–2.

[4] 'Macbeth and the word "strange"', *ibid.* (October 1954), p. 425.

[5] 'Echoes of the Bible Story in *Macbeth*', *ibid.* (April 1955), pp. 142–3.

[6] '"Out, out, brief candle" and the Jacobean understanding', *ibid.* (April 1955), pp. 143–5.

[7] 'An Approach to *Julius Caesar*', *Shakespeare Quarterly*, V (Summer 1954), 259–70.

[8] '"Julius Caesar"—an Earlier Play, and an Interpretation', *Modern Language Review*, L (April 1955), 135–41.

[9] 'Flavius teases his Audience', *Notes and Queries* (April 1954), pp. 149–50.

[10] 'The Tragedy of Shakespeare's Brutus', *ELH, A Journal of English Literary History*, XXII (March 1955), 1–15.

[11] 'A Plot Chain in *Antony and Cleopatra*', *Notes and Queries* (September 1954), pp. 379–80.

[12] 'The Characterization of Shakespeare's Cleopatra', *Shakespeare Quarterly*, VI (Winter 1955), 67–88.

[13] 'Shakespeare and the Lonely Dragon', *University of Toronto Quarterly*, XXIV (January 1955), 109–20.

[14] 'Coriolanus: Boy of Tears', *Essays in Criticism*, V (January 1955), 18–31.

[15] 'In Defence of the Tribunes', *ibid.* IV (July 1954), 331–3.

The plays of the last period are the subject of two books. Horst Oppel maintains[1] that there is a shift of emphasis rather than a complete break with Shakespeare's earlier work, and he supports his reasonable contention by a detailed analysis of two passages in *Macbeth* and *The Tempest*. Oppel then discusses briefly the relative functions of metaphor and symbol in Shakespeare's plays, and insists on the organic nature of the imagery. D. A. Traversi's book[2] is at once valuable and disappointing. He argues that the last plays have a symbolic unity, that though they are unrealistic they possess "the concreteness proper to great poetry", and that they are vehicles of a profoundly personal reading of life. *Pericles* and *Cymbeline* are treated as experiments which led the way to the final masterpieces, the central theme of *The Tempest* being judgement. Traversi's analysis of the four plays is subtle and impressive, though not all will agree with some of his criticisms of the verse of *Cymbeline*, or with his view that Prospero's forgiveness is essentially Christian, for it might equally be regarded as Senecan. The book, good as it is, does not quite satisfy the expectations aroused by Traversi's articles. It is written almost without reference to previous books on the subject and in some ways he has been forestalled by Knight's *The Crown of Life*. His method of interpretation deliberately ignores the dramatic value of the plays, and one or two slips, unimportant in themselves, suggest that symbolic interpretation may take the critic too far from the plays interpreted. Traversi marries Marina to Cerimon and rechristens the Duke of *Measure for Measure* as Vincenzo. A more serious fault is that Traversi, who is generally sensitive to the poetic texture of the plays, is sometimes led by his general interpretations to an unhappy attitude to individual speeches. Few will agree that Perdita's flower-catalogue displays "a certain pathetic weakness, a kind of wilting from life" or that the "beauty of these lines is devoid of strength". Nevertheless it must be emphasized that the book contains much fine criticism.

José García Lora compares[3] *Pericles* with the treatment of the same story in the medieval *Libro de Apolonio* and he discusses the performance of Shakespeare's play at the Birmingham Repertory Theatre. J. A. Bryant Jr. carries the allegorical method[4] to extremes in his interpretation of *The Winter's Tale*. He thinks that Hermione represents Christ, Leontes the Jews, Mamillius the Jewish Church, and Perdita the Christian Church, so that Leontes's reconciliation with Perdita may be interpreted as "regenerated Jewry's expected reconciliation to the body of true believers". This, I am afraid,

> Must be a faith that reason without miracle
> Should never plant in me.

Hermann Heuer gives[5] a perceptive discussion of the mingling in *The Tempest* of metaphors suggestive of the world of dreams and of metaphors of a homely and realistic cast, to express the two opposed worlds of the play. Finally Carol Jones Carlisle provides[6] an account of William Macready's comments on the Shakespearian roles in which he appeared.

---

[1] *Shakespeares Tragödien und Romanzen: Kontinuität oder Umbruch?* (Wiesbaden: Franz Steiner Verlag, für die Akademie der Wissenschaften und der Literatur in Mainz, 1954).

[2] *Shakespeare, The Last Phase* (London: Hollis and Carter, 1954).

[3] 'Pericles y Apolonio', *Insula*, 15 March 1955, Suplemento, 1–2.

[4] 'Shakespeare's Allegory: *The Winter's Tale*', *The Sewanee Review*, LXIII (Spring 1955), 202–22.

[5] 'Traumwelt und Wirklichkeit in der Sprache des Tempest', *Shakespeare Jahrbuch*, XC (1954), 210–28.

[6] 'William Macready as a Shakespearean Critic', Allan H. Gilbert, *op. cit.* pp. 30–9.

2. SHAKESPEARE'S LIFE, TIMES AND STAGE

reviewed by R. A. FOAKES

The mystery of Shakespeare's life seems to provoke a monstrous deal of speculation for each poor pennyworth of fact. Those who enjoy pure speculation may derive pleasure from Arthur Field's *Recent Discoveries Relating to the Life and Works of William Shakespeare*,[1] which makes some staggering claims, based largely on marginal notes in copies of old books, which, if the 'facsimiles' provided are accurate, are neither intelligible nor Elizabethan. Jean Paris cleverly presents a picture of Shakespeare, his age, and his treatment of various themes in carefully chosen quotations from the plays and poems. *Shakespeare par lui-même*[2] is lavishly illustrated with photographs and facsimiles, and the author's commentary gives the essential facts, but also airs again the Baconian and other heresies; Abel Lefranc and Percy Allen are named in the bibliography, but not E. K. Chambers.[3] One or two further details relating to Shakespeare have been put forward in articles and notes. H. A. Shield[4] identifies the five people associated with Shakespeare in a complaint of 1615 against Matthew Bacon, and finds a tenuous connexion between one of them and Grafton, Northants, which gave its name to a portrait of the playwright. Sir Giles Isham[5] supports G. M. Young's suggestion[6] that the story of *Lear* may be related to the life of Brian Annesley (died 1604), whose youngest daughter of three he now shows was called Cordelia.

The most fruitful lines of investigation seem to lie at the moment in the study of the background of Shakespeare's art and the interpretation of clues in his works. It is coming to be realized more and more clearly just how inaccurate was the eighteenth-century notion of an untutored Shakespeare. Kenneth Muir[7] points out that the later plays show not a rejection of the rhetorical devices used in the early work, but a masterly use of them, and Gladys Willcock[8] sets this view in perspective in her excellent analysis of the state of the language in the lifetime of Shakespeare, when it was possible "to combine a maximum of Art with a minimum of inhibition". Mario Praz[9] reviews Shakespeare's knowledge of Italy as revealed in the plays, and concludes that he had a superficial acquaintance with Italian literature, and mentioned enough details of local colour relating to the area between Venice and Milan to show either that he travelled to Italy or that he consulted an Italian, possibly John Florio.

Further evidence to suggest that Shakespeare had some Italian is put forward by Helen A. Kaufman,[10] who notes interesting parallels which seem to indicate that in writing *Twelfth Night*

---

[1] Mitre Press, 1954. [2] Paris: Éditions du Seuil, 1954.

[3] A survey of the growth of the heresies and a critique of some recent work in support of them is provided by Harald Gyller, 'Dimmor Kring Shakespeare', *Bonniers litterära magasin* (July 1954), pp. 378–82, and Sidney L. Gulick Jr. has fun in what he describes as a satire on pseudo-scholarship, 'Was "Shakespeare" a Woman?', *College English*, xv (May 1954), 445–9. [4] 'Links with Shakespeare XII', *Notes and Queries* (March 1955), 94–7.

[5] 'The Prototypes of King Lear and his Daughters', *Notes and Queries* (April 1954), pp. 150–1.

[6] 'Shakespeare and the Termers', *Proceedings of the British Academy*, XXXIII (1947), 96.

[7] 'Shakespeare and Rhetoric', *Shakespeare Jahrbuch*, XC (1954), 49–68.

[8] 'Shakespeare and Elizabethan English', *Shakespeare Survey*, 7 (1954), 12–24.

[9] 'Shakespeare's Italy', *Shakespeare Survey*, 7 (1954), 95–106.

[10] 'Nicolò Secchi as a Source of *Twelfth Night*', *Shakespeare Quarterly*, v (Summer 1954), 271–80.

he consulted not only Nicolò Secchi's *Gl'Inganni* but his *L'interesse*, a play not translated into English until about 1660. H. G. Wright[1] claims, less convincingly, that for *All's Well* Shakespeare read the *Decameron* in a French translation, while Percy Simpson[2] amply demonstrates Shakespeare's considerable use of Latin authors in a comprehensive guide to his direct borrowings. In his study of the sources of *Troilus and Cressida*, Robert K. Presson[3] hints that Shakespeare may even have read some Homer in the original, although his main purpose is to attack the notion that the play reflects a 'medieval' conception of the Troy story; he shows that while Shakespeare consulted Chaucer for the love story, Lydgate and Caxton's *Recuyell*, his main source for the camp scenes was Chapman's *Seauen Bookes of the Iliades* (1598). The evidence for this is strong, but the conclusions drawn from it, that the play reflects Chapman's concern with the passions and their control by the judgement and is organic in the development of the tragedies, are less likely to meet with acceptance; they seem to involve seeing Achilles as a tragic hero.

The recognition that Shakespeare may have been able to read in several foreign languages is matched by an increasing assurance that he read very widely in his own. Presson and Miss Kaufman incidentally illustrate his use of a number of sources for a single play, and Kenneth Muir, who has done much to foster the idea that most of the plays are indebted to multiple sources, contributes further evidence,[4] not all of it convincing, but strong enough to carry his main point, for the Pyramus and Thisbe interlude in *A Midsummer Night's Dream*. In this he thinks Shakespeare was deliberately parodying bad poetry. E. A. J. Honigmann seeks to establish with more certainty than has hitherto been allowed to them three secondary sources for *The Winter's Tale*[5] besides *Pandosto*, and numerous researchers have noted further parallels between passages in the plays and a variety of earlier books. Abbie Findlay Potts's argument that Shakespeare was influenced by the *Faerie Queene* in writing *Hamlet* seems more ingenious than sound,[6] but Karl Hammerle sees an interesting parallel between the Bower of Bliss and the Gardens of Adonis in Spenser's poem on the one hand, and Titania's bower on the other,[7] all of which he relates to a traditional type of 'pleasure garden'. Rolf Soellner finds a source in Erasmus for a passage in *Romeo and Juliet*,[8] and Kenneth Muir draws attention to further similarities between *Twelfth Night* and Riche's *Farewell to Military Profession*, and between *Troilus and Cressida* and Greene's *Euphues his Censure to Philautus*.[9] In addition to these, Shakespeare may have known

[1] 'How did Shakespeare come to know the "Decameron"?', *Modern Language Review*, L (January 1955), 45–8.

[2] 'Shakespeare's Use of Latin Authors' in *Studies in Elizabethan Drama* (Oxford: The Clarendon Press, 1955); this volume also contains an important and fully documented account of 'The Official Control of Tudor and Stuart Printing', together with a record of piracy between 1550 and 1640, a brief survey of 'Shakespeare's Versification' for the general reader, and reprints a number of articles which have appeared in periodicals.

[3] *Shakespeare's Troilus and Cressida and the Legends of Troy* (Madison, Wisconsin: University of Wisconsin Press, 1953).

[4] 'Pyramus and Thisbe: A Study in Shakespeare's Method', *Shakespeare Quarterly*, V (Spring 1954), 141–53, and 'Shakespeare as Parodist', *Notes and Queries* (November 1954), pp. 467–8.

[5] 'Secondary Sources of *The Winter's Tale*', *Philological Quarterly*, XXXIV (January 1955), 27–38.

[6] 'Hamlet and Gloriana's Knights', *Shakespeare Quarterly*, VI (Winter 1955), 31–43.

[7] 'Das Titanialager des Sommernachtstraumes als Nachhall des Topos vom "Locus Amoenus"', *Shakespeare-Jahrbuch*, XC (1954), 279–81.

[8] 'Shakespeare and the "Consolatio"', *Notes and Queries* (March 1954), pp. 108–9.

[9] 'The Sources of *Twelfth Night*', *Notes and Queries* (March 1955), p. 94; 'Greene and *Troilus and Cressida*', *Notes and Queries* (April 1955), pp. 141–2.

the anonymous *Caesar's Revenge*,[1] the Catholic burial service,[2] *Gorboduc*,[3] and books by Nashe, Greene and Sir Thomas Wilson,[4] though the evidence is not overwhelming in any one case. The only voice of dissension from this multiplication of sources is that of Georges Bonnard, who falls back on a postulated common source as a way out of difficulties.[5] Bonnard notes that many features of *Timon of Athens* are not found in Plutarch, Lucian or other possible sources, but only in the anonymous play of *Timon*, and suggests that a common source may be found in a Latin or Italian version of the Timon story enriched with Byzantine elements, like certain imitations of Lucian in the Bibliothèque Nationale. This is a most interesting article, but it is based on a belief that Shakespeare used one work as a source, "Nous avons peine à croire, en effet, qu'il ait lui-même rassemblé des matériaux de provenance très diverse".

The study of sources is bound up with questions of chronology and authorship. All are involved in an important article[6] by E. A. J. Honigmann, who argues strongly that there is no need to look for lost source plays for *Henry VI*, *Hamlet* or *The Merchant of Venice*, and that the inferior versions of other plays like *Richard III* and *John* antedated Shakespeare's; he notes that these belonged to the Queen's Men, who are known to have reconstructed prompt-copies. In addition to suggesting radical changes in the accepted chronology of Shakespeare's early plays, Honigmann offers a new interpretation of the "upstart crow" passage in Greene's *Groatsworth of Wit*. Robert Adger Law shows that 2 and 3 *Henry VI* follow the chronicles much more closely than Part I, and concludes that Part I is "fundamentally a Talbot play revised by Shakespeare" after the others were written.[7] There is no reason to doubt the evidence he presents, but it could be interpreted differently. From a study of *Sir Thomas More* J. M. Nosworthy[8] concludes that Additions II and III are Shakespeare's, that they show correspondences with his verbal habits of 1598–1602, and that they were written *c.* 1601–2, a little after Munday, Chettle and Dekker had collaborated in the main text. The verbal parallels are not too convincing (there are too many in early and late plays) and it seems odd that a history play of the Elizabethan genre should be written so long after the main vogue had come to an end round about 1598. Abbie Findlay Potts pleads that Shakespeare studied Jonson's *Cynthia's Revels* and *Poetaster* carefully in writing *Troilus and Cressida*;[9] the evidence is not clear, although some comparison between the latter and *Poetaster* seems justified. More general 'background' studies include a long article by D. C. Boughner[10] which seeks to show that Falstaff is a composite

---

[1] Ernest Schanzer, 'A Neglected Source of *Julius Caesar*', *Notes and Queries* (May 1954), pp. 196–7.

[2] Maurice J. Quinlan, 'Shakespeare and the Catholic Burial Services', *Shakespeare Quarterly*, v (Summer 1954), 303–6.

[3] Joan Rees, 'A Passage in *Henry VI*, Part 3', *Notes and Queries* (May 1954), pp. 195–6.

[4] Frank W. Bradbrook, 'Thomas Nashe and Shakespeare', *Notes and Queries* (November 1954), p. 470; 'Shakespeare and Daniel's "Letter from Octavia"', *Notes and Queries* (February 1955), pp. 56–7; Douglas L. Peterson, 'A Probable Source for Shakespeare's Sonnet CXXIX', *Shakespeare Quarterly*, v (Autumn 1954), 381–4.

[5] 'Note sur les Sources de *Timon of Athens*', *Études Anglaises*, VII (January 1954), 59–69. C. A. Greer, 'Shakespeare's Use of "The Famous Victories of Henry the Fifth"', *Notes and Queries* (June 1954), pp. 238–41, raises the old bogy of a lost common source for *Henry V* and *The Famous Victories*.

[6] 'Shakespeare's Lost Source-Plays', *Modern Language Review*, XLIX (July 1954), 293–307.

[7] 'The Chronicles and the *Three Parts of Henry VI*', *University of Texas Studies in English*, XXXIII (1954), 13–32.

[8] 'Shakespeare and Sir Thomas More', *Review of English Studies*, n.s. VI (January 1955), 12–25.

[9] '*Cynthia's Revels*, *Poetaster*, and *Troilus and Cressida*', *Shakespeare Quarterly*, v (Summer 1955), 297–302.

[10] 'Vice, Braggart and Falstaff', *Anglia*, LXXII (1954), 35–61.

figure derived from both the Vice of the morality tradition and the braggart of Latin and Italian comedy; an interesting suggestion[1] by Roy F. Montgomery that an image in *The Merry Wives* may refer to the rebuilding of the Globe in 1598; and another by S. G. E. Lythe[2] that Elsinore was chosen as the location for *Hamlet* because, as the site of the Danish custom-house, it would have been a familiar name to Londoners. E. M. Trehern[3] draws attention to the use Shakespeare makes of an Elizabethan commonplace in the idea of popular support for a victim preventing the execution of tyranny. Allusions by Shakespeare to whales are shown by Roger J. Trienens to reflect a widespread belief in their lustfulness.[4]

The accumulation of detailed knowledge enriches our understanding of Shakespeare and his age, and makes a fresh critical assessment necessary and valuable every few years. This year the second volume in the 'Penguin' guide to English literature, *The Age of Shakespeare*, has appeared.[5] It opens with surveys of the 'social setting' and literary background, in which L. D. Salingar compresses very well a mass of information around the rather overworked idea of 'civility' as distinguishing the renaissance in England. These are followed by essays of varying quality and by different authors on the novel, Daniel and Raleigh, the stage and acting, Marlowe, various aspects of Shakespeare's plays, Chapman, Tourneur, Bacon, Elizabethan music, and comedy. The list is pretty comprehensive, but omits Spenser, discussed in the first volume, and Donne, who, apparently will take pride of place in the third; Daniel and Raleigh were perhaps included to make up the deficiency, though the choice of these poets seems an adventitious one. The best critical essays are those by L. C. Knights on *Lear* and the great tragedies, and on Ben Jonson, by J. C. Maxwell on Marlowe, by L. D. Salingar on Tourneur and revenge tragedy, and by Wilfrid Mellers on the union of words and music. These and other sections have all the best qualities of the kind of critical outlook which used to be associated with *Scrutiny*; a serious concern with the functions of language, imagery and style, a stress on moral implications, and a full evaluation of tragic themes. They well deserve to be widely read, as they certainly will be, and will make many of us think again about, for instance, the merits of *Sejanus*, of Webster's plays, of *Troilus and Cressida* and *Coriolanus*. But one feels that a note of warning should have been inserted for the undergraduate (the essays are rather too scholarly, and some of them too turgid, for the general reader) that the critical approach is a very literary and a very moral one; that the theatre is represented only by B. L. Joseph unrepentantly depicting again a "stylized Elizabethan actor", and that comedy receives very short shrift indeed. Shakespeare's career is seen as a development towards the crowning fulfilment of *Lear* and the last plays, which are interpreted as philosophical patterns, and the early comedies are dismissed in a sentence or two as mere entertainment. Kenneth Muir's well-balanced contribution on 'Changing Interpretations of Shakespeare' may help to set in critical perspective the judgements offered in the rest of the book, and should perhaps be read first. Another excellent little guide to the history of

---

[1] 'A Fair House Built on Another Man's Ground', *Shakespeare Quarterly*, V (Summer 1954), 207–8.

[2] 'The Locale of "Hamlet"', *Notes and Queries* (March 1954), pp. 111–12.

[3] 'Dear, They Durst Not...', *English*, X (Summer 1954), 59–60.

[4] 'The Symbolic Cloud in *Hamlet*', *Shakespeare Quarterly*, V (Spring 1954), 211–13. Robert Adger Law's discussion of the use Shakespeare makes in three plays of a single passage in Hall's chronicle also deserves notice, 'Edmund Mortimer in Shakespeare and Hall', *Shakespeare Quarterly*, V (Autumn 1954), 425–6.

[5] Ed. by Boris Ford (Penguin Books, 1955).

Shakespeare criticism is provided in C. J. Sisson's *Shakespeare*,[1] which contains a valuable bibliography by J. R. Brown.

The year's most controversial book on Shakespeare is Leslie Hotson's *The First Night of Twelfth Night*,[2] which brings brilliantly to life a festive occasion at the court of Queen Elizabeth, when she entertained a Muscovite ambassador and Don Virginio Orsino, Duke of Bracciano. Once again Hotson has discovered some important documents, and builds a fascinating story out of the evidence they provide, successfully communicating his excitement to the reader. But the mixture of fact, conjecture and generalization he offers is not sufficient to support his two major conclusions, that the play performed on 6 January 1600/1 before Don Virginio was *Twelfth Night*, commissioned and written within ten or twelve days, and that the performance was staged in the centre of the great hall at Whitehall, with the audience on all four sides:

The Elizabethans...show us reality: the play being acted openly *out in the middle of the floor*—an island of drama surrounded by crowded scaffolds on all sides.... The first performance of *Twelfth Night*, presented by Shakespeare completely 'in the round'.

In none of the documents is the title of the play performed before Don Virginio cited, and it is not easy to believe that Shakespeare wrote his polished *Twelfth Night* at short notice to compliment him and Queen Elizabeth, and to satirize members of the court. Hotson supports this assertion with some fanciful and many ingenious new interpretations of passages in this play, which will give future editors pause; if, as a whole, they do not carry conviction, it is because they apply to details or to characters at certain moments and do not seem to affect the structure or dramatic interest of what has always been considered, in its own right, as a comic masterpiece.

Other aspects of the book have already provoked much comment and criticism. Attention has been drawn to an uncertainty over the year in which the performance took place.[3] More importantly, William Empson and M. St Clare Byrne[4] have severely criticized Hotson's interpretation of Don Virginio's "atorno atorno" as describing an audience on four sides; Empson suggests that it could be a loose description of an audience on three sides of the stage, Miss Byrne that it includes the spectators in the public gallery at the rear as the fourth side. Both note discrepancies between the descriptions of the stage in documents and Hotson's reconstruction, and observe that the phrase "in the middle of the hall" may indicate the middle of one side, or a stage extending to the middle from one end, rather than an area isolated in the centre of the hall, as Hotson supposes. Miss Byrne also claims that his generalizations about stage procedure would not stand up to practical realization. He extends his argument for 'arena' staging to the public theatres, and asserts that there was no inner or upper stage, and that tents "or collapsed scenic *houses* were carried out on the stage to be set up before the performance". His

[1] Writers and their Work Series (Longmans, for The British Council, 1955).
[2] Hart-Davis, 1954.
[3] By W. W. Greg and J. W. Lever, *Times Literary Supplement*, 31 December 1954, 28 January and 18 February 1955, and Sydney Race, 'The First Night of "Twelfth Night"', *Notes and Queries* (February 1955), pp. 52–5; Hotson replied to Greg in *Times Literary Supplement*, 21 January 1955.
[4] 'The Elizabethan Stage', *Times Literary Supplement*, 10 December 1954; 'Twelfth Night "In the Round"', *Theatre Notebook*, IX (January–March 1955), 46–52.

book will make everyone think again about the Elizabethan stage, but his case is very far from being proved; however, he promises new evidence in a further book which, he is confident, will convince the reader.[1]

Meanwhile the staging of 'difficult' scenes in Shakespeare's plays is being investigated, and the views of J. C. Adams, who located many scenes entirely on the inner or upper stages, are being more and more discredited. Richard Hosley re-interprets the staging of three scenes in *Romeo and Juliet*,[2] III, v, where Juliet is upbraided by her mother, and IV, iii and iv, where a bed is required, in terms of action flowing from the upper or inner stage on to the main platform. In an article based on a number of references to rails running round the platform stage, J. W. Saunders[3] suggests that the problems offered by certain scenes could have been solved by the use of the stage rails in conjunction with an alley through the pit alongside the stage giving access to the tiring-rooms: the monument in *Antony and Cleopatra* could then have been represented by the platform stage, and the body of Antony have been brought in through the pit. Whether one agrees or not with his view of the staging of this scene and others in *Pericles*, *Romeo and Juliet* and *Henry VIII*, the general emphasis on bringing the action "further into the midst" of the audience is probably right.

More general studies of the Elizabethan stage include a brilliantly summarized account of the present state of our knowledge by F. P. Wilson,[4] who also presents some new information from documents. Perhaps the most interesting point he makes concerns Hotson's argument for 'arena' staging:

Again he is presuming a consistency of usage for which I see no justification. Apart from the two documents which he quotes I find no other information about stages in the middle of a hall in the declared accounts of some 50 years, and I have a suspicion that in these two years the situation of the stage may have been mentioned because it was exceptional.

In his survey of the development of the stage in the sixteenth century, A. M. Nagler[5] makes the point that medieval and renaissance stages persisted side by side, so that the age must be regarded as transitional. *Theater Pictorial*,[6] a lavish and fascinating history of world theatre in drawings and photographs, includes many relating to this period which are not otherwise easily available; among them are the plans for the Lucerne passion play of 1583 and the setting of the St Laurentius play at Cologne in 1581. One could wish that the provenance and dates of the illustrations were given in more detail, but this is perhaps to cavil. Davis P. Harding[7] eloquently evokes a visit to the theatre in 1600, in order to make the point that we should be very careful about our assumptions regarding Shakespeare's audience, which, he argues, was unusually

[1] *Times Literary Supplement*, 7 January 1955.

[2] 'The Use of the Upper Stage in *Romeo and Juliet*', *Shakespeare Quarterly*, v (Autumn 1954), 371–9.

[3] 'Vaulting the Rails', *Shakespeare Survey*, 7 (1954), 69–81.

[4] 'The Elizabethan Theatre', *Neophilologus*, XXXIX (January 1955), 40–58.

[5] 'Sixteenth-Century Continental Stages', *Shakespeare Quarterly*, v (Autumn 1954), 359–70.

[6] Ed. by George Altman, Ralph Freud, Kenneth MacGowan and William Melnitz (Berkeley: University of California Press; Cambridge University Press, 1953).

[7] 'Shakespeare the Elizabethan' in *Shakespeare: of an Age and for All Time*, The Yale Shakespeare Festival Lectures, edited by C. T. Prouty (The Shoe String Press, 1954), pp. 11–32.

heterogeneous in its make-up. Richard Southern analyses in more detail[1] a print of an indoor stage found in a book of 1635 describing the Hague fair; the arrangement of the stage, in a building which he thinks may have been a tennis-court, shows interesting points of similarity with what is known about the Elizabethan theatre. Important new material revealing in considerable detail the history of the Red Bull theatre and Queen Anne's Men has been brought to light by C. J. Sisson:[2] this is particularly interesting for the insight it provides into the lives of famous actors such as Christopher Beeston, Richard Baxter and Richard Perkins.

The growth of interest in Elizabethan actors and acting is reflected in several articles. Joseph Allen Bryant Jr.[3] seeks to explain Kemp's departure from the King's Men in 1599 or so as due not to a quarrel but to the creation of Falstaff, who usurped "the basic devices with which the unencumbered clown had for so long enchanted his audiences", and made a new type of fool necessary. William A. Armstrong refutes the often-repeated charge that Edward Alleyn was representative of a bombastic style of acting,[4] and stresses the contemporary comparisons between him and Burbage which claim that both acted to the life. Two articles, one by Marvin Rosenberg, one by the present writer, continue the discussion provoked by B. L. Joseph's *Elizabethan Acting*;[5] both attack the latter's view that this was stylized and rhetorical, and Rosenberg points out that even if "the Elizabethan idea of natural acting was not exactly the same as ours", there is no reason to believe that acting was formal; the evidence is strong that it was regarded as realistic.

Modern acting and productions of Shakespeare's plays receive so much attention that the future historian will be glutted with material. The more notable reviews include Richard David's survey of 'Stratford 1954',[6] T. C. Kemp's report on a number of British productions,[7] and the account of the Mermaid Theatre productions by Bernard Miles and Josephine Wilson.[8] Alan S. Downer describes some of the six productions of *Hamlet* staged in Scandinavia in 1953–4,[9] and A. C. Sprague reports the New York season.[10] Guy Boas, the headmaster of the Sloane School, presents in *Shakespeare and the Young Actor*[11] a history of performances by his boys; it is not always easy to understand now why they should have generated such enthusiasm as the reviews he quotes show.

A much needed full-length study of William Poel and his work has at last appeared in Robert Speaight's biography,[12] which portrays a man who never received adequate recognition

---

[1] 'A Seventeenth-Century Indoor Stage', *Theatre Notebook*, IX (October–December 1954), 5–11.

[2] 'The Red Bull Company and the Importunate Widow', *Shakespeare Survey*, 7 (1954), 57–68.

[3] 'Shakespeare's Falstaff and the Mantle of Dick Tarlton', *Studies in Philology*, LI (April 1954), 149–62.

[4] 'Shakespeare and the Acting of Edward Alleyn', *Shakespeare Survey*, 7 (1954), 82–9.

[5] 'Elizabethan Actors: Men or Marionettes', *PMLA*, LXIX (September 1954), 915–27; 'The Player's Passion, Some Notes on Elizabethan Psychology and Acting', *Essays and Studies*, VII (1954), 62–77. B. L. Joseph's book was reviewed in *Shakespeare Survey*, 5 (1952).

[6] *Shakespeare Quarterly*, V (Autumn 1954), 385–94. [7] *Shakespeare Survey*, 7 (1954), 121–7.

[8] *Shakespeare Quarterly*, V (Summer 1954), 307–10. [9] *Shakespeare Quarterly*, V (Spring 1954), 155–65.

[10] *Shakespeare Quarterly*, V (Summer 1954), 311–15; Wolfgang Stroedel's account of the productions associated with the 90th anniversary celebrations of the Deutsche Shakespeare Gesellschaft, *ibid.* pp. 317–22, is also worth noting.

[11] Rockliff, 1955.

[12] *William Poel and the Elizabethan Revival* (Heinemann, for The Society for Theatre Research, 1954).

in his lifetime, partly through his own wilfulness, reflected in his hatred of the press and his addiction to casting women in male parts. The story of the development of his views on staging, and of his principle of speaking Shakespeare's poetry with a musical intonation and stress on key-words, is fascinating. Two aspects of his character, his fanaticism and his pioneer daring, the latter represented in his use of an apron stage, and his revival of unpopular or unknown plays, among them *Faustus* and *Measure for Measure*, are well brought out. Perhaps too much space is devoted to Poel's mistakes and faults; it could have been a more exciting book. Frank McMullan[1] writes well on 'Producing Shakespeare'; he recalls the modern progress towards simplicity of staging under the stimulus of Poel and others, and goes on to criticize, from a practical point of view, both J. C. Adams's reconstruction of the Globe, and Leslie Hotson's conjectured 'arena' stage.

Finally, a group of articles on nineteenth-century interpretations of Shakespeare deserves notice. Carol Jones Carlisle[2] shows from their writings that the great actors of the period, with the exception of Fanny Kemble, did not share the view of the romantic critics that the plays suffered in performance. Francis J. Nock[3] illustrates the influence of Shakespeare on E. T. A. Hoffmann, and René Taupin[4] contributes a fascinating study of the development from Delacroix through Mallarmé and Laforgue of 'Hamletisme', a view of the play as a tragedy of adolescence, in which the central problem was "to accept the world, or to save one's being for one's intimate enjoyment".

3. TEXTUAL STUDIES

reviewed by JAMES G. McMANAWAY

In a time like this of feverish activity in the study of Shakespearian texts, it is well to pause for an evaluation of the present state of scholarship and a co-ordination and consolidation of recent discoveries. This is the more necessary because many of the most rewarding investigations have been of a highly technical nature, requiring the discovery and application of new and ever more rigorous bibliographical techniques and an appalling amount of sheer drudgery. The published results of these researches are likely to be caviare to the general. Indeed, the serious scholar who has not had the time to read all the literature of the subject may find the going heavy. He would not, however, be justified in wondering whether the investigators were indulging in intellectual gymnastics for their own pleasure. Should he be tempted to entertain such a frivolous thought, he would be well advised to read Sir Walter Greg's monumental book about the First Folio.[5]

From the first chapter, entitled 'Planning the Collection', to the last, dealing with 'The Printing', the author asks all the questions that can be imagined, presents and weighs the evidence, and pronounces judgement with the utmost modesty and admirable detachment. It

[1] *Shakespeare: Of an Age and for All Time*, pp. 53–77.

[2] 'The Nineteenth-Century Actors Versus the Closet Critics of Shakespeare', *Studies in Philology*, LI (October 1954), 599–615.

[3] 'E. T. A. Hoffmann and Shakespeare', *Journal of English and Germanic Philology*, LIII (July 1954), 369–82.

[4] 'The Myth of Hamlet in France in Mallarmé's Generation', *Modern Language Quarterly*, XIV (December 1953), 432–47.

[5] *The Shakespeare First Folio, Its Bibliographical and Textual History* (Oxford University Press, 1955).

need hardly be said that no one else has the author's intimate knowledge of English Renaissance drama, whether in manuscript or print; but it should be gratefully recorded that Greg has a lively, pungent style, and is completely at ease in the exposition of the most complicated problems. Thus in Chapter IV, 'Editorial Problems 2', he writes:

The question whether a particular Folio text was set up from a manuscript or from an earlier print is one which sufficiently patient and minute examination should be able to answer definitely, although in a few cases critics are not yet agreed. But when we probe beyond this comparatively superficial problem, and ask what sort of manuscript was handed to the Folio printer or lay behind the printed edition supplied, or in some cases what sort of manuscript it was by comparison with which that edition was corrected before being used as copy for the Folio, we enter an altogether different field of criticism, a misty mid region of Weir, a land of shadowy shapes and melting outlines, where not even the most patient inquiry and the most penetrating analysis can hope to arrive at any but tentative and proximate conclusions. But if what song the Sirens sang is a question not beyond all conjecture, we may at least hope to form an idea of the manuscripts behind the transmitted texts of Shakespeare's plays that can claim to be reasonable and to possess a measure of plausibility. We shall be wise to pitch our expectation no higher (pp. 105–6).

The Shakespeare First Folio epitomizes the scholarship of half a century and blocks out the problems that must be solved in the years ahead.

How those problems are to be solved is the chief concern of Fredson Bowers[1] in his Rosenbach Lectures in Bibliography. It must be largely in terms of the nature and authority of the manuscripts from which the plays were printed and of the processes of the printing shops and the characteristics of the printers who converted copy to type and read the proofs. Bowers is not content simply to describe and illustrate the known methods of bibliographical-textual research; he seeks, as always, to penetrate the textual mysteries that yet baffle us. And in so doing, he does not hesitate to challenge received opinion. The characteristics of certain texts have hitherto been most satisfactorily explained as originating in the use of Shakespeare's foul sheets as copy. Bowers demands proof that an Elizabethan playwright ever turned his foul papers over to a company of actors that bought his play.[2] Instead, he argues that the author delivered a fair copy, of which a transcript was then made that served as prompt book, and that it was this author's fair copy that was on occasion turned over to the printer. The suggestion has its attractions, one of which is that such a fair copy might receive partial editorial annotations before the prompt book was prepared. But no such fair copy is known, and Bowers is on unsure ground when he cites the publication by Heywood, Marston and others of some of their own plays. The fact is that we do not know how these playwrights arranged to put their plays in print and are unlikely at this date to find any new evidence.

It is not clear to me that Bowers takes sufficiently into account the need to have play manuscripts licensed by the Master of the Revels. With so many plays in repertory, is it likely that players' parts would be copied out and the cast required to memorize them before the prompt

---

[1] *On Editing Shakespeare* (Rosenbach Lectures in Bibliography). University of Pennsylvania Press, 1955.

[2] May it not be pertinent that a portion of text missing from *Bonduca* (B.M. Add. MS. 36758) was by Edward Knight, book-keeper of the King's Men, "transcrib'd from the foule papers of the Authors wᶜʰ were found"?

book was ready and *licensed*? It is dangerous to argue from one case, as Bowers does from Daborne's notes to Henslowe.

The book is full of illustrations, many of them drawn from work in progress of which there are otherwise no published accounts. One of these relates to the printing of the Good Quarto of *Hamlet*. He is confident that compositor X set sheets B–D (Act I) while Y started on sheet E. Thereafter X set F I N O and Y set G H K L M. This leads him to the inference that while X used the Bad Quarto in conjunction with manuscript copy, Y worked exclusively with manuscript, so that there are no Bad Quarto corruptions whatever in sheets E G H K L M. This may be true, but it seems incapable of proof; we cannot know all the circumstances of printing. On any given day, X may have been ill, and Y may have looked at the copy of the Bad Quarto X had used in B–D—and probably kept at hand—or Y may at any time have walked across the room and checked or confirmed a reading. It is hazardous to speak in absolute terms.

Two years ago, Dover Wilson began a series of essays in response to a plea for a "Textual Introduction to Shakespeare without Tears". The first,[1] as a brief account of how textual study is practised today, is comparatively easy reading. In the second[2] the needs and limitations of the general reader are subordinated to the desire to state at length the textual hypothesis upon which the author and his collaborating editor have made their text of *Romeo and Juliet*[3] in the latest volume of the New Cambridge Shakespeare.

Before commenting on these essays, it will be profitable to glance at a lecture delivered by Wilson at Stratford-upon-Avon under the auspices of the Governors of the Memorial Theatre.[4] A few details need correction or qualification, but otherwise the lecture is for many readers a better statement than the first two essays of the series.

These it will be advantageous to consider together, along with the New Cambridge *Romeo* and the edition of this play by Richard Hosley.[5] It is now the belief of Wilson and Duthie that the copy for the Good Quarto 2 was printed directly from a copy of the Bad Quarto 1, in which interlineations, marginal additions, and loose slips of paper had been inserted bearing corrections of the text secured from collation with Shakespeare's foul sheets. They were driven to this desperate position by their decision that direct bibliographical links are to be found between Q2 and every one of the ten sheets of Q1. It is likely, I think, that minute examination of the evidence will incline readers to favour Hosley's acceptance of the more conservative opinion that, except for certain specific passages demonstrably printed from Q1, the copy for Q2 was basically Shakespeare's foul sheets. Certain minor bibliographical links noted by Wilson and Duthie suggest, however, that the compositor(s) of Q2 did refer sporadically to Q1 to verify or clarify a difficult manuscript reading. This is an unhappy situation, but there seems no help for it. It is regrettable that neither edition is able to contribute new information about the agency that reported the Q1 text or the purpose for which the text was prepared.

---

[1] 'The New Way with Shakespeare's Texts: an Introduction to Lay Readers. I. The Foundations', *Shakespeare Survey*, 7, pp. 48–56.

[2] 'II. Recent Work on the Text of *Romeo and Juliet*', *Shakespeare Survey*, 8, pp. 81–99.

[3] *Romeo and Juliet*, ed. John Dover Wilson and George Ian Duthie (Cambridge University Press, 1955).

[4] 'On Editing Shakespeare, with Special Reference to the Problems of *Richard III*', in *Talking of Shakespeare*, ed. John Garrett (Hodder and Stoughton with Max Reinhardt, 1954).

[5] *The Tragedy of Romeo and Juliet* (Yale Shakespeare), ed. Richard Hosley. New Haven: Yale University Press, 1954.

During the year three volumes of the New Arden Shakespeare have been published and four (in addition to *Romeo*) of the New Yale edition. Frank Kermode is resolutely conservative in dating *The Tempest*[1] and rejecting suggestions of multiple authorship or extensive authorial revision. The mislineation of prose as verse and verse as prose troubles him, partly because he thinks that Shakespeare's ideas about decorum and the distribution among the dramatis personae of prose and verse in comedy have not yet been apprehended. Acting on the unpublished suggestions of Harold F. Brooks, the Advisory Editor of the series, he observes that in some places, notably in Folio pages 4 and 9, there is relation between unorthodox lineation and the compositor's need to save—or fill up—space. This is a shrewd anticipation of Charlton Hinman's discovery that did not appear in print until more than a year later.[2]

In his edition of *King John*,[3] E. A. J. Honigmann keeps the promise implied in his discussion of Shakespeare's early plays[4] and boldly dating his play 1590–91 asserts that it precedes and is the source of *The Troublesome Raigne* (Q 1591). The supporting argument is too long and complicated to be rehearsed in detail, and it might carry conviction were it not for the evident maturity of much of the verse in *John* and, what is of greater moment, the effect on the accepted chronology of the plays up to *Henry IV*. If it could be granted that by the spring of 1591 Shakespeare had already produced at least one version not only of *Richard III*, *Titus Andronicus*, the Ur-*Hamlet* and the plays about *Henry VI* and would in the next year or two add *Richard II*, *Love's Labour's Lost*, *Romeo*, and *Midsummer Night's Dream*, what would be the effect on our ideas of Shakespeare's development as a poet and playwright? Shakespeare's middle years, as we have understood the term, when he should have been actively creative, are made to seem to have been devoted largely to the rewriting of youthful exercises. Honigmann is a redoubtable champion of his cause, and he has found new and amusing evidence to support it; the odds will remain against him, however, until each play in question can be assigned its chronological place in the canon. His treatment of the text of *John* is independent and deserves respectful consideration, as in his reassignment of lines at II, i, 149–51, his new act division at III, i, 75, and his restoration of Folio readings that earlier editors have emended. The comments on punctuation, certain "old" spellings, and the retention of "-ed" and "-d" are dubious.

Cymbeline[5] is called by its editor "an experimental romance". Nosworthy believes that the sometimes colourless and even trivial lines and the occasional weaknesses in construction are associated with the fact that Shakespeare had to work out for himself the technique of writing a new kind of play and are not to be considered evidence of collaboration or of revision by another hand. He finds no reason to propose a different date of composition (1609–10) than that generally agreed upon, and he is convinced that this was early enough for the play to have influenced the writing of *Philaster*. The cleanness of the text and the transition from laconic stage directions in the early scenes to long, detailed descriptive directions towards the end are, he thinks, best explained by Miss Alice Walker's privately communicated suggestion that copy for the Folio was a scribe's careful transcription of foul papers, with casual adjustments by the

---

[1] *The Tempest* (New Arden Shakespeare), ed. Frank Kermode. Methuen, 1954.
[2] 'Cast-off Copy in the First Folio of Shakespeare', *Shakespeare Quarterly*, VI, 259–73.
[3] *King John* (New Arden Shakespeare), ed. E. A. J. Honigmann. Methuen, 1954.
[4] 'Shakespeare's "Lost Source-Plays"', *Modern Language Review*, XLIX, 293–307. This will be discussed below.
[5] *Cymbeline* (New Arden Shakespeare), ed. J. M. Nosworthy. Methuen, 1955.

bookkeeper. It might come closer to the facts to conjecture that the bookkeeper started marking a fair copy of the foul sheets, striking out the author's stage directions and inserting theatrical notations (exclusive of those for music and sound effects, as Nosworthy observes), but broke off in the midst of his labours.

In these volumes the special editors have been granted a latitude in their treatment of text that was not enjoyed by the editors of the first volumes of the edition, but the resultant lack of uniformity is more than compensated by the new independence.

The Yale Shakespeare, originally edited by the late C. F. Tucker Brooke, is now in process of revision under the general editorship of Helge Kökeritz and Charles T. Prouty. The pocket-sized, clearly printed volumes, one to a play, are convenient for private reading and for class use. There is in such volumes a minimum of space for annotation and criticism, but this little is allocated by each special editor according to the needs of the play and his particular interests. The first four plays [1] are known only in the First Folio text; the fifth, *Romeo*, mentioned above, has behind it also a Bad and a Good Quarto. It should be noted that Waith has grappled courageously with the problem of erratic lineation in *Macbeth*, following the Folio where he thinks the irregularities may be linked with stage business and regularizing other passages as best he may. Readers of *The Shrew* may be disappointed that Bergin does not reprint in an appendix the conclusion of the Induction from *A Shrew*, for this is not readily come by though frequently included in modern productions. All the texts seem to be printed accurately. It would help in future volumes to extend the Reading List.

The most recent addition to the Penguin Shakespeare is *Measure for Measure*.[2] The text, prefaced by Harrison's succinct accounts of Shakespeare, the Elizabethan theatre, and the play, retains the Folio lineation and punctuation "except where they seemed definitely wrong".

It is a convenience to distinguish between what may be called theoretical and practical studies in textual bibliography. Miss Alice Walker, who has been a very active practitioner of the former, makes two more contributions this year. The first[3] has special importance for editors of old-spelling texts, with its demonstration, for example, of why an old-spelling *Hamlet* must read "lonelines" at III, i, 46 and never "lonelinesse". Its general value is that it provides the theory of compositor determination, reinforced by illustrations, so that future investigators may avoid the false assumptions that in the past have led to a wasteful beating about of brains.

In the second article[4] Miss Walker accepts as proved that Roberts's compositors X and Y set the Fisher Quarto of *The Merchant of Venice* and the Creede Quarto (1604–5) of *Hamlet*, both supposed to have been printed from Shakespeare's foul papers, and inquires what can be learned from a study of the emendations found in the eclectic texts of the Old Cambridge editors, Dover Wilson, Alexander, and Sisson. One thing is that the *Hamlet* MS. was probably more difficult to read than *Merchant*; another, that unknown conditions affected the setting of *Hamlet*— haste was probably one of these, but the others are unknowable; and a third, that reference to

---

[1] *As You Like It*, ed. S. C. Burchill; *Twelfth Night*, ed. William P. Holden; *Macbeth*, ed. Eugene M. Waith; and *The Taming of the Shrew*, ed. Thomas G. Bergin (Yale Shakespeare). Yale University Press, 1954.

[2] *Measure for Measure* (Penguin Shakespeare, B25), ed. G. B. Harrison. Melbourne, London, Baltimore, 1954.

[3] 'Compositor Determination and Other Problems in Shakespearian Texts', in *Studies in Bibliography*, VII, 3–15 (Charlottesville, Virginia: Bibliographical Society of the University of Virginia, 1955).

[4] 'Collateral Substantive Texts (with Special Reference to *Hamlet*)', *loc. cit.* pp. 51–67.

collateral texts enables a good editor to emend even the better of his texts with greater assurance than if, as in *Merchant*, his authority is single.

An example of the practical study of text by bibliographical methods is Bowers's 'The Printing of *Hamlet*, Q2'.[1] This traces the introduction and reappearance of the units of running-titles through the Quarto and confirms, and is confirmed by, the pattern described by John Russell Brown[2] in another 'practical' study of the work of Roberts's compositors *X* and *Y* in setting *Hamlet* Q2 and *The Merchant of Venice*. These may seem to be no more than intellectual exercises in determining what happened to particular books in a particular shop, but as Brown points out his researches enable us to discard the notion that *Hamlet* was set by a bungling, inexperienced compositor and to differentiate between the stints of two men whose characteristics can be tabulated and whose relative skill can be determined. This is of enormous value, for it helps the eclectic editor to isolate and evaluate doubtful readings. Bowers illustrates the potential value of specific information about compositors and press work by his suggestion elsewhere that compositor *X*, who used the Bad Quarto in his first stint on Quarto 2 in setting sheets B–D, probably retained the book so that none of the sheets (after the conclusion of Act I in sheet E) set by *Y* were subject to contamination.[3] Thus the theoretical studies have practical utility, and the practical studies contribute to the formulation of theory.

The records of Shakespeare's early years in London are scanty. He was an unknown provincial trying to make his fortune in the theatrical world that was itself still in the second or third day of creation. Many men whose names even are unknown to us wrote plays that for the most part did not survive in manuscript or print and were performed by actors of whom as individuals or companies we know next to nothing. It is hardly a figure of speech to say that conditions were chaotic. If it is true, as we are told, that the early history of the moving picture is hard to document, even in this age when everything great or trivial seems to get into print, should there be wonder at the paucity of records of playwrights, actors, and their plays, or dismay that such as did survive are frequently ambiguous or baffling? Two scholars with antipodal points of view have attempted to supplement and reinterpret the data relating the titles and dates of some of Shakespeare's early plays. E. A. J. Honigmann[4] adds a few hitherto unnoted details to the discussion of Greene's famous attack upon Shake-scene, the upstart Crow, that help towards the final rejection of the charge of plagiarism as framed by Malone and revived by Dover Wilson. In so doing, he re-examines Nashe's reference to the Ur-*Hamlet* and Gosson's to a play about usurers, but finds no compulsion to the belief that Nashe was attributing *Hamlet* to Thomas Kyd or that the play mentioned by Gosson had either a casket story or a bond. To put the matter differently, there is no necessity for thinking that Shakespeare used a lost play as the source of *The Merchant of Venice* and there is some possibility that Shakespeare wrote the Ur-*Hamlet*. Honigmann's opinions about the 'source-plays' of *The Shrew*, *Richard III*, *King John*, and *Henry IV–Henry V*, are likewise iconoclastic. They are in the direction of adding to the canon and of starting Shakespeare's career very early.

From the opposite direction, Charles T. Prouty rejects "the idea of Shakespeare, early in his

---

[1] Fredson Bowers, in *Studies in Bibliography*, VII, 41–50.
[2] 'Compositors of *Hamlet* Q2 and *The Merchant of Venice*', *loc. cit.* pp. 17–40.
[3] But see above, p. 150.
[4] In 'Shakespeare's "Lost Source-Plays"', for which see p. 151.

career, writing popular original plays dealing with English history"[1]. The focus of his attack is *2 Henry VI*, which he follows Malone and Feuillerat, to name one early and one late commentator, in considering Shakespeare's revision of an early play (*The First Part of the Contention betwixt the Two Famous Houses of Yorke and Lancaster*, 1594) written by two unidentifiable poets. The book is characterized by the asking of shrewd questions. These relate to the staging of the two versions, the differences in style, the authors' concepts of certain of the characters, and the structure of the two plays, and their purpose is to establish that Q cannot be a reported version of F. The Folio text is freely conceded to be superior as poetry, but in other respects Prouty unwittingly forces himself into the position of arguing that by 1599 (by which date "we can be reasonably sure that Shakespeare had revised the old plays") Shakespeare, in the revision of a play that would never attract attention on its own merits, could do no better than falsify the facts of history, foul the action, weaken the structure, and confuse the characterization. This of the playwright who had fashioned the plot of *Romeo*, manipulated the historical events in the reign of Henry IV, and created Falstaff! The point at issue is not Shakespeare idolatry—whether it was unworthy of Shakespeare to begin his career by revising old plays or irreverent of us to think he did—though the dialectics of the book would so imply. Prouty's error is that he did not ask more questions, such as these. What kind of manuscript was used in printing the *Contention*—prompt-book, author's fair copy, foul sheets, or what? For what purpose had it been prepared—for performance in London or in the provinces, or for sale to a publisher? If for performance, on what kind of stage? Then the same questions should have been asked about the Folio text, which is obviously not printed from the prompt-book used about 1599 or even from Shakespeare's original fair copy as partly annotated by a book-keeper. Once these questions had been answered, Prouty, if still reluctant to agree that *The Contention* is a reported text, should have asked the significance of the descriptive stage directions in *The Contention* and sought an explanation of its anticipations and recollections. In a word, vital evidence is ignored and the book attempts to compare two texts without proper regard for their nature. In a long and important review,[2] G. Blakemore Evans, whose private opinion is that Shakespeare's *2 Henry VI* is a revision of a lost play, rejects Prouty's theory because he finds abundant proof that *The Contention* is a reported text of *2 Henry VI*.

Considerable attention has been given to Miss Alice Walker's attempts to prove that the Folio texts of several plays, *Hamlet* and *2 Henry IV* among them, were set from corrected copies of Good Quartos, and that, in consequence, the F texts have much less authority than has been accorded them. Her conclusions have not gone unchallenged. Two painstaking studies, independently pursued but written upon the same basic assumptions and employing essentially the same methods, reassess Miss Walker's evidence for *2 Henry IV*[3] and *Hamlet*[4] and arrive at conclusions diametrically opposed to hers.[5] Shaaber grants the existence of certain identities in spelling and punctuation between Folio and Quarto texts but is more impressed by the dif-

[1] '*The Contention*' and Shakespeare's '*2 Henry VI*', *A Comparative Study* (Yale University Press, 1954).

[2] *J.E.G.P.* LIII, 628–37. [3] M. A. Shaaber, 'The Folio Text of *2 Henry IV*', *Shakespeare Quarterly*, VI, 134–44.

[4] Harold Jenkins, 'The Relation between the Second Quarto and the Folio Text of *Hamlet*', *Studies in Bibliography*, VII, 69–83.

[5] See also the dissenting reviews of M. A. Shaaber, *M.L.N.* LXIX, 436–8, and G. Blakemore Evans, *J.E.G.P.* LIII, 473–6.

ferences. "I think", he writes, "there is reason to expect a certain amount of agreement, perhaps a good deal, in two texts derived by different lines of transmission from the same original." He is unwilling to concede that Q was referred to by the scribe who, he thinks, made a transcript of the playhouse MS. for use by the printer (and I judge he would object equally to the suggestion that the compositors of F consulted Q, as has been suggested in the case of *Romeo*). Jenkins goes further. Admitting that a number of identical readings listed by Miss Walker are proof that Q2 of *Hamlet* is occasionally the source of F's text, he produces weighty evidence that the F text is wrong in a greater number of readings because Q2 was not followed consistently, and he concludes that a corrected copy of Q2 could not have been used as printer's copy for F. He believes that Heminges and Condell were not satisfied with the Q2 text and accordingly supplied Jaggard with a transcript of the playhouse MS., and further, that the scribe consulted a copy of Q2 sporadically. This, with the very important substitution of scribe for compositor, is the same position as for *Romeo*, which Jenkins describes in a gem of understatement as "very inconvenient". "If neither the nature nor the extent of the consultation can be defined," he continues, "it leaves the position of the modern editor hazy and insecure."

Two remarkable copies of the Second Folio in the Folger Shakespeare Library, one that has no colophon, and another that has the usual colophon and also an impression of the colophon from the same type overprinted on the text of page 3 d 2, suggest[1] that the publishers of this edition planned to bring it out without a colophon. An even more remarkable copy of the Third Folio has come to attention in the library of Mr John Francis Neylan of San Francisco. It contains the normal pages of text of *1 Henry IV* and two inserted leaves containing the first three pages of the play printed by a different shop and reproducing the text of Q 1639. The conjectured explanation[2] is that a misunderstanding occurred arising out of the fact that copy (quires of the Second Folio) had been distributed to three different printers.

The discrepancies in *Henry V* between the text on the one hand and, on the other, its Prologue and choruses and the Epilogue to *2 Henry IV* have been the cause of much controversy. This is given a new turn by Warren D. Smith,[3] who denies Shakespearian authorship, conjectures that they were written for a performance at court, and possibly after the publication of the Bad Quarto of 1600, and identifies "the general of our gracious empress", not as the Earl of Essex but as Charles Blount, Lord Mountjoy, who succeeded Essex in the campaign against Tyrone and won a brilliant victory. Let us consider these in reverse order. The case for Blount is incapable of proof and would probably not have been considered except as a support for the late date (Essex by that time being in disgrace or dead). A court performance is suggested by the reference to "this cockpit" and "unworthy scaffolds" in the Prologue and by the salutation of the audience as "gentles all", a term that would not be strictly accurate in a public theatre.[4] The denial of the lines to Shakespeare rests insecurely upon his known aversion to prologues and to the occurrence of a large number of words that are not used elsewhere in the plays.

---

[1] James G. McManaway, 'The Colophon of the Second Folio of Shakespeare', *The Library*, ser. 5, IX, 199–200.

[2] James G. McManaway, 'A Miscalculation in the Printing of the Third Folio', *loc. cit.* pp. 129–33.

[3] 'The *Henry V* Choruses in the First Folio', *J.E.G.P.* LIII, 38–57.

[4] This latter point is supported by the argument that a Globe audience would be puzzled by the references to the inadequacies of the splendid new stage and would fail utterly to comprehend the apology for violations of unities of place and time.

11-2

Admitting the discrepancies between choruses and play, I remain unconvinced, if only because there was no one else who could write such poetry. I think Smith may read some of the lines too literally, and I suggest that the explanation lies in the imperfect text that has been preserved. The prompt book, I suspect, differed considerably from the foul sheets that were used in printing the Folio.

First Folios of Shakespeare being very costly and difficult of access, most people who want to read the plays as printed in 1623 use one of the four facsimiles. The one most widely distributed, both because of its modest cost and its diminished size, is that issued by James O. Halliwell-Phillipps about 1875. It will continue to be a handy volume for the general reader, but scholars have been warned by Charlton Hinman[1] against reliance upon it in textual or bibliographical work. It proves to be based partly on what is now Folio No. 33 in the Folger Shakespeare Library and partly on the Staunton facsimile of 1866. Furthermore, the Staunton facsimile was derived from two copies of the First Folio. And, to make all worse, there was serious tampering with the Staunton plates before a copy of this facsimile was used to supplement Folger 33, and the plates of the reduced facsimile were also tampered with before and in the course of printing. Caveat editor!

[1] 'The "Halliwell-Phillipps Facsimile" of the First Folio', *Shakespeare Quarterly*, v, 395–401.

BOOKS RECEIVED

[Inclusion of a book in this list does not preclude its review in a subsequent volume]

ALEXANDER, PETER. *Hamlet Father and Son* (Oxford: Clarendon Press, 1955).

ALTMAN, GEORGE, FREUD, RALPH and MACGOWAN, KENNETH. *Theater Pictorial* (Berkley and Los Angeles: California University Press, 1953).

BOAS, C. VAN EMDE. *Shakespeare's Sonnetten en hun Verband met de Travesti: Double Spelen.* (Amsterdam-Antwerpen: Wereld-Bibliotheek, 1951).

BOAS, GUY. *Shakespeare and the Young Actor* (London: Rockliff, 1955).

CLEMEN, WOLFGANG. *Die Tragödie vor Shakespeare*, Schriftenreihe der Deutschen Shakespeare-Gesellschaft, Neue Folge, Band V (Heidelberg: Quelle & Meyer, 1955).

ECKHOFF, LORENTZ. *Shakespeare Spokesman of the Third Estate* (Oslo: Akademisk forlag; Oxford: Basil Blackwell, 1954).

FIELD, ARTHUR. *Recent Discoveries Relating to the Life and Works of William Shakespeare* (London: The Mitre Press, 1954).

FORD, BORIS (Editor). *The Age of Shakespeare: A Guide to English Literature*, vol. II (London: Penguin Books, 1955).

GARRETT, JOHN (Editor). *Talking of Shakespeare* (London: Hodder and Stoughton in association with Max Reinhardt, 1954).

GILBERT, ALLAN H. (Editor). *Renaissance Papers* (a selection of papers presented at the Renaissance Meeting in the Southeastern States, Duke University 23–24 April 1954) (South Carolina University Press, 1954).

GREG, W. W. *The Shakespeare First Folio* (Oxford: Clarendon Press; London: Geoffrey Cumberlege, 1955).

HALLIDAY, F. E. *The Poetry of Shakespeare's Plays* (London: Duckworth, 1954).

HOTSON, LESLIE. *The First Night of Twelfth Night* (London: Rupert Hart-Davis, 1954).

ISAACS, J. *Shakespeare's Earliest Years in the Theatre.* Annual Shakespeare Lecture of the British Academy, 1953 (London: Geoffrey Cumberlege, n.d.).

KIRSCHBAUM, LEO. *Shakespeare and the Stationers* (Columbus: Ohio State University Press, 1955).

KNIGHT, G. WILSON. *The Mutual Flame* (London: Methuen, 1955).

KOSZUL, A. *Fête chez le Cordonnier.* Text and translation of *The Shoemaker's Holiday.* Collection du Théâtre Anglais de la Renaissance (Paris: La Société d'Édition Les Belles Lettres, 1955).

LONG, JOHN H. *Shakespeare's Use of Music* (Gainesville: Florida University Press, 1955).

MARÍN, LUIS ASTRANA. *Obras Completas de William Shakespeare. I. Macbeth, Trabajos de Amor Perdidos, Mucho Ruido Para Nada.* Edición Bilingüe Ilustrada (Madrid: Ediciones de la Universidad de Puerto Rico, 1955).

MASEFIELD, JOHN. *William Shakespeare* (London: Heinemann, 1954).

NICOLL, ALLARDYCE. *Cooperation in Shakespearian Scholarship.* Annual Shakespeare Lecture of the British Academy, 1952 (London: Geoffrey Cumberlege, 1954).

OPPEL, HORST. *Shakespeares Tragödien und Romanzen: Kontinuität oder Umbruch.* Akademie der Wissenschaften und der Literatur in Mainz (Wiesbaden: Franz Steiner Verlag, 1954).

PARIS, JEAN. *Shakespeare par lui-même* (Paris: Éditions du Seuil, 1954).

PONGETTI, HENRIQUE and KELLER, WILLY. *A Comédia dos Equívocos* (Rio de Janeiro: Depart. de Imprensa Nacional, 1955).

PRESSON, ROBERT K. *Shakespeare's 'Troilus and Cressida' and the Legends of Troy* (Madison: Wisconsin University Press, 1954).

PROUTY, C. T. (Editor). *Shakespeare: of an Age and for All Time.* The Yale Shakespeare Festival Lectures (Hamden, Connecticut: The Shoe String Press, 1954).

SAUVAGE, F. and KOSZUL, A. *Le Roi Henri VI.* Text and translation of *Henry VI*, Part I. Collection Shakespeare (Paris: La Société d'Édition Les Belles Lettres, 1955).

Shakespeare Jahrbuch, Band 90 (Heidelberg: Quelle & Meyer, 1954).

Shakespeare Quarterly, vol. V (New York: Shakespeare Association of America, 1954).

SHAKESPEARE, WILLIAM. *As You Like It.* The Yale Shakespeare, revised edition. Edited by S. C. Burchell (New Haven: Yale University Press; London: Geoffrey Cumberlege, 1954).

SHAKESPEARE, WILLIAM. *Cymbeline.* New Arden Shakespeare. Edited by J. M. Nosworthy (London: Methuen, 1955).

SHAKESPEARE, WILLIAM. *King John.* New Arden Shakespeare. Edited by E. A. J. Honigmann (London: Methuen, 1954).

SHAKESPEARE, WILLIAM. *Macbeth.* The Yale Shakespeare, revised edition. Edited by Eugene M. Waith (New Haven: Yale University Press; London: Geoffrey Cumberlege, 1954).

SHAKESPEARE, WILLIAM. *Measure for Measure.* The Penguin Shakespeare. Edited by G. B. Harrison (London: Penguin Books, 1954).

SHAKESPEARE, WILLIAM. *The Merchant of Venice.* New Arden Shakespeare. Edited by J. R. Brown (London: Methuen, 1955).

SHAKESPEARE, WILLIAM. *Romeo and Juliet.* The Yale Shakespeare, revised edition. Edited by Richard Hosley (New Haven: Yale University Press; London: Geoffrey Cumberlege, 1954).

SHAKESPEARE, WILLIAM. *Romeo and Juliet.* New Cambridge Shakespeare. Edited by J. Dover Wilson and G. I. Duthie (Cambridge University Press, 1955).

SHAKESPEARE, WILLIAM. *The Taming of the Shrew.* The Yale Shakespeare, revised edition. Edited by Thomas G. Bergin (New Haven: Yale University Press; London: Geoffrey Cumberlege, 1954).

SHAKESPEARE, WILLIAM. *The Tempest.* New Arden Shakespeare. Edited by Frank Kermode (London: Methuen, 1954).

SHAKESPEARE, WILLIAM. *Twelfth Night.* The Yale Shakespeare, revised edition. Edited by William P. Holden (New Haven: Yale University Press; London: Geoffrey Cumberlege, 1954).

SIMPSON, PERCY. *Studies in Elizabethan Drama* (Oxford: Clarendon Press, 1955).

SPEAIGHT, ROBERT. *Nature in Shakespearian Tragedy* (London: Hollis and Carter, 1955).

SPEAIGHT, ROBERT. *William Poel and the Elizabethan Revival* (London: Heinemann, 1954).

TRAVERSI, D. A. *The Last Phase* (London: Hollis and Carter, 1954).

INDEX

INDEX

INDEX

INDEX

INDEX